Sentencing Discretion and the Constitution

OXFORD MONOGRAPHS ON CRIMINAL LAW AND JUSTICE

This series aims to cover all aspects of criminal law and procedure including criminal evidence. The scope of this series is wide, encompassing both practical and theoretical works.

OTHER TITLES IN THIS SERIES

How Juries Work
And How They Could Work Better
Rebecca K. Helm

Civil Recovery of Criminal Property
Colin King and Jennifer Hendry

The Insanity Defence
International and Comparative Perspectives
Ronnie Mackay and Warren Brookbanks

Justice In-Between
A Study of Intermediate Criminal Verdicts
Federico Picinali

Criminal Fraud and Election Disinformation
Law and Politics
Jeremy Horder

Policing the Borders Within
Ana Aliverti

Criminalizing Sex
A Unified Liberal Theory
Stuart P. Green

Reasons to Doubt
Wrongful Convictions and the Criminal Cases Review Commission
Carolyn Hoyle and Mai Sato

Fitness to Plead
International and Comparative Perspectives
Ronnie Mackay and Warren Brookbanks

Criminal Misconducts in Office
Law and Politics
Jeremy Horder

The Preventive Turn in Criminal Law
Henrique Carvalho

Criminal Justice and Taxation
Peter Alldridge

In Search of Criminal Responsibility
Ideas, Interests, and Institutions
Nicola Lacey

Preventive Justice
Andrew Ashworth and Lucia Zedner

Character in the Criminal Trial
Mike Redmayne

Homicide and the Politics of Law Reform
Jeremy Horder

The Insecurity State
Vulnerable Autonomy and the Right to Security in the Criminal Law
Peter Ramsay

Manifest Madness
Mental Incapacity in the Criminal Law
Arlie Loughnan

The Ethics of Plea Bargaining
Richard L. Lippke

Prosecuting Domestic Violence
A Philosophical Analysis
Michelle Madden Dempsey

Sentencing Discretion and the Constitution

Due Process of Time

DONALD A. DRIPPS

Class of 1975 Endowed Professor,
University of San Diego School of Law, USA

OXFORD
UNIVERSITY PRESS

OXFORD
UNIVERSITY PRESS

Oxford University Press is a department of the University of Oxford. It furthers the University's objective of excellence in research, scholarship, and education by publishing worldwide. Oxford is a registered trade mark of Oxford University Press in the UK and in certain other countries.

Published in the United States of America by Oxford University Press
198 Madison Avenue, New York, NY 10016, United States of America.

Library of Congress Cataloging-in-Publication Data
Names: Dripps, Donald A., 1957– author
Title: Sentencing discretion and the constitution : due process of time / Donald A. Dripps.
Description: New York : Oxford University Press, 2025. |
Series: Ox mono on criminal law justice series |
Includes bibliographical references and index.
Identifiers: LCCN 2025037767 (print) | LCCN 2025037768 (ebook) |
ISBN 9780197830369 hardback | ISBN 9780197830383 updf |
ISBN 9780197830390 online | ISBN 9780197830376 epub
Subjects: LCSH: Sentences (Criminal procedure) | Judicial discretion |
Judicial error | Punishment | Due process of law | Constitutional law
Classification: LCC K5121 .D75 2026 (print) | LCC K5121 (ebook) |
DDC 345/.0772—dc23/eng/20250814
LC record available at https://lccn.loc.gov/2025037767
LC ebook record available at https://lccn.loc.gov/2025037768

DOI: 10.1093/9780197830390.001.0001

Printed by Marquis Book Printing, Canada

The manufacturer's authorized representative in the EU for product safety is Oxford University Press España S.A. of Parque Empresarial San Fernando de Henares, Avenida de Castilla, 2–28830 Madrid (www.oup.es/en or product.safety@oup.com). OUP España S.A. also acts as importer into Spain of products made by the manufacturer.

Note to Readers

This publication is designed to provide accurate and authoritative information in regard to the subject matter covered. It is based upon sources believed to be accurate and reliable and is intended to be current as of the time it was written. It is sold with the understanding that the publisher is not engaged in rendering legal, accounting, or other professional services. If legal advice or other expert assistance is required, the services of a competent professional person should be sought. Also, to confirm that the information has not been affected or changed by recent developments, traditional legal research techniques should be used, including checking primary sources where appropriate.

(Based on the Declaration of Principles jointly adopted by a Committee of the American Bar Association and a Committee of Publishers and Associations.)

To the memory of Yale Kamisar, 1929–2022

Contents

Acknowledgments

I have worked on this project since at least 2016, when I benefited greatly from comments on a preliminary paper at a conference on Philosophical Perspectives on Criminal Procedure at the University of Toronto in November 2016. I am grateful to the organizers, Vincent Chiao, Chad Flanders, and Stephen Galoob, for including me, and from the insightful comments from the participants.

I owe a similar debt to the organizers and participants in a Southwest Crim conference held at the University of Nevada at Las Vegas in October 2018. I benefited in particular from the comments of Carissa Hessick, Justin Morneau, and Anders Kaye.

The University of San Diego has supported this project in countless ways. Four chapters were drafted during a research leave in 2018. Another leave, in 2025, permitted preparation of a final manuscript. The support of the librarians at USD's Legal Research Center was consistently superb. I give special thanks to Sasha Nunez for help on finalizing the footnotes.

Thanks to Mark Osler, Erik Luna, and George Fisher for valuable responses to research queries.

I am quite grateful for comments I received from those who reviewed the proposal for the press. If they compare their comments with the published volume, they will see just how constructive I found those comments.

Perhaps my greatest debt is to my colleagues at USD, in particular, Larry Alexander and Kevin Cole.

Given the book's long gestation period, it is probable I have omitted many others who deserve to be acknowledged. My apologies, in advance, for all such omissions.

Table of Cases

PART I
THE DOCTRINAL PROBLEM

1

The Problem of Prosecutorial Sentencing

A. Two Thought Experiments: *Prosecutorial Sentencing* versus *Theft in 229 Degrees*

Prosecutorial sentencing now poses the central problem in adjudicatory criminal procedure. To specialists on criminal justice, "prosecutorial sentencing" is an ordinary phrase referring to an everyday phenomenon. To others—even to lawyers who specialize in other fields—the phrase may seem alien and even something of an oxymoron.

Prosecutors decide whether to bring charges and then manage the presentation of the government's case. If the proceedings result in a conviction, sentencing is for the judge, not the prosecutor. That's how the process is commonly understood. The reality is very different. How do prosecutors determine sentences? Consider two, apparently artificial, thought experiments.

How is it possible for prosecutors, rather than judges, to exercise sentencing discretion? Call the first statute *Prosecutorial Sentencing*:

> §1 Grand theft, definition. Whoever exerts unauthorized control over property having a value in excess of $10,000, with the intent to permanently deprive the owner, commits grand theft, a felony.
>
> §2 Penalty. Grand theft is punishable by a term of imprisonment, to be determined, conclusively, by the attorney for the government, of not less than 12 nor more than 240 months.

Now compare another hypothetical statute, this one called *Theft in 229 Degrees*:

> §1 Grand theft, definition. Whoever exerts unauthorized control over property having a value in excess of $10,000, with the intent to permanently deprive the owner, commits grand theft, a felony.
>
> §2. Penalty. Grand theft shall be punished according to the degree of the offense.

Sentencing Discretion and the Constitution. Donald A. Dripps, Oxford University Press.
 DOI: 10.1093/9780197830390.003.0001

(a) Degrees of grand theft

1. Grand theft in the 229th degree is theft of property valued in excess of $10,000.00.
2. Grand theft in the 228th degree is theft of property valued in excess of $10,000.01.
3. Grand theft in the 227th degree is theft of property valued in excess of $10,000.02. . . .

229. Grand theft in the first degree is theft of property valued in excess of $10,002.40.

(b) Penalties.

1. Grand theft in the 229th degree shall be punished by 12 months imprisonment.
2. Grand theft in the 228th degree shall be punished by 13 months imprisonment.
3. Grand theft in the 227th degree shall be punished by 14 months imprisonment. . . .

229. Grand theft in the 1st degree shall be punished by 240 months imprisonment.

For purposes of this thought experiment, I shall posit some further institutional features of the criminal justice system in the jurisdiction where the statutes apply. First, in this jurisdiction the public prosecutor is an executive official and monopolizes the charging function. Private prosecution is unknown, and there are no other sovereigns with authority to punish crime as there might be in a federal system. Second, trial courts may not return a conviction for a more serious offense than the one charged, even if the evidence proves the higher charge to a practical certainty. Third, the courts will return a conviction on a lesser offense only when the evidence fails to prove the greater one charged.

I will stipulate one more fact. Not one case in a million will involve a theft of property with a value of more than $10,000 and less than $10,002.40.

The statute's operation is now easy to understand. When police have gathered enough evidence to convict a suspect of grand theft, the sentence imposed will be determined by the degree of the offense. The degree of the offense cannot exceed the degree charged by the prosecutor (because the courts may not convict of greater including offenses). Nor can the degree of the offense be less than that selected by the prosecutor, because the courts must convict of the offense charged if that offense is proved, even if the proof also shows less serious offenses. The prosecutor's finding of guilt can be challenged at a trial, but if the trial ends in a conviction, the sentence, up to the maximum penalty for theft in the first degree, is determined—completely determined—by the charge.

In some cases, there is no dispute about factual guilt. Suppose, for example, that after arrest, the suspect makes a voluntary confession. The confession admits the theft and directs the police to the location of the stolen goods. The goods were offered on an active market with a list price of $15,000, and inventory moved rapidly at this price. Absent some further quite extraordinary facts, the evidence proves grand theft in any of the 229 degrees the prosecutor chooses to charge.

In *229 Degrees*, the prosecutor's chosen sentence will be executed only following a conviction. By contrast, in *Prosecutorial Sentencing*, the prosecutor chooses the sentence after the conviction. There is, nonetheless, no practical difference between the two hypothetical statutes. No case comes out differently under one or the other. Where guilt is admitted or the proof conclusive, the prosecutor selects the sentence, including the discount for pleading guilty. Where the outcome of a trial is not certain, a plea deal would be worked out by agreeing to the sentence under the first statute and agreeing to the charge under the second. Either way, the risks and costs of trial would net out to the same sentence under both schemes.

Is *Prosecutorial Sentencing* constitutional? Even if we leave separation-of-powers issues aside, and even if we assume that indeterminate sentences are not vulnerable to challenge under the void-for-vagueness doctrine, there is an obvious due process problem. If "liberty" includes freedom from incarceration, and if "due process" means at least the right to be heard by a neutral tribunal, the answer would seem to be no.

A good law student who had taken the course in constitutional law, but not in criminal procedure—adjudication, would likely conclude that if the first statute is unconstitutional, the second statute must also be unconstitutional. As this last sentence implies, however, such a view would be naïve. Current doctrine insists on neutrality and regularity in adjudication, but not in charging decisions that have adjudicatory consequences. As we will see in the rest of this chapter, the actual system in the United States bears a close resemblance to *Theft in 229 Degrees*. Yet the basic elements of the system have survived constitutional challenge.

In the prosecutorial discretion cases, the Court's baseline for assessing prosecutorial charging decisions is the maximum penalty for the offender's conduct authorized by the legislature. When discretionary decisions about sentencing are made by other officials—judges, parole boards, and probation authorities—prevailing constitutional doctrine mirrors a long-standing legal commitment to a different baseline. Outside of charging decisions by prosecutors, discretionary decisions about incarceration are measured against a baseline of fair procedure.

The offender has no constitutional right to any particular sentence within a range, but does have a constitutional right to have discretion over the range exercised by a neutral decision maker after an opportunity to be heard. The Court compares prosecutorial decisions to the maximum penalty authorized by the entire penal code, but compares judicial decisions within statutory ranges to the outcomes produced by fair procedure. To illustrate the difference between them, let us reconsider our two hypothetical statutes.

From the code perspective, *229 Degrees* is permissible, since the prosecutor's charge selection does not deprive guilty defendants of any liberty they justly retain. It follows that secret decisions, without explanation, by one party to the case, are acceptable procedures for imposing decades of incarceration. There being no consequential difference between *229 Degrees* and *Prosecutorial Sentencing*, it follows further that plenary discretion over a nineteen-year range, by the initiator of the suit, without notice or reasons, is acceptable when exercised by prosecutors (even though neither the constitutional nor the statute law would permit judges or parole boards to proceed in this way).

By contrast, measured against the baseline set by fair procedure, *Prosecutorial Sentencing* is clearly unconstitutional, simply because conclusive discretion over liberty is exercised by a partisan. Neutral discretion should be, and nowadays typically is, exercised with the guidance of general standards and checked by appellate review. In unusual cases, the neutral sentence may end up harsher than the prosecutor's preference. A procedural baseline, however, is still a baseline, not an outcome. If a neutral decision pursuant to established guidelines survives appellate review, the procedural baseline gives the accused no right to a lesser penalty just because the prosecutor joins the appeal.

Given the equivalence between *Prosecutorial Sentencing* and *229 Degrees*, the procedural baseline, like the code one, leads to the same result for both statutes. From the procedural perspective, *229 Degrees* is unconstitutional because, while the offender has no right to any particular sentence below the legislative maximum, delegating determination of the precise sentence to the prosecutor still violates the right to a neutral decision after fair hearing. The only difference is the nominal one between "charging" and "sentencing."

These conclusions should disturb us. The code baseline is at odds with established law and widespread intuitions requiring judicial hearings before sentencing. The notion that sentencing could be transferred to prosecutors (or, for that matter, police) without violating due process seems implausible, even repugnant. On the other hand, the procedural baseline's condemnation of prosecutorial charging decisions with conclusive sentencing consequences is likewise at odds with prevailing law and seems in conflict with the executive's responsibility for law enforcement. Prevailing opinion and legal doctrine respecting charging and sentencing differ dramatically. Yet the hypotheticals show that under certain conditions, this bifurcation of charging and sentencing is counterfactual, either a fiction or a delusion.

B. A Story from the Real World

I initially described our hypotheticals as "apparently artificial." In fact, *229 Degrees* bears a close relationship to prevailing practice. Consider one illustrative case story.

In 2015, federal agents investigated methamphetamine distribution in Great Falls, Montana.[1] After undercover purchases from a local dealer, surveillance showed the dealer procuring methamphetamine from Tony Amato, a Great Falls roofer, age fifty. Surveillance of Amato determined that Amato went to Helena, ninety miles away, to procure additional inventory to resell in Great Falls.

Officers stopped Amato as he drove back to Great Falls from Helena. A search discovered 110.3 grams of 97.8 percent pure methamphetamine (for sentencing purposes, 107.8 grams of "actual methamphetamine"). Amato told investigators that Amato had obtained the methamphetamine from "a guy named Scott" in Helena. Amato identified a photograph of Scott Mitchell Bummer as Scott, Amato's supplier.

After obtaining a warrant, officers found a scale, plastic bags, and a safe in Bummer's home. The safe proved to contain a loaded revolver, another

[1] The facts are drawn from *United States v. Bummer*, No. 19-CV-00030, 2020 WL 33129 (D. Mont. Jan. 2, 2020), and the U.S. Attorney's Office Press Release. *See* Press Release, *Great Falls Roofer Sentenced to Seven Years in Prison*, U.S. Att'y Off., D. Mont. (Jan. 7, 2016), https://www.justice.gov/usao-mt/pr/great-falls-roofer-sentenced-seven-years-prison [https://perma.cc/CTR2-A7VY].

pistol, more than $7,000 in cash, a list of names with phone numbers, and 120.6 grams of 98 percent pure methamphetamine (118.1 grams of actual methamphetamine).

The rest of the story requires some background on the applicable law. The Controlled Substances Act (CSA) prohibits possessing methamphetamine with the intent to distribute. The CSA also includes a separate conspiracy provision. The penalties for both PWID (possession with intent to deliver) and conspiracy depend on the quantity of the illegal drug. For methamphetamine, the CSA provides a five-year minimum and a forty-year maximum for trafficking in more than five grams, and a ten-year minimum and a maximum of life for more than fifty grams.

The US Attorney's Office obtained an indictment charging both Amato and Bummer with two counts. Count I charged conspiracy to distribute fifty or more grams, and Count II charged possessing with intent to distribute fifty or more grams. Each count carries a ten-year minimum. Under the CSA and the Federal Sentencing Guidelines, convictions on both counts would not run consecutively unless the judge determined that the defendants deserved more than the maximum for one count—in this case, life. The judge, however, could not impose a sentence less than ten years, even if the sentences on each count were to run concurrently.

The prosecution offered both defendants the opportunity to plead guilty to a single count of possession with intent to distribute of five or more grams. Of course, both possessed more than fifty. Supreme Court precedent, however, holds that statutes creating minimum sentences based on drug quantity create distinct crimes. Unless the indictment includes an allegation of drug quantity, conviction does not require a minimum sentence. Instead, the judge will choose a sentence based on the federal guidelines. Again, under Supreme Court precedent, the judge has discretion to impose a sentence within the range advised by the guidelines.

On the drug charges, the prosecutors had discretion to choose one of three possible minimum sentences. If they elected to charge possession of fifty grams or more, the minimum would be ten years. If they elected to charge five grams or more, the minimum would be five years. If they alleged no quantity at all, there would be no minimum. Under the guidelines, a hundred grams of methamphetamine triggers Offense Level 30, which, for a first offender given full credit for "accepting responsibility," calls for seventy to eighty-seven months.

Amato pleaded guilty to possessing with intent to distribute more than five grams. The judge sentenced Amato to eighty-eight months. Amato's sentence was at the high range of the guidelines but significantly less than the ten-year mandatory minimum that would have applied if the government had put "fifty or more" instead of "five or more" grams in the indictment.

Bummer refused to plead guilty. In response, the government proceeded to trial on the two-count indictment alleging fifty grams, carrying a ten-year minimum. The government also added one count of possessing firearms in furtherance of a drug trafficking felony, based on the guns found in Bummer's safe. Conviction for a violation of this notorious "924(c)" statute triggers another five-year minimum, but by statute, the 924(c) sentence runs consecutively to the time imposed for all other counts.

Given the guns found with the meth in Bummer's safe, the government could choose among five different minimum sentences. The government could choose no minimum by not alleging drug quantity at all, or a five-year minimum by alleging five or more grams, or a ten-year minimum by alleging fifty grams. One 924(c) count would add another consecutive five years to the minimum for the drug convictions.

Bummer, however, had two guns next to the drugs and the cash. Ninth Circuit precedent permits multiple 924(c) convictions based on the possession of different guns, as long as each 924(c) charge is predicated on a different drug trafficking felony. Conspiracy and possession with intent to distribute are separate offenses, even if they relate to the same stash of drugs. So by predicating one gun charge on the PWID, and another on the conspiracy, the government could add ten years, consecutive, to the sentence on the drug charges.[2]

So, depending on what prosecutors chose to put in the indictment, Bummer might have faced no minimum, a five-year minimum, a ten-year minimum, a fifteen-year minimum, or a twenty-year minimum. As it happened, the government alleged fifty grams and one firearms violation for both guns. Bummer was convicted at trial in 2016. Even though the guidelines recommended *more* than ten years on the drug charges, the judge imposed "only" the ten-year minimum, plus the five consecutive years for the

[2] United States v. Lopez, 37 F.3d 565, 569 (9th Cir. 1994) ("the firearm charged in count four was linked to the possession with intent to distribute charged in count three. And the firearms charged in count five were linked to the conspiracy charged in count one. Therefore, each firearm was tied to a separate offense."), *vacated on other grounds*, 516 U.S. 1022 (1995). Whether a single gun possessed in furtherance of a single discrete act that violated two different statutes would support two convictions under 924(c) is doubtful. *See* United States v. Andrade, 993 F. Supp. 2d 1269, 1285–86 (D. Nev. 2014). *Lopez*, however, remains good law. United States v. Lopez, 100 F.3d 98, 105 (9th Cir. 1996) (affirming on remand the linked charges of counts three and four, *Lopez*, 37 F.3d 565). In Bummer's case, there were two predicate offenses and two guns.

gun charge. In March 2025, a query to the Federal Bureau of Prisons website showed an expected release date for Scott Mitchell Bummer, now age sixty, of June 2, 2028.[3]

We began this chapter with theoretical examples that now appear very real. Prosecutors, not judges, decided that Tony Amato would serve seven years and Scott Bummer would serve fifteen years for the same conspiracy. Even the prosecutors did not believe either defendant deserved fifteen years. If they had believed that, they wouldn't have offered the five-gram plea deal to both Amato and Bummer. Yet under current law, the government was free to threaten fifteen years (or even twenty) because those minimum sentences were below the maximum set by the entire penal code for the defendants' conduct.

As a doctrinal matter, "real world" sentencing looks very close to *229 Degrees*. *229 Degrees* is indistinguishable from *Prosecutorial Sentencing*. And *Prosecutorial Sentencing* is unconstitutional—obviously unconstitutional.

C. Three Hard Problems

Prosecutorial sentencing raises three connected (and very difficult) problems. The first is a doctrinal problem. When judges exercise sentencing discretion, the Supreme Court's decisions require adversary hearings where the defendant has the right to counsel. If a prosecutor communicates information about sentencing, or a recommendation as to sentence, without contemporaneous notice to the defense, due process requires vacating the sentence.[4] Even if the same information is made available to the defense before imposition of sentence, a prosecutor who tries, secretly, to influence the sentencing judge violates due process.[5]

[3] *Federal Inmates by Name*, FED. BUREAU OF PRISONS, https://www.bop.gov/mobile/find_inmate/byname.jsp [https://perma.cc/U7LD-QYT7].

[4] *See* Haller v. Robbins, 409 F.2d 857 (1st Cir. 1969) (remand for rehearing to develop evidence as to the truth of the allegations in the prosecution's pre-sentence ex parte communication); United States v. Solomon, 422 F.2d 1110 (7th Cir. 1970) (formulation of prospective rule requiring disclosure to the defendant of prosecution's pre-sentence memorandum); United States v. Rosner, 485 F.2d 1213 (2d Cir. 1973) (remand for resentencing by a newly drawn judge, when the original sentencing judge had received ex parte a pre-sentence memorandum from the prosecution and had not disclosed the voluminous contents to the defendant until immediately before announcement of the sentence).

[5] *Haller*, 409 F.2d at 860 ("Having in mind that the prosecutor would later be permitted to make the same statement in open court, the presiding judge may well have regarded a premature disclosure as a pardonable informality. It is not.").

Yet the same prosecutors who are forbidden to influence in secret the exercise of judicial discretion have their own discretion to make decisions that actually *control* the sentence. In general, "so long as the prosecutor has probable cause to believe that the accused committed an offense defined by statute, the decision whether or not to prosecute, and what charge to file or bring before a grand jury, generally rests entirely in his discretion."[6] When the defendant's conduct meets the terms of two statutes, one requiring a higher penalty than the other, discretion over "what charge to file or bring before a grand jury" amounts to prosecutorial sentencing discretion.

Two theoretical problems, common to many systems around the world, underlie the contradiction in American constitutional doctrine. One is the baseline problem in criminal procedure. Our criminal procedure relies on guilty pleas for more than 90 percent of convictions. Defendants plead guilty to obtain a reduction in their expected sentences. In many cases, the gap between the sentence likely after conviction by plea and the sentence likely after conviction by trial can be measured not just by years but by decades of imprisonment. The Supreme Court characterizes these pleas as voluntary, even though, as a commonsense matter, doing anything to avoid years in prison sounds coerced.

If, however, we characterize the baseline for assessing voluntariness as the maximum sentence permitted by the applicable statutes, the defendant is not entitled to the plea offer. For clarity, I'll call the menu of all possible offenses the prosecutor might allege for the defendant's conduct the "code maximum." I'll use "statutory maximum" to refer to the maximum sentence a judge can select for a particular offense of conviction. When prosecutors decline to charge every offense the code permits, or judges impose a sentence below the statutory maximum for the offense of conviction, the defendant is getting a break, rather than being strong-armed. So says the Court. But this is a fiction.

Typical penal codes create multiple offenses, each carrying severe maximum penalties. Legislatures do not intend to inflict all these penalties. They do not vote for the appropriations that would be required even to attempt this. Our penal codes create so many crimes and authorize so many penalties that prosecutors and judges make almost all decisions about how severely offenders will be punished. The Supreme Court's mantra that legislatures

[6] Bordenkircher v. Hayes, 434 U.S. 357, 364 (1978).

should define crimes and fix penalties is a fig leaf that quite fails to conceal the reality.

The challenge to those who criticize the current guilty plea system is to justify a baseline other than the code and statutory maximums. The alternatives thus far on offer, however, are subject to familiar and powerful objections. The logical baseline is the set of charges under the code maximum, and the sentence under the statutory maxima, that is proportionate to the defendant's culpability. It is common ground that the maximum allowed by the array of charges our penal codes include far exceeds the defendant's culpability.

Yet this approach to the baseline problem runs into the other intractable theoretical problem—proportionality. We might say that Scott Bummer's fifteen-year sentence was excessive by reference to Tony Amato's seven-year sentence. We might with equal logic say that by reference to Bummer's sentence, Amato's was too lenient. Do the guns in Bummer's home justify a sentence twice as long, when they were not, as far as we know, ever carried in public, let alone brandished or fired? What responsibility does Amato bear for Bummer's guns, given their ongoing and mutually profitable business venture? Bummer struck his lawyers as worthy of an examination to determine his competence to stand trial. Amato was a man no longer young. How, if at all, should these variations among offenses and offenders be reduced to some index of culpability? And by what moral metric could any assessment of culpability justify some precise punishment—no more and no less—as condign?

The literature on the substantive criminal law offers no standard view of just what punishment proportionate to culpability means. There is, in fact, something of a consensus that proportioning punishments to culpability is not just elusive but unachievable. That's a conclusion quite as shocking as the guilty-pleas-are-voluntary doctrine. Without some sense of proportionality, how can we justify treating some torts as crimes, some crimes as felonies, and some felonies as categorically more serious than others?

Indeed, proportionality's role in criminal law theory has become fundamental. For retributivists, the purpose of criminal law *is* simply to impose punishment commensurate with desert.[7] Utilitarians, faced with the more

[7] *See, e.g.*, LARRY ALEXANDER & KIMBERLY KESSLER FERZAN, CRIME AND CULPABILITY 18 (2009) ("[T]he criminal law should be primarily structured to ensure to a considerable degree that actors are not punished in the criminal law more than they deserve but are punished to the extent that they deserve.").

sinister implications of cost-benefit analysis, generally have adopted retributive proportionality as an upper limit on sentences otherwise justified by favorable consequences.[8] Expressivists acknowledge that the law's moral message depends in part on the consistency of sentences with prevailing opinions about proportionate punishment.[9]

One might say that the defendant is entitled to the set of charges and the usual penalty that would be predicted based on prior cases. Agnosticism about proportionality infects this alternative, too. How do we know that the punishments imposed on previous cases even resemble justice if we can't justify a proportionality metric?

If the Justices really were committed to the statutory-maximum baseline, they wouldn't—as they have in a well-established line of cases—require adversary sentencing hearings. According to the plea bargaining cases, the conviction extinguishes the offender's right to liberty up to the statutory maximum. If the defendant had a free-standing right to a fair procedure, the sentencing hearing cases make sense. But whence comes this right, if not from the risk that at least some sentences within the statutory range would be unjust?

Both bodies of criminal law—the substantive and the procedural—contradict their fundamental principles. Innocent people can (and do) decide quite rationally to plead guilty. Some offenders receive penalties more severe than even the most exaggerated description of their culpability. The most culpable are the most likely recipients of favorable plea deals. Those highest up in criminal hierarchies have information that can be very valuable to prosecutors. Others, less culpable, do not.

[8] Hart published his influential characterization of general purpose subject to limiting principles in 1968. H. L. A. Hart, Punishment and Responsibility 9 (1968) ("it is perfectly consistent to assert *both* that the General Justifying Aim of the practice of punishment is its beneficial consequences and that the pursuit of this General Justifying Aim should be qualified or restricted out of deference to principles of Distribution which require that the punishment should only of an offender for an offence."). Hart himself was not explicitly utilitarian, but modern utilitarians generally have embraced his mixed-theory model. *See, e.g.*, Andrew von Hirsch, Doing Justice: The Choice of Punishments 51 (1976) ("while deterrence accounts for why punishment is socially useful, desert is necessary to explain why that utility may justly be pursued at the offender's expense") (footnote omitted). In collaboration with Andrew Ashworth, Andrew von Hirsch has now moved to a censure theory that incorporates expressivist and crime control elements. *See* Andrew von Hirsch and Andrew Ashworth, Proportionate Sentencing: Exploring the Principles (2005).

[9] *See* R. A. Duff, Trials and Punishments 280–81 (1986).

D. Overview of the Argument

The relationship between our three problems is apparent. The doctrinal problem results from the theoretical failure to justify a baseline in criminal procedure. Deciding cases ad hoc, the Supreme Court has adopted a procedural baseline for assessing judicial sentencing discretion, but a different baseline, set by the maximum sentence permitted by the penal code, for assessing prosecutorial sentencing discretion. Without a satisfactory account of proportioning punishment to desert, there is no normative basis for either the procedural or the positive-law baseline.

The book proposes a resolution of all three problems by characterizing the right against disproportionate punishment as a right to procedural justice. Every justice system will convict innocent people. Deontologists have given different justifications for fallible systems, but all of them depend on procedural justice in the sense that when meticulously fair procedures convict the innocent, enforcing the apparently true but factually false conviction inflicts *undeserved* yet *justified* suffering. Proponents of this view include John Rawls and Ronald Dworkin.

The book adopts such a procedural justice understanding of the individual offender's right against disproportionate punishment, by treating punishment exceeding desert as morally equivalent to convicting the innocent. If meticulously fair procedures justify systems that convict the innocent, they likewise justify systems that inflict disproportionate punishment. By "meticulously fair," I mean procedures that do more to protect the individual against injustice than would the procedures called for by distribution-indifferent calculations of costs and benefits.

If that account succeeds, the baseline for distinguishing threats and offers in the plea bargaining process is the right against disproportionate punishment. If that right is best understood in terms of procedural justice, the system is justified in inflicting undeserved (because excessive) punishment as long as fair procedures lead to the sentence. This account offers a moral grounding for the procedural baseline. As long as fair procedures set the limit of an offender's retributive desert, society has satisfied the offender's right against disproportionate punishment. If the book's arguments are persuasive, important consequences would follow in the real world of criminal justice.

Part I develops, in depth, the doctrinal problem presented by legislative delegations of sentencing discretion to prosecutors. Chapter 5, the last chapter in Part I, shows in considerable detail that the doctrinal problem cannot be solved by invoking tradition, because prosecutorial sentencing has no deep roots in history. Part II explains the theoretical challenges that have made the doctrinal problem so stubborn. Part III defends an account of proportionate punishment as procedural justice.

2
The Anomaly of Prosecutorial Sentencing Discretion

A. Bentham versus Beccaria: Is Delegation of Sentencing Discretion Inevitable?

Liberal democracies trust elected legislatures, despite their flaws, with defining crimes and assigning punishments. "Whatever views may be entertained regarding severity of punishment, whether one believes in its efficacy or its futility, these are peculiarly questions of legislative policy."[1] Legislatures, however, have no capacity to specify the precise penalty for every possible combination of offenses and offenders.

We cannot say this view is unanimous, because one eccentric figure argued for legislation defining specific discrete offenses, and affixing to each a single discrete penalty. If this lone dissenter were a lesser figure than Cesare Beccaria, it might be unnecessary to seriously consider the premise that legislatures have no choice but to delegate substantial discretion over sentencing. Beccaria's views, even when time has passed them by, deserve a serious hearing.

Beccaria condemned judicial interpretation of penal laws,[2] claims of situational excuse,[3] and executive clemency.[4] The code he imagined would consist of mutually exclusive offenses, each with a single specific penalty:

[1] Gore v. United States, 357 U.S. 386, 393 (1958) (citation omitted).

[2] Cesare Beccaria, An Essay on Crimes and Punishments 16 (Piccadilly, J. Almon 1767) ("The disorders, that may arise from a rigorous observance of penal laws, are not to be compared with those produced by the interpretation of them.").

[3] *Id.* at 26–27:

> THEY err, therefore, who imagine, that a crime is greater, or less, according to the intention of the person by whom it is committed; for this will depend on the actual impression of objects on the senses, and on the previous disposition of the mind; both which will vary in different persons, and even in the same person at different times, according to the succession of ideas, passions, and circumstances. Upon that system, it would be necessary to form, not only a particular code for every individual, but a new penal law for every crime.

[4] *Id.* at 176:

Sentencing Discretion and the Constitution. Donald A. Dripps, Oxford University Press.
 DOI: 10.1093/9780197830390.003.0002

> IN every criminal cause the judge should reason syllogistically. The *major* should be the general law; the *minor*, the conformity of the action, or its opposition to the laws; the *conclusion*, liberty, or punishment. If the judge be obliged by the imperfection of the laws, or chuses, to make any other, or more syllogisms than this, it will be an introduction to uncertainty.[5]

Jeremy Bentham, on much else, Beccaria's disciple and an intemperate critic of judicial discretion generally, made the case against such "syllogistic" jurisprudence.

Bentham agreed that the legislature should "as much as possible, . . . determine everything relating to punishments, for two reasons: that they may be *certain*, and *impartial*."[6] Moreover, judges might find it too "arduous" to do the psychologically taxing work of measuring punishment case by case. To specify every sentence for every case by general legislation, however, was not within the realm of what is "possible."

"There may, however, often arise, either with regard to offences themselves, or the person of the delinquent, unforeseen and particular circumstances, which would be productive of great inconveniences, if the law were altogether inflexible."[7] Offenders are not all equally responsible or dangerous, nor do all experience identical punishments with the same degree of pain. "Other circumstances may render it expedient to change the kind of punishment: that which has been directed by the law may be incapable of application, or it may be less suitable in other respects."[8]

Systems around the world delegate sentencing discretion. Typically, however, sentencing discretion is delegated to judges rather than to prosecutors. Bentham, as we will see later, left most sentences to discretion, but only when discretion was informed by legislatively defined circumstances of aggravation and mitigation, and exercised by neutral, transparent tribunals. The doctrinal problem in the United States follows from the relatively recent

> Clemency is a virtue which belongs to the legislator, and not to the executor of the laws; a virtue which ought to shine in the code, and not in private judgment. To shew mankind, that crimes are sometimes pardoned, and that punishment is not the necessary consequence, is to nourish the flattering hope of impunity, and is the cause of their considering every punishment inflicted as an act of injustice and oppression.

[5] *Id.* at 14.

[6] Jeremy Bentham, *Principles of Penal Law*, in 1 THE WORKS OF JEREMY BENTHAM 365, 516 (John Bowring ed., 1843).

[7] *Id.* at 517.

[8] *Id.*

delegation of general sentencing discretion to prosecutors. How did this happen, and why does it continue?

B. How Prosecutorial Sentencing Discretion Emerged in the "Steroid Era" of Criminal Justice

In the United States today, *229 Degrees* bears a close resemblance to the everyday operation of the criminal justice system. It follows that the choice between the statutory and procedural baselines is more than theoretically interesting. The decision to embrace the statutory baseline for charging decisions has had profound practical consequences, as would a fresh decision to apply to charging decisions the procedural baseline that governs sentencing decisions.

American sports fans remember the 1990s as Major League Baseball's "steroid era."[9] During this period, the use of performance-enhancing drugs led to massive physiques and more, longer, home runs. After a period of exhilaration, fans turned against the players who had broken both league policy and federal criminal law. Baseball is still coping with the long-term damage players did to themselves, and the problem of assessing records achieved during the now generally reviled "steroid era."

This same period saw a steroid era in criminal justice. The system's executive muscle—police at the front end of the process and corrections at the back end—grew rapidly. The resources devoted to adjudication—judges, prosecutors, and public defenders—grew very little. In effect, the system splurged on crime control and scrimped on due process. To begin with policing:

> From 1992 . . . to 2004, State and local law enforcement agencies added about 230,400 full-time employees, including 123,800 sworn officers and 106,600 nonsworn employees. During this time the number of violent crimes handled by law enforcement agencies nationwide decreased by more than 565,000.[10]

[9] This section was initially published in D. A. Dripps, *Guilt, Innocence and Due Process of Plea Bargaining*, 57 Wm. & Mary L. Rev. 1343 (2016), and is used by permission.

[10] Bureau of Just. Stat., U.S. Dep't of Just., BJS Bull. NCJ 212749, Census of State and Local Law Enforcement Agencies, 2004, at 3 (June 2007) (figures omitted), https://bjs.ojp.gov/content/pub/pdf/csllea04.pdf [https://perma.cc/84WW-WXYY].

That amounts to a 27.2 percent increase in overall employees and a 20.4 percent increase in the number of sworn officers.

Not only did law enforcement agencies deploy more officers, but those officers also made more arrests than they had before. In 1980, police made 9,703,181 arrests.[11] In 2000, there were 13,980,297, roughly 40 percent more than in 1980.[12] During the 1990s, crime fell sharply. The homicide rate per 100,000 population was 20.2 in 1980, 9.4 in 1990, and 5.5 in 2000.[13]

The higher arrest rate translated into more prosecutions. From 1987 to 2004, state criminal court filings rose by 67 percent.[14] The incarceration rate rose too, from 139 prisoners per 100,000 population in 1980 to 292 in 1990 to 478 in 2000.[15] So during a period of falling crime rates, the number of prosecutions and the number of prisoners per capita rose by roughly two-thirds.

The resources devoted to adjudicating criminal cases failed to keep pace. From 1987 to 2004, "State trial courts increased judicial staffing by 11% overall, adding 2600 judges in courts across the country."[16] Between 1992 and 2001, the number of state prosecutors rose 39 percent.[17] The system's neglected stepchild, indigent defense, has not fared that well. "From 1999 to 2007, public defender program caseloads increased by 20% while staffing increased by 4%."[18]

An increasing reliance on guilty pleas enabled the system to cope with caseloads that rose far faster than the resources for adjudication. In the federal system, in 1980, "one defendant went to trial for every four who pled guilty. By 1999, that ratio fell to one in twenty."[19] Defendants, however, have

11 Fed. Bureau of Investigation, U.S. Dep't of Just., Crime in the United States 1980, at 200 tbl.32 (1981).

12 Fed. Bureau of Investigation, U.S. Dep't of Just., Crime in the United States 2000, at 216 tbl.29 (2001).

13 Homicide data are from the FBI's Uniform Crime Reporting Statistics, available at https://www.fbi.gov/how-we-can-help-you/more-fbi-services-and-information/ucr/publications.

14 Bureau of Just. Stat., U.S. Dep't of Just., BJS Special Rep. NCJ 217996, State Court Organization, 1987-2004, at 2 (Oct. 2007), https://bjs.ojp.gov/content/pub/pdf/sco8704.pdf [https://perma.cc/DM73-DTFD].

15 The incarceration rates are taken from BJS Sourcebook of Criminal Justice Statistics Online table 6.29.2012 available at https://wayback.archive-it.org/org-652/20230414115855/https://www.albany.edu/sourcebook/pdf/t6292012.pdf.

16 State Court Organization, *supra* note 14, at 2.

17 Bureau of Just. Stat., U.S. Dep't of Just., BJS Bull. NCJ 193441, National Survey of Prosecutors: Prosecutors in State Courts, 2001, at 2 (May 2002), https://bjs.ojp.gov/content/pub/pdf/psc01.pdf [https://perma.cc/Y9XG-9RPA].

18 Bureau of Just. Stat., U.S. Dep't of Just., BJS Special Rep. NCJ 228229, State Public Defender Programs, 2007, at 17 (Sept. 2010), https://bjs.ojp.gov/content/pub/pdf/spdp07.pdf [https://perma.cc/WX54-Q8EG].

19 Irwin H. Schwartz, *Consequences of the Disappearing Criminal Jury Trial*, Champion, Nov. 2001, at 7.

a constitutional right to trial, and under *Jones v. Barnes*,[20] they are not required to accept the advice of counsel to plead guilty. How did the system induce defendants to plead at much higher rates than had prevailed hitherto? Prosecutors needed more leverage, and they got it.

The two key developments were sentencing guidelines and statutory mandatory minimum sentences.[21] The prosecutor's selection of the charges came to control the sentence imposed, as long as the prosecution could credibly threaten conviction at trial. By charging possessory offenses that can be established solely by officer testimony—"proxy crimes" such as possession with intent to distribute and felon-in-possession-of-a-firearm—prosecutors could avoid the perils of civilian witnesses susceptible to either threats or claims of loyalty. Absent judicial discretion over sentencing, which guidelines and mandatory minimums curtailed, prosecutors could credibly threaten catastrophic consequences based on charges that could be proved beyond reasonable doubt with officer testimony.

The discretionary power of state prosecutors is less complete than that of their federal counterparts but still substantial. About half of the states have sentencing guidelines, and all of them have mandatory minimums for some offenses.[22] In the state courts, guilty pleas account for 95 percent of felony convictions.[23]

In this world of guilty pleas, charge selection, in a great many cases, is not the beginning of an adversarial process but the outcome of the case, practically speaking. More than ample evidence points to the guilt of the typical defendant. Catastrophic trial penalties make the prosecution's plea offer all but inevitable.

[20] 463 U.S. 745 (1983).

[21] *See, e.g.*, Ronald F. Wright, *Trial Distortion and the End of Innocence in Federal Criminal Justice*, 154 U. PA. L. REV. 79, 85 (2005):

> The federal system over the last three decades has featured increasingly severe sentences, and the adoption of federal sentencing guidelines in the late 1980s enhanced the power of prosecutors and judges to reward cooperation from defendants. In those districts where prosecutors took full advantage of the tools available to them under the sentencing laws, it became more expensive than ever for a federal defendant to insist on a trial; fewer paid the price each year.

[22] *See* Ben Trachtenberg, *State Sentencing and New Prison Admissions*, 38 U. MICH. J. L. REF. 479, 487 (2005).

[23] Wright, *supra* note 21, at 90 n.36.

C. Case Examples

Some examples illustrate how charging has taken over sentencing. Begin with *Harmelin v. Michigan*,[24] the leading Supreme Court precedent upholding long mandatory sentences against attack under the Eighth Amendment's Cruel and Unusual Punishments Clause. Police stopped Harmelin for a traffic offense and subsequently discovered evidence of drug dealing, including 672.5 grams of powder cocaine, in Harmelin's car. At the time, Michigan's "650-lifer" law required judges to impose a sentence of life without parole on anyone convicted of possessing more than 650 grams of cocaine. The statute attempted to prevent plea bargaining by requiring that any dismissal of charges after arraignment on motion of the prosecutor be with prejudice.[25]

The legislature's attempt to prevent plea bargaining was unsuccessful. The parties could negotiate before arraignment. Even after arraignment, apparently it was possible for prosecutors to dismiss the 650-gram charge and then bring a new charge of some non-included lesser offense, such as conspiracy to distribute.[26]

Tim Allen, the now-famous television celebrity, could have been prosecuted under the 650-lifer law. He was arrested transporting more than 650 grams.[27] In exchange for information about other dealers, the

[24] Harmelin v. Michigan, 501 U.S. 957 (1991).

[25] *See* People v. Matthews, 371 N.W.2d 887, 896 (Mich. Ct. App. 1985) ("Section 7415(1) provides that upon arraignment of a defendant on certain drug offenses, the 'examining magistrate shall not dismiss the case upon motion of the prosecuting attorney unless the dismissal is with prejudice,' and that the magistrate may not permit the prosecutor to reduce the charge against the defendant."); People v. Kidd, 328 N.W.2d 394, 395 (Mich. Ct. App. 1982) ("Section 7415 was enacted to foreclose the use of a reduction in charges in negotiating guilty pleas.").

[26] *See* People v. Siebert, 507 N.W.2d 211 (Mich. Ct. App. 1993). In *Siebert*, the prosecutor dismissed the delivery of a 650-gram charge and filed a fresh information charging conspiracy to distribute between 225 and 650 grams. Conspiracy requires an agreement with another but not actual possession, and the possession charge did not require any agreement. The dismissal of the possession charge with prejudice, therefore, did not bar the conspiracy charge. Most such agreements would not be reported. *Siebert* was unusual in that the sentencing judge came in below the sentences prescribed by the agreement, and the prosecution then moved, ultimately successfully, to set the agreement aside.

[27] *See* Heather Waugh, *"I'm Not the Same Guy": Tim Allen Recalls His Time in Prison for Drug Trafficking as He Says, "I'm Extremely Grateful for Where I Am Today,"* Daily Mail (Mar. 31, 2017), http://www.dailymail.co.uk/tvshowbiz/article-4368640/Tim-Allen-recalls-prison-stint-drug-trafficking.html [https://perma.cc/VX58-72DM]; *see also* Laura Sager, *Advocating for Change in Mandatory Minimum Sentencing*, 16 T.M. Cooley L. Rev. 27, 32 (1999):

> Tim Allen, the star of Home Improvement . . . was arrested in Michigan for delivery of well over 650 grams of cocaine. If he had been charged as a '650 defendant,' he would still be in prison. But, he had information to trade and instead he spent two and one-half years in federal prison.

prosecution agreed to refer him for federal prosecution and not to charge him under Michigan law.[28] Allen served two years in federal prison and went on to great success. Harmelin either had no comparable information or refused to share what he knew. Either way, the choice between two years and life without parole was made, practically speaking, by executive branch officials who were more interested in law enforcement than in just deserts. In cases like Harmelin's, charge selection doesn't just set parameters for sentencing. In functional terms, charge selection simply *is* sentencing.

Federal prosecutors generally have at least as much control over sentencing as their state counterparts. The Sentencing Guidelines constrain federal judges. Those guidelines are now advisory, but they exert considerable gravitational force. Moreover, the US Attorney's offices have discretion to charge violations of numerous statutes carrying mandatory minimum sentences.

One notorious example is *United States v. Angelos.*[29] According to an informant, the defendant, Weldon Angelos, sold eight ounces of marijuana to the informant on three occasions. The informant saw a gun at two of these sales. Agents found additional firearms at the home of Angelos and his girlfriend. Under 18 U.S.C. § 924(c), carrying a firearm during and in relation to any drug trafficking is subject to a mandatory five-year minimum sentence for the first offense, and a mandatory twenty-five-year minimum sentence for each subsequent offense, with probation disallowed and all sentences to run consecutively.

The US Attorney's office charged three distribution counts, one 924(c) count and two lesser charges. The government told the defense that

> if he pled guilty to the drug distribution count and the § 924(c) count, the government would agree to drop all other charges, not supersede the indictment with additional counts, and recommend a prison sentence of 15 years. The government made clear to Mr. Angelos that if he rejected the offer, the government would obtain a new superseding indictment adding several § 924(c) counts that could lead to Mr. Angelos facing more than 100 years of mandatory prison time.[30]

When the defendant refused to plead, the government then "obtained two superseding indictments, eventually charging twenty total counts, including

[28] Sager, *supra* note 27, at 32.
[29] 345 F. Supp. 2d 1227 (D. Utah 2004) (Cassell, J.).
[30] *Id.* at 1231.

five § 924(c) counts which alone carried a potential minimum mandatory sentence of 105 years."[31] The prosecution rebuffed subsequent defense efforts to reopen plea discussions, and after a trial, the jury convicted on sixteen counts, including three 924(c) charges.[32]

Angelos had no significant criminal history, so on the drug charges, the Guidelines prescribed a range of seventy-eight to ninety-seven months.[33] The 924(c) mandatory minimums, however, added fifty-five years (five years on the first count, and twenty-five each on the second and third counts, which the government added only after the refusal to plead). With manifest reluctance, Judge Cassell rejected the defendant's Eighth Amendment challenge to the sentence.[34]

Angelos was lucky enough to be resentenced and released in 2016.[35] Under the original sentence, if he lived long enough to serve it, he would have been released in November 2051.[36] As it happened, his "release allowed Angelos to see the son he left at age 7 graduate from high school[.]"[37]

The First Step Act, adopted after Angelos was released, limits the mandatory sentence for each 924(c) count to five years (the twenty-five-year sentence still applies if the defendant had a final 924(c) conviction prior to the instant prosecution).[38] Under the current law, three 924(c) convictions would add "only" fifteen years, mandatory and consecutive to any sentences for drug trafficking.

The case of Edward Lamar Young is another notorious example. According to the appellate court that upheld his sentence:

> Edward Young received a mandatory fifteen-year prison sentence for the crime of possessing seven shotgun shells in a drawer. He came into possession of the shells while helping a neighbor sell her late husband's possessions. When he eventually discovered them, he did not realize that

[31] *Id.* at 1232.
[32] *Id.*
[33] *Id.*
[34] *Id.* at 1256–60.
[35] Greg Jaffe & Sari Horwitz, *Utah Man Whose Long Drug Sentence Stirred Controversy Is Released*, WASH. POST (June 3, 2016), https://www.washingtonpost.com/politics/president-obama-just-commuted-the-sentences-of-42-people-here-are-their-names/2016/06/03/08f23b7c-29c3-11e6-a3c4-0724e8e24f3f_story.html.
[36] *See Angelos*, 345 F. Supp. 2d at 1239.
[37] Jaffe & Horwitz, *supra* note 35.
[38] *See, e.g.*, U.S. SENT'G COMM'N, THE FIRST STEP ACT OF 2018: ONE YEAR OF IMPLEMENTATION 34–35 (2020), https://www.ussc.gov/sites/default/files/pdf/research-and-publications/research-publications/2020/20200831_First-Step-Report.pdf [https://perma.cc/XCU4-4LKZ].

> his legal disability against possessing firearms—resulting from felonies committed some twenty years earlier—extended to ammunition. *See* 18 U.S.C. § 922(g)(1). Under the Armed Career Criminal Act (ACCA), Young received a mandatory fifteen-year sentence.[39]

Young's record included burglaries committed twenty years earlier, in some of which he stole, inter alia, firearms. Young, however, "owned no compatible gun, and there is no evidence that he intended to use the shells in a crime, had ever used any weapon in any crime, or would provide the shells to someone who would use them in a crime."[40]

Like Judge Cassell in *Angelos*, the judges in *Young* condemned the sentence the law compelled them to impose. They quoted this language from a prior decision: "'The striking and troublesome harshness [of a fifteen-year sentence for felon in possession of a firearm] . . . is but a particularly clear example of our sometimes difficult duty to apply the policy choices of Congress, rather than our own.'"[41] The truth, however, is that the judges were applying the policy choices of the US Attorney's office.

Prosecutorial sentencing is commonplace in state prosecutions, too. Despite some welcome but modest recent retrenchment, the states have mandatory recidivism enhancements as well as specific statutory minimum sentences based on factors such as drug quantity or use of a firearm.[42] For example, Idaho punishes the possession of explicit child pornography by up to ten years, with no minimum. If, however, the offender has a prior conviction for similar offenses, a separate statute provides a mandatory minimum and consecutive sentence of fifteen years.[43]

Idaho, like many jurisdictions, counts each child-pornographic image as a separate offense.[44] Because offenders typically possess multiple images, the recidivism statute enables prosecutorial sentencing. If the prosecutor does not allege the prior conviction, the judge has discretion to sentence up to ten years on each count, and to make the sentences on multiple counts run concurrently. In the alternative, the prosecutor can allege the prior conviction and as many specific images as the evidence supports. The menu then includes zero-to-ten, zero-to-ten plus fifteen maximum and consecutive,

39 United States v. Young, 766 F.3d 621, 623 (6th Cir. 2014) (per curiam).
40 *Id.* at 627.
41 *Id.* at 628 (citation omitted).
42 *See, e.g.*, John B. Meixner Jr., *Shocking Sentences*, 100 Ind. L. J. 137, 153–59 (2024).
43 Idaho Code Ann. §§18-1507(3), 19-2520G (West 2025).
44 State v. Gillespie, 316 P.3d 126 (Idaho Ct. App. 2013).

zero-to-ten plus thirty maximum and consecutive, and so on. The Idaho Supreme Court rejected a separation-of-powers challenge to this arrangement.[45] Due process is another matter.

D. The Institutional Architecture of Prosecutorial Sentencing Discretion

(1) How the Legislature Gets Cut Out: Delegation

In the United States, criminal codes now include (1) laws that define forbidden conduct broadly to include conduct that does not threaten the harm the law aims to prevent, including minimal participation as an accomplice or conspirator; (2) multiple statutory offenses, with different penalties, including mandatory minimums, applicable to the same conduct; and (3) authorize sentences higher than the legislature expects to be imposed. The paradigm of these pathologies is federal criminal law, which is not a unitary code but rather one list of offenses in U.S. Code Title 18, plus dozens of other crimes, many serious, spread throughout the rest of the federal statutes. For example, drug trafficking crimes, including mandatory minimum sentences based on drug quantity, are defined by the Controlled Substances Act, located in U.S. Code Title 21, "Food and Drugs."

In federal law, examples of sweeping legislative delegations to federal prosecutors abound. Congress has not *required* prosecution under any of these overbroad and draconian statutes. Congress *authorized* prosecutors to file (or not to file) the 924(c) charges in *Angelos*. In *Young*, the federal felon-in-possession charge automatically triggered the fifteen-year minimum if, at sentencing, his criminal history included the required prior convictions. The government, however, was not required to charge Young with any federal offense at all. He was facing multiple burglary charges in state court, which were dropped after the federal prosecution.[46] What was exceptional in Young's case was not the overlap of more punitive federal law and less punitive state law but the decision to proceed federally in the particular case.

[45] State v. Barr, 555 P.3d 1082 (Idaho 2024).

[46] Todd South, *A Few Shotgun Shells Landed a Man 15 Years in Prison*, Chattanooga (TN) Times Free Press (July 21, 2013), http://www.timesfreepress.com/news/local/story/2013/jul/21/a-few-shotgun-shells-landed-a-man-15/113861/ [https://perma.cc/49D3-CQJU].

"Most drug and weapons crimes amenable to federal mandatory minimums are actually prosecuted in state courts pursuant to state laws carrying much lower sentences."[47]

The state systems prosecute the great majority of offenders. In general, state codes also feature overbroad, overlapping statutes carrying potentially severe penalties. If there is a generalizable difference between the powers of state and federal prosecutors, it is a difference of degree.

A 2015 survey of state legislation found that although twenty-nine states have ameliorated mandatory minimum sentences since 2000, mandatory minimum sentences "are in place in every state."[48] These laws "shifted discretion from sentencing courts to prosecutors" who "choose whether to charge a defendant with an offense that carries a mandatory term or to offer a plea bargain to a lesser crime that does not carry a mandatory sentence."[49]

The delegation of practical sentencing power to the executive is not confined to politically conservative states. Florida provides mandatory minimums for drug offenses based on drug quantity; so does Illinois.[50] Florida also has a separate offense of possessing a gun during the commission of some other offense; so does New Jersey.[51]

Efforts to either compel or prevent punitive charging decisions by prosecutors have consistently failed. Michigan tried to force prosecutions such as Harmelin's, and California sought to compel charging recidivism counts under the three-strikes law. These "mandatory" minimums nonetheless became prosecutorial options. When the executive branch brought the charge, the statute bound the courts. The decision to bring the charge, however, remained discretionary with the executive.

To present another example, Minnesota places more limits on charging than does federal law. Minnesota has a sentencing merger rule that permits convictions on multiple counts for the same conduct but sentencing only for the most serious one.[52] That sounds like it might prevent charge stacking.

[47] Erik Luna & Paul G. Cassell, *Mandatory Minimalism*, 32 Cardozo L. Rev. 1, 16 (2010) (footnote omitted).

[48] Alison Lawrence, NCSL, Making Sense of Sentencing: State Systems and Policies 8 (2015), https://documents.ncsl.org/wwwncsl/Criminal-Justice/sentencing.pdf [https://perma.cc/V5LT-SLXK]; *see also* Meixner, *supra* note 42, at 153–59.

[49] Lawrence, *supra* note 48, at 1.

[50] *Compare* Valera-Rodriguez v. State, 294 So. 3d 990 (Fla. Dist. Ct. App. 2020) *with* People v. McCarty, 858 N.E.2d 15 (Ill. 2006).

[51] *Compare* Fla. Stat. Ann. § 775.087 (West 2024) *with* N.J. Stat. Ann. § 2C:43-6(c) (West 2025).

[52] Minn. Stat. § 609.035 (with certain exceptions, "if a person's conduct constitutes more than one offense under the laws of this state, the person may be punished for only one of the offenses").

The rule, however, is limited to particular criminal episodes, so that four different drug sales to the same undercover agent on four different days can be sentenced as four offenses, not one.[53] Moreover, Minnesota also provides a firearms offense exception so that illegal gun possession can be punished in addition to a simultaneous drug, robbery, or assault conviction.[54] The rule leaves Minnesota prosecutors with discretion over whether to file a firearms count or multiple incidents, with corresponding sentencing consequences.[55]

Minimum sentences that are mandatory not just in court but also for the prosecutor are conceptually possible. Writing after the adoption of the federal sentencing guidelines, and before the Supreme Court's *Booker* decision, Stephen Schulhofer distinguished such "mandatory mandatories" from "discretionary mandatories."[56] If the statute directs the courts and the corrections bureaucracy to inquire in each case about whether the factual trigger for a mandatory minimum was present or not, prosecutors could not offer to forgo the minimum. This goal inspired the Sentencing Commission's initial efforts to base the defendant's sentence, in substantial part, on the offender's "real offense" conduct rather than the charge of conviction.

The effort was not successful. Because the offense of conviction sets the base offense level, prosecutors could manipulate the guidelines range by selecting a less or more serious charge from the many permitted by the overbroad substantive law. Moreover, because prosecutors often could manipulate the sentencing court's fact-finding, plea bargains could be struck to conceal true facts or stipulate to false ones. Attempting to enforce a policy of

[53] *See, e.g.*, State v. Soto, 562 N.W.2d 299 (Minn. 1997). *Soto* held that each of the four sales to one buyer over a month were separate "behavioral incidents" so that the defendant's criminal history on the fourth count included convictions on the other three. The result was to increase the presumptive sentence from 98 months to 161 months.

[54] State v. Williams, 757 N.W.2d 504, 511 (Minn. Ct. App. 2008) ("Therefore, where a defendant's multiple offenses arise from a single behavioral incident and include ineligible possession of a firearm, the defendant can be sentenced for the ineligible-possession offense in addition to being sentenced for one of the other offenses, and the offense that occurred first can be sentenced first and included in the defendant's criminal-history score to determine the presumptive sentence for the second offense.").

[55] *See, e.g.*, *Soto*, 562 N.W.2d at 302 ("Soto was charged with one count of sale of cocaine in the first degree and the state agreed not to charge him with three additional counts if he would testify against two other accomplices. However, Soto declined the offer and the state amended their complaint by adding the three additional counts for sale of cocaine in the first degree.").

[56] Stephen J. Schulhofer, *Rethinking Mandatory Minimums*, 28 Wake Forest L. Rev. 199, 202 (1993) ("Mandatories require the judge to impose a given minimum sentence upon conviction under a specified charge, but they do not necessarily obligate prosecutors to bring such a charge just because the facts support it. Therefore, the most important question in any mandatory minimum statute concerns the prosecutor's role: Does the statute entail a mandate to prosecute or merely an option to bargain?").

real-offense sentencing, Attorney General Thornburgh announced a policy of bringing the most serious possible charge.[57]

If this policy had been followed for many years, Congress probably would have responded to rising prison populations and public reaction to draconian penalties. Maybe Congress would have recodified federal criminal law in a way that limited the menu of charges available to prosecutors. More likely, given the fear of being seen as "soft on crime," the political branches would have reverted to a regime of unconstrained prosecutorial discretion.

This is, in fact, just what happened. Even though the Thornburgh policy had little practical effect, Janet Reno, President Clinton's first Attorney General, rescinded it. President Clinton was anything but "soft on crime." He signed the notorious 1994 crime bill (including the five-year mandatory minimum for five grams of crack) before an audience of uniformed police officers.[58]

If truly mandatory minimums were at least imaginable before *Booker*,[59] they are now all but unimaginable. *Booker* held that the right to jury trial applies to every fact that, by itself, automatically triggers a higher sentence, without any possibility of discretionary intervention by the sentencing court. One solution to the problem is sentencing by juries, and a few states have long followed this practice.[60] *Booker*'s solution was to sever the provisions of the sentencing guidelines that deprived judges of discretion to depart below the guidelines' minimum. A corollary of *Booker* is that statutes purporting to bypass *prosecutorial* discretion over mandatory minimum sentences by directing independent fact-finding by probation officers or judges have become impermissible.

The jury is not permitted to convict on a charge not filed. Greater charges include lesser, but if the government does not charge, for example, a firearms

[57] *See* Jeffrey Standen, *Plea Bargaining in the Shadow of the Guidelines*, 81 Calif. L. Rev. 1471, 1506–12 (1993) (explaining how charge selection controls the guidelines range); Deborah J. Daniels, *Sentencing Guidelines and Prosecutorial Discretion: The Justice Department's "Clarification" of the Thornburgh Memo*, 6 Fed. Sent'g Rep. 302–3 (1994) (noting prosecutorial power to manipulate sentencing facts, and discussing the Thornburgh memorandum).

[58] Lauren-Brooke Eisen, *The 1994 Crime Bill and Beyond: How Federal Funding Shapes the Criminal Justice System*, Brennan Ctr. for Just. (Sept. 9, 2019), https://www.brennancenter.org/our-work/analysis-opinion/1994-crime-bill-and-beyond-how-federal-funding-shapes-criminal-justice [https://perma.cc/M57V-G6F5].

[59] United States v. Booker, 543 U.S. 220, 244 (2005).

[60] Melissa Carrington, *Applying* Apprendi *to Jury Sentencing: Why State Felony Jury Sentencing Threatens the Right to Jury Trial*, 2011 U. Ill. L. Rev. 1359, 1360 ("In six states, however, the jury's sentencing purview extends beyond the death penalty and into the broader context of general felony sentencing.").

enhancement, the jury cannot consider it. If an enhancement is not subject to jury trial, it cannot bind the courts under *Booker*. It might still be possible for a statute to provide minimum penalties and then install oversight mechanisms such as case audits—but only if the triggering facts were submitted to a jury. After *Booker*, absent some such extraordinary oversight process, "mandatory" minimum sentences apply only when prosecutors elect to charge the offense to which the "mandatory" penalties apply.

The *Booker* line of cases still retains an important exception for prior convictions that trigger higher minimum sentences under recidivism statutes.[61] If the recidivism statute requires the prosecution to allege the priors, the prosecution, of course, controls whether or not the higher sentence applies. Even when the statute imposes an independent duty on the courts to enhance the sentence based on priors, selecting a different charge in the instant case often can avoid the enhancement. For example, in Lamar Hunt's case, his prior record required the court to impose the mandatory minimum because he was convicted of a federal firearms offense. The U.S. Attorney's Office, however, could have referred the case for state prosecution even if the evidence showed no alternative federal crime.

(2) How Grand Juries Get Cut Out: Institutional Competence

Technically, federal criminal charges are not brought by the US Attorney. The Fifth Amendment declares that "[n]o person shall be held to answer for a capital, or otherwise infamous crimes, unless on a presentment or indictment of a Grand Jury," military cases excepted. Federal indictments still begin with "The Grand Jury for the District . . . charges: . . ." Indictments are endorsed by both the attorney for the government and the foreperson of the grand jury.[62]

As discussed more fully in Chapter 5, there was a time when grand juries nullified prosecutions supported by strong evidence because they objected to the law (including sentences seen as disproportionate) rather than the evidence. Urbanization in the nineteenth century spelled the end of the self-informing grand jury. Critics of the institution pointed out that because the jurors heard only evidence presented by the public prosecutor, they had

[61] *See, e.g.*, Nancy J. King, *Sentencing and Prior Convictions: The Past, the Future, and the End of the Prior-Conviction Exception to* Apprendi, 97 Marq. L. Rev. 523 (2014).

[62] For a sample indictment, see, e.g., Indictment, United States v. Manafort et al., 1:17-cr-00201 (D.D.C. Oct. 27, 2017), https://www.politico.com/f/?id=0000015f-6d73-d751-af7f-7f735cc70000.

ceased to serve any useful purpose.[63] When some states authorized charging felonies by information, having the same content as an indictment but filed directly by the prosecutor, the Supreme Court ruled that the Fourteenth Amendment did not require the grand jury procedure.[64]

Today, felony prosecutions require indictment by a grand jury in about half the states, and in federal cases, where the Fifth Amendment grand jury clause establishes a constitutional requirement. Grand juries remain impotent checks on prosecutorial charging decisions for two different reasons. One is the prosecutor's control of the evidence the jurors hear. While the standard grand jurors apply to the evidence before indicting was a subject of dispute for centuries, the established standard today is probable cause.[65] The grand jurors are asked whether a trial jury might rationally convict if the trial jurors believe the prosecution's witnesses. With no independent source of either information or legal advice, indictment is all but inevitable.[66] As Professor Leipold puts it, the "root cause of the institution's inability to screen is the jurors' lack of competence to perform their task."[67]

The second reason grand juries fail to check prosecutors is that when they are certain to see the judge, the judge tells them not to. The Federal Judicial Center's model charge includes some strong language stressing the grand jury's independence,[68] but it requires only probable cause to indict[69] and

[63] *See, e.g.*, Report of the Judiciary Committee of the House of Representatives on Recommending the Passage of the Bill to Provide for the Trial of Offences upon Information, H. Doc. No. 4, at 10 (Mich. 1859) ("The experience of all large cities has demonstrated the necessity of local criminal courts, with power to impose a speedy and summary trial, and without the intervention of a grand jury."); *id.* at 31–34 (defending the superiority of the information/preliminary examination system for screening unfounded charges).

[64] Hurtado v. California, 110 U.S. 516 (1884).

[65] *See* Barbara Shapiro, Beyond Reasonable Doubt and Probable Cause 42–113 (1991); *id.* at 102 ("Probable cause is now the prevailing grand jury evidentiary standard.").

[66] *See* Andrew Leipold, *Why Grand Juries Do Not (and Cannot) Protect the Accused*, 80 Cornell L. Rev. 260, 264 (1995):

> Rather than being asked to find facts and apply those facts to the law, the jurors are presented with a single set of facts, instructed on the law by the prosecutor, and asked to decide whether those undisputed facts are sufficient to satisfy a specific legal test—the probable cause standard.

[67] *Id.*

[68] Fed. Jud. Ctr., *Grand Jury Selection and Instructions*, *in* Benchbook for U.S. District Court Judges 251 (6th ed. 2013) ("The determination of whether a witness is telling the truth is something you must decide."); *id.* at 253 ("If the facts suggest that you should not indict, then you should not do so, even in the face of the opposition or statements of the government attorney.").

[69] *Id.* at 252:

> To return an indictment charging an individual with an offense, it is not necessary that you find that individual guilty beyond a reasonable doubt. . . . To put it another way, you should vote to indict where the evidence presented to you is sufficiently strong to warrant a reasonable person's belief that the person being investigated is probably guilty of the offense charged.

expressly tells the jurors that the wisdom of the law and the severity of punishment are not to be considered.[70] Prosecutors have the license to "judge the wisdom of the criminal laws enacted by Congress" by prosecuting some cases and not others. Prosecutors are keenly interested in "punishment in the event of a conviction." These are the most controversial decisions prosecutors make. The grand jury can review these critical decisions only by defying the court's instructions.

(3) How Juries and Judges Get Cut Out: Guilty Pleas, Guidelines, and Mandatory Minimums

We have already seen how charges lead to sentences without the independent judgment of either juries or judges. Almost all cases are resolved by guilty pleas, so no trial jury is empaneled. Given the sentencing prospects facing defendants (most of them guilty in fact), almost all of them enter a "knowing and voluntary" guilty plea to avoid harsher punishment after conviction at trial. Sentencing guidelines constrain judicial sentencing discretion. Mandatory minimums curtail it.

To be sure, the sentencing consequences of charging decisions are contingent upon a conviction. This obvious fact does not change the practical, moral, or legal equivalence of modern charging and sentencing. As a practical matter, charge selection has by far the greatest impact on the sentences actually received by the guilty. It is precisely this practical importance of charge selection that empowers prosecutors to induce guilty pleas.

No single decision in the criminal justice process conclusively determines from within the statutory range how severely the offender will be punished. Sentences imposed after conviction, by judge or by jury, are contingent not only upon a conviction ex ante, but also on avoiding reversal on appeal. Trial convictions may be reversed for procedural error or insufficiency of the evidence. Whether the conviction followed a trial or a guilty plea, the sentence itself is subject to appeal (although this was not always the case). More

[70] *Id.* at 249:

> You cannot judge the wisdom of the criminal laws enacted by Congress, that is, whether or not there should or should not be a federal law designating certain activity as criminal. That is to be determined by Congress and not by you. . . . Furthermore, when deciding whether or not to indict, you should not consider punishment in the event of conviction.

remote but not trivial contingencies attend even sentences that survive appeal. The convict may die, escape, obtain post-conviction relief in the courts, or benefit from executive clemency.

While the statistics are a little hard to parse, the risk of acquittal at trial seems no greater than the risk of reversal on appeal. The data from the Bureau of Justice Statistics (BJS) survey of state courts in the most populous counties show that 2 percent of felony charges lead to trial, and 1 percent of felony charges end in acquittal.[71] About a fourth are dismissed, about a tenth end in diversion, and the rest end in guilty pleas.[72] In the federal system the percentages of trials are slightly higher and the rate of acquittals lower.[73]

In 2025, the circuit courts of appeal terminated 23,155 criminal appeals, and reversed 1,736—or 7.8 percent. They remanded 337 others.[74] So, of the 23,155 appeals, the courts provided some relief in 2,073 cases, 9 percent of the total. That's more than a trivial success rate, but it is not the percentage of sentences imposed that are later modified on appeal.

Most convictions come on pleas, and most who plead guilty do not try to undo the deal later. This year's appeals come from convictions rendered earlier, so a precise comparison is impossible. If, however, we compare the 2,073 successful appeals in 2024 with the 71,578 convictions and sentences in the district courts, we get a much better picture of the contingencies created by the appeals process. Slightly fewer than 3 percent of federal convictions are disturbed on appeal. That sounds more modest, but it is still about ten times higher than the probability that a federal defendant will be acquitted at a trial.[75]

In the state systems, for year 2010 the BJS reported 69,348 criminal appeals, and that in "12% of appeals, appellate courts reversed, remanded,

[71] Bureau of Just. Stat., U.S. Dep't of State, BJS Stat. Tables NCJ 243777, Felony Defendants in Large Urban Counties, 2009, at 24, tbl.21 (Dec. 2013), https://bjs.ojp.gov/content/pub/pdf/fdluc09.pdf [https://perma.cc/B76W-E7B7]. As of March 2025, the BJS has not published newer data on state court processing statistics.

[72] *Id.*

[73] *Statistical Tables for the Federal Judiciary*: Table D-4, Admin. Off. of the U.S. Courts (Dec. 31, 2024), https://www.uscourts.gov/data-news/data-tables/2024/12/31/statistical-tables-federal-judiciary/d-4 (reporting 76,734 defendants charged, 71,578 convicted and sentenced). 4,941 had their cases dismissed, leaving 71,793 for adjudication. Of these, 70,014—97.5 percent—entered guilty pleas. In the 1,799 trial cases, juries convicted 1,348 and acquitted 154, and judges at bench trials convicted 216 and acquitted 61. Counting bench and jury trials together, the 215 acquittals made up 12 percent of the trial cases.

[74] *Statistical Tables for the Federal Judiciary*: *Table B-5*, Admin. Off. of the U.S. Courts (Dec. 31, 2024), https://www.uscourts.gov/data-news/data-tables/2024/12/31/statistical-tables-federal-judiciary/b-5.

[75] Per Table D-4, there were 76,734 indicted defendants. Of these, 215 were acquitted, either by a jury or the court. The chance that a federal defendant will be acquitted at trial works out to about one-third of 1 percent.

or modified a component of the trial court decision."[76] The fraction of convictions appealed depends on the total number of convictions. In 2006, the BJS reported 1,132,290 felony convictions in state courts but discontinued the data series.[77] The number probably fell between 2006 and 2010. On the other hand, misdemeanor convictions are subject to appeal, although appeals are more common in more serious cases.

In serious criminal cases, the reversal rate was higher than the reversal rate for all appeals. "In 2010, appellate courts reversed 23% of appeals for drug trafficking, 23% for larceny or theft, 21% for sex offenses, and 17% for murder."[78] Even if only one drug conviction in twenty was appealed, the chance of a trial court sentence being reversed would still be higher than the 1 percent chance a trial acquittal will prevent a charge from becoming a conviction.

So we cannot distinguish *Prosecutorial Sentencing* from *229 Degrees* based on the contingent effect of the charging decision on the actual sentence in *229 Degrees.* In the modern system, the effect of charge selection on the ultimate punishment inflicted is no more—and probably even less—contingent than the effect of judicial sentencing. The contingency of charge effect on punishment is at most a distinction without a difference. Fairly considered, it is not even a distinction at all.

E. The Disconnect from Due Process

The descriptive claims made thus far are neither terribly novel nor terribly controversial. They echo the opinions of many distinguished judges and scholars. Ron Wright says that sentencing guidelines, together with "far-reaching and duplicative criminal codes, relatively few resources available for trial, and nondiscretionary sentencing laws," collectively "give prosecutors extraordinary power—maybe unsurpassed power—in the American criminal justice system."[79] Stephanos Bibas, citing a pathbreaking article by

[76] Bureau of Just. Stat., U.S. Dep't of Just., BJS Bull. NCJ 248874, Criminal Appeals in State Courts 1 (Sept. 2015), https://bjs.ojp.gov/content/pub/pdf/casc.pdf [https://perma.cc/3LNH-B2X6]. Again, newer data are not available from the BJS as of March 2025.

[77] Bureau of Just. Stat., U.S. Dep't of Just., BJS Stat. Tables NCJ 226846, Felony Sentences in State Courts, 2006—Statistical Tables 3, tbl.1.1 (rev. Nov. 2010), https://bjs.ojp.gov/content/pub/pdf/fssc06st.pdf [https://perma.cc/F6JC-T6A5].

[78] Criminal Appeals in State Courts, *supra* note 76, at 1.

[79] Ronald F. Wright, *Sentencing Commissions as Provocateurs of Prosecutorial Self-Regulation*, 105 Colum. L. Rev. 1010, 1011–12 (2005).

Gerard Lynch, says that in "essence, the prosecutor is the only adjudicator."[80] Jed Rakoff wrote that "prosecutors, rather than judges, now effectively determine the sentences to be imposed in most cases."[81] I select these informed opinions from among a host of others because Professor Wright, Judge Bibas, Judge Lynch, and Judge Rakoff all at some point served as prosecutors.

This next section makes a normative and legal argument. The scale of executive control over sentencing is at odds with fundamental principles of due process. Indeed, in other contexts within the criminal justice system, such as issuing search warrants, determining probable cause to bind suspects over for trial, and at trial, prosecutorial participation in adjudication, let alone control of adjudication, is a constitutional anathema.

(1) Due Process 101

The Fifth Amendment declares that "[n]o person shall be . . . deprived of life, liberty, or property, without due process of law[.]" In parallel language, the Fourteenth Amendment adds "nor shall State deprive any person of life, liberty, or property, without due process of law[.] These provisions guarantee that the government is subject to the rule of law.

The quintessential denial of due process is punishment without trial, the abuse attributed to the infamous King John, whom rebellious barons compelled to agree to the Magna Carta's famous Chapter 39. There, King John pledged not to kill, imprison, fine, or dispossess any free man except "per legale judicium parium suorum vel per legem terrae." There are some slight disagreements about the precise translation, but "by a lawful judgment of peers or the law of the land" is widely accepted.

English monarchs reissued Magna Carta, with some abridgements. In 1225, Chapter 39 became Chapter 29 and is often cited as such.[82] As Parliament evolved into a legislature, it adopted statutes confirming the

[80] Stephanos Bibas, *Designing Plea Bargaining from the Ground Up: Accuracy and Fairness Without Trials as Backstops*, 57 Wm. & Mary L. Rev. 1055, 1066 (2016) (citing Gerard E. Lynch, *Our Administrative System of Criminal Justice*, 66 Fordham L. Rev. 2117, 2118–23 (1998)).

[81] Jed S. Rakoff, *Why Prosecutors Rule the Criminal Justice System—And What Can Be Done About It*, 111 Nw. U. L. Rev. 1429, 1432 (2017).

[82] *Magna Carta: Muse and Mentor—Due Process of Law*, Library of Congress, http://www.loc.gov/exhibits/magna-carta-muse-and-mentor/due-process-of-law.html [https://perma.cc/5FHT-UR5R] (last visited June 28, 2025).

Great Charter.[83] The earliest recorded reference to "due process of law" appears in one such statute, in 1354.[84]

Charter and statutes notwithstanding, until the English revolution in 1688, British monarchs had asserted crown power over ordinary laws (the "royal prerogative") and subverted the rule of law by sacking judges and fabricating evidence. Henry VIII's confiscation of the monasteries and Charles I's indefinite imprisonment of subjects who refused to pay forced "loans" afforded salient examples.[85] "Due process of law" played an important role in the struggle between Parliament and the Stuart Kings in the seventeenth century. Edward Coke quoted the statute in his second *Institute* on Magna Charta[86] and in the Petition of Right, which Charles I granted "by grace" rather than "of right" in 1628.[87]

American patriots protesting taxation without representation and writs of assistance invoked Magna Carta and the confirming acts as trumps on ordinary statutes.[88] State constitutions adopted after independence typically incorporated Chapter 39 using "law of the land" language.[89] The federal Fifth Amendment uses the due process formula, perhaps because the New York ratification message, calling for a bill of rights, used "due process" language.[90] Or it may be that James Madison, who drafted the Bill of Rights, reached back directly to Coke and the Petition of Right. American jurists generally have understood the two formulations to express the same principle.

That superficially simple principle, however, turns out to be quite complex. Just what official actions count as "deprivations" of "life, liberty or

[83] J. C. Holt, Magna Carta 39–40 (3d ed. 2015).

[84] Liberty of Subject Act 1354, 28 Edw. 3, c. 3.

[85] See Darnell's Case (1627) 3 How. St. Tr. 1 (KB) (holding royal prerogative a good return to a writ of habeas corpus). The Petition of Right did not prevent Charles I from charging parliamentary opponents for sedition, an accusation that could be filed by information rather than indictment, was not automatically bailable, and could be tried without a jury in the common-law courts where the judges served at the king's pleasure. R v. Eliot (1629) 79 Eng. Rep. 759, 3 How. St. Tr. 294 (KB).

[86] Edward Coke, The Second Part of the Institutes of the Lawes of England 50 (1642).

[87] Petition of Right 1628, 3 Cha. 1, ch. 1, http://www.legislation.gov.uk/aep/Cha1/3/1/ [https://perma.cc/8GNW-FJ8N].

[88] For fuller discussion, see Donald A. Dripps, *Due Process: A Unified Understanding*, *in* The Cambridge Companion to the United States Constitution 46–48 (Karen Orren & John W. Compton eds., 2018).

[89] For example, the 1780 Massachusetts Constitution is representative: "And no subject shall be arrested, imprisoned, despoiled, or deprived of his property, immunities, or privileges, put out of the protection of the law, exiled, or deprived of his life, liberty, or estate; but by the judgment of his peers, or the law of the land." Mass. Const. of 1780, pt. 1, art. XII,

[90] *Ratification of the Constitution by the State of New York; July 26, 1788*, Avalon Project, http://avalon.law.yale.edu/18th_century/ratny.asp [https://perma.cc/XV7V-7UER] (from U.S. Dep't of State, 2 Documentary History of the Constitution of the United States of America: 1786–1780, at 190–203 (1894).

property"? Even when "deprivation" is clear, as in criminal punishment by death or imprisonment, deep issues remain. The trial requirement presupposes some issue to be tried, some legal rule that governs the case, and some dispute about whether, in fact, that rule was followed. A trial on the issue of whether the King has condemned the accused to death would do nothing to enforce the rule of law. Likewise, a show trial on a trumped-up treason charge could (and often did) nullify due process.

It follows from the American doctrine of judicial review that deprivations, legality, and fair process are not whatever the legislature decrees them to be. Daniel Webster gave the classic exposition of the relationship between "the law of the land" and statutory law in *Trustees of Dartmouth College v. Woodward*.[91] The New Hampshire legislature adopted a statute replacing the college's trustees, who held their posts under a royal charter issued by George III. The state court rejected the trustees' reliance on the state constitution's "law of the land" clause. Webster challenged that ruling in the US Supreme Court:

> By the law of the land, is most clearly intended, the general law; a law, which hears before it condemns; which proceeds upon inquiry, and renders judgment only after trial. The meaning is, that every citizen shall hold his life, liberty, property and immunities, under the protection of the general rules which govern society. Everything which may pass under the form of an enactment, is not, therefore, to be considered the law of the land. If this were so, acts of attainder, bills of pains and penalties, acts of confiscation, acts reversing judgments, and acts directly transferring one man's estate to another, legislative judgments, decrees and forfeitures, in all possible forms, would be the law of the land. Such a strange construction would render constitutional provisions, of the highest importance, completely inoperative and void.[92]

The legislature has no authority to define liberty or property out of existence, to make arbitrary deprivations lawful, or to conclusively determine the fairness of trials.

[91] 17 U.S. 518 (1819).

[92] *Id.* at 581–82. The Court refused to overrule the state court on the meaning of the state constitution, but ruled for Dartmouth based on Webster's alternative argument based on the impairment-of-contracts clause in art. I, §10.

Due process, then, requires that when the government seriously injures an individual, it must act pursuant to law and after a fair hearing. The general principle, although complex, is not controversial. Article 6, section 1 of the European Convention on Human Rights provides that in "the determination of his civil rights and obligations or of any criminal charge against him, everyone is entitled to a fair and public hearing within a reasonable time by an independent and impartial tribunal established by law." The free nations of the world have endorsed the United Nations *Universal Declaration of Human Rights*. According to Article 10 of the declaration, "Everyone is entitled in full equality to a fair and public hearing by an independent and impartial tribunal, in the determination of his rights and obligations and of any criminal charge against him."

(2) Pretrial Investigations: Searches and Arrests

In criminal cases, the "deprivation" component of due process is clear. Liberty or property is always on the line, and in capital cases, the issue is "life." It follows that before punishing an offender for a crime, due process requires that a fair trial find that the accused had violated some valid, preexisting law.

For centuries, Anglo-American lawyers have seen the very paradigm of due process violations in a law making one party judge of the case.[93] In Judge Friendly's famous taxonomy of due process hearing rights, item number one is "an unbiased tribunal."[94] Proof of actual bias establishes a due process violation in administrative proceedings imposing liabilities such as occupational license revocations,[95] public employment,[96] or even public school suspensions.[97] In the administrative law cases, bias is not always presumed from the combination of prosecutorial and adjudicatory functions.[98]

[93] *See, e.g.*, Day v. Savadge (1614) 80 Eng. Rep. 235, 237 (KB) ("even an Act of Parliament, made against natural equity, as to make a man Judge in his own case, is void in it self, for *jura naturae sunt immutabilia*").

[94] Henry J. Friendly, *Some Kind of Hearing*, 123 U. Pa. L. Rev. 1267, 1279 (1975).

[95] Withrow v. Larkin, 421 U.S. 35, 47 (1975) ("Not only is a biased decisionmaker constitutionally unacceptable but 'our system of law has always endeavored to prevent even the probability of unfairness.'") (citation omitted).

[96] Cleveland Bd. of Educ. v. Loudermill, 470 U.S. 532 (1985).

[97] Goss v. Lopez, 419 U.S. 565 (1975).

[98] *Withrow*, 421 U.S. 35.

Due process, independent of the Bill of Rights, continues to play a vital role in criminal procedure doctrine. In these "free-standing due process" cases, the Court has not used administrative law's balancing test but instead consulted the more general test of "fundamental fairness." Under this rubric, the Supreme Court has consistently found unconstitutional partiality without proof of case-specific bias. Executive branch officials, no matter how fair in fact, may not adjudicate. Judicial officers, no matter how fair in fact, may not serve in an executive capacity or have even a trivial financial stake in the outcome. Judicial tolerance of prosecutorial charging decisions is a curious outlier. We will explore this exception and the reasons given for it at the end of the chapter. We turn first to an exposition of the Supreme Court's jurisprudence requiring neutral decision makers in the criminal process.

Searches and arrests are "deprivations of liberty." The Constitution's Fourth Amendment, applicable to the states by force of the Fourteenth Amendment's Due Process Clause, requires that police decisions to search or arrest be reviewed by a "neutral and detached" magistrate. In *Coolidge v. New Hampshire*,[99] the defendant challenged the validity of a search warrant issued by the state attorney general, who held a dual commission as a justice of the peace (JP). The record showed that in other cases, police officers holding JP commissions issued search warrants.

The Supreme Court held the "warrant" invalid because "the state official who was the chief investigator and prosecutor in this case . . . was not the neutral and detached magistrate required by the Constitution[.]"[100] Ergo, the search stood "on no firmer ground than if there had been no warrant at all."[101] The ample showing of probable cause could not rescue the flawed procedure because "prosecutors and policemen simply cannot be asked to maintain the requisite neutrality with regard to their own investigations—the 'competitive enterprise' that must rightly engage their single-minded attention."[102]

Just as police officers may not act as judges, judges may not act as police officers. In *Lo-Ji Sales, Inc. v. New York*,[103] a justice of the peace issued a warrant to search the defendant business for obscene materials. The warrant did not specify the items to be seized. Instead, the justice accompanied the police and reviewed the materials at the site. Arguably, the justice's participation in

[99] 403 U.S. 443 (1971).
[100] *Id.* at 453.
[101] *Id.*
[102] *Id.* at 450 (footnote omitted).
[103] 442 U.S. 319 (1979).

the search protected the *First* Amendment by providing a judicial determination of obscenity before any seizures.

The Supreme Court, however, saw the case very differently:

> The Town Justice did not manifest that neutrality and detachment demanded of a judicial officer when presented with a warrant application for a search and seizure. [citing *Coolidge*]. We need not question the subjective belief of the Town Justice in the propriety of his actions, but the objective facts of record manifest an erosion of whatever neutral and detached posture existed at the outset. He allowed himself to become a member, if not the leader, of the search party which was essentially a police operation. Once in the store, he conducted a generalized search under authority of an invalid warrant; he was not acting as a judicial officer but as an adjunct law enforcement officer.[104]

As in *Coolidge*, the search pursuant to the pseudo-warrant was a warrantless search, and, in the absence of an emergency, unconstitutional.

Indeed, the Court has held that neutrality is more important than expertise. In *Shadwick v. City of Tampa*,[105] the justices approved arrest warrants issued by the clerk of the court rather than by a commissioned judge. "Whatever else neutrality and detachment might entail, it is clear that they require severance and disengagement from activities of law enforcement. There has been no showing whatever here of partiality, or affiliation of these clerks with prosecutors or police."[106]

To be sure, most searches and arrests are made without warrants, authorized by one of the many exceptions to the warrant requirement. In these cases, however, when judicial review is not available ex ante it is available ex post. Following a warrantless search, the Fourth Amendment requires the police to bring the suspect into court for a judicial determination of probable cause. A "policeman's on-the-scene assessment of probable cause provides legal justification for arresting a person suspected of crime, and for a brief period of detention to take the administrative steps incident to arrest. Once the suspect is in custody, however, the reasons that justify dispensing with the magistrate's neutral judgment evaporate."[107]

[104] *Id.* at 326–27.
[105] 407 U.S. 345 (1972).
[106] *Id.* at 350.
[107] Gerstein v. Pugh, 420 U.S. 103, 113–14 (1975).

Ex post remedies are second-best, not just for unjustified arrests but also for unjustified searches. The exclusionary rule and damages actions both have limitations. Surely, however, a statute authorizing the police chief or the state's attorney to decide suppression motions would be unconstitutional, either because the Fourth Amendment requires neutral review or because due process forbids partisan adjudication. The Fourth Amendment, after all, is more a specification of due process than a world unto itself. "The security of one's privacy against arbitrary intrusion by the police—which is at the core of the Fourth Amendment—is basic to a free society. It is therefore implicit in 'the concept of ordered liberty' and as such enforceable against the States through the Due Process Clause."[108]

(3) Due Process at Trial

Even without the Sixth Amendment's "impartial jury" requirement, elementary due process requires a neutral decision maker. If an executive branch officer participates in the investigation or prosecution of the case, the neutrality requirement bars that same official from any later role in adjudicating the case. Surreal extreme cases, such as police officers ruling on suppression motions or prosecutors' ruling on the admissibility of trial testimony, are too lurid to have been attempted in liberal democracies. Many subtler cases have reached the courts. The Supreme Court has insisted on excluding those who investigate and accuse from those who adjudicate.

If state law assigns an individual judge to conduct investigations by exercising the power of a grand jury, the same judge is presumed conclusively to be not impartial when sitting as the trial judge of a contempt prosecution based on conduct during the judge's investigative proceedings.[109] In 2016, the Supreme Court held that the prosecutor who authorized seeking the death penalty against a homicide defendant violates due process by sitting, decades later, on an appellate court hearing that defendant's post-conviction petition.[110] In criminal cases, the performance of prosecutorial functions is

[108] *See* Wolf v. Colorado, 338 U.S. 25, 27–28 (1949). The Court has never questioned *Wolf*'s incorporation holding, although *Mapp v. Ohio*, 367 U.S. 643 (1961), overruled that portion of *Wolf* that held the exclusionary remedy inapplicable to the states.

[109] *In re* Murchison, 349 U.S. 133, 136 (1955) ("A fair trial in a fair tribunal is a basic requirement of due process. Fairness of course requires an absence of actual bias in the trial of cases. But our system of law has always endeavored to prevent even the probability of unfairness.").

[110] Williams v. Pennsylvania, 579 U.S. 1 (2016).

inconsistent with the impartiality required by due process in subsequent judicial proceedings in the case.

We will consider the role of due process in judicial and administrative sentencing procedures in the next chapter. Even at this point, however, the disconnect between general due process principles and prosecutorial control over sentences should be apparent. A prosecutor may not issue arrest warrants that might impose a night in jail. Yet the same prosecutor can decide to add decades of prison time to an offender's sentence by exercising the charging power.

This disconnect from due process calls for explanation. How can a free society with a robust respect for civil liberties justify turning the sentencing of so many defendants over to the executive branch of the government? How can the courts of such a society require strict procedural fairness when judges issue warrants or conduct trials, but not when law enforcement officers determine the crimes to which the accused will confess, and the penalty to be inflicted?

As a matter of legal doctrine, the explanation is that courts use a procedural baseline to test the exercise of discretion by judges and parole boards but a penal code baseline when testing the exercise of prosecutorial discretion. If, as argued here, charging now determines sentencing, we need to reconsider this division of constitutional labor. Chapters 3 and 4 examine the evolution of the constitutional doctrine applicable to sentencing and charging decisions, respectively.

3
The Supreme Court and Judicial Sentencing Discretion

A. Introduction

We saw in Chapter 2 how overbroad, overlapping, and overpunitive penal codes authorize catastrophic differences in dispositions. Ronald Harmelin received a life sentence for the same offense as Tim Allen, who served two years. Weldon Angelos could have avoided fifty years of his sentence by pleading guilty. We also saw that the officials who determined these outcomes were in the executive, rather than the judicial, branch—prosecutors, not judges.

Despite the written constitution's command that officials deciding to deprive people of their liberty must observe due process, and despite the US doctrine of judicial review, the executive branch now largely controls criminal justice outcomes. We now explore what I call "the due process disconnect" between charging and sentencing. One substantial line of Supreme Court decisions requires neutral adjudicators, a right to be heard through counsel, and a statement of reasons for post-conviction sentencing determinations. Another substantial line rejects constitutional challenges to pre-conviction charging decisions having catastrophic sentencing consequences.

The sentencing cases proceed on the premise that every exercise of sentencing discretion potentially deprives the offender of liberty, property, or both. Accordingly, minimal due process—neutrality, notice, and a right to be heard—attend every exercise of this discretion. That tracks preanalytical common sense. You don't need a law degree to see that where the law subjects the offender to a five-year maximum, the person who decides the individual's actual sentence shouldn't be the chief of police.

The charging decisions proceed on the quite different premise that the legislature has authorized every charge supported by the evidence. Again, as a matter of untutored intuition, if the executive seems obscenely out of place at sentencing, so judges seem obscenely out of place in making law

Sentencing Discretion and the Constitution. Donald A. Dripps, Oxford University Press.
 DOI: 10.1093/9780197830390.003.0003

enforcement decisions. The Supreme Court's horror at the judge who issued the warrant and then led the search party in *Lo Ji Sales* is illustrative.

The two lines of precedent show that powerful considerations of institutional competence substantiate these intuitions. Judges are better for sentencing because they are neutral and hear both sides. The post-conviction sentencing process benefits from better information about both the offender and limited correctional assets. Prosecutors are better judges of how to deploy limited resources in light of intelligence about crime, knowledge of case strength, and accountability to the community's concerns about public safety.

But when charging decisions are sentencing decisions, as is so often the case, this attractive dichotomy breaks down. This chapter surveys the cases on due process rights in judicial sentencing proceedings. The Supreme Court itself has never approved prosecutorial sentencing. These cases initially reasoned from a positive-law baseline, but ultimately discarded the focus on statutory maximum sentences in favor of a baseline set by fair procedures.

B. The Origins of Sentencing Law

The common law formally prohibited felony defendants from being heard through counsel except on collateral points of law.[1] America repudiated the rule against counsel,[2] but the federal constitutional right to appointed counsel for the indigent in state felony prosecutions was not recognized until *Gideon* in 1963.[3] Even without counsel, however, from time immemorial, the convicted prisoner was asked what was to be said on his behalf before the court pronounced sentence.[4] Although there were some exceptional grounds for arresting judgment that might appear at allocution,[5] allocution was primarily a ritual—a post-trial ritual in an age when guilty pleas were rare. The eighteenth-century felony trial itself functioned much as a sentencing hearing, where juries weighed whether to nullify the death penalty and judges pondered pardon recommendations.[6]

[1] 4 William Blackstone, Commentaries *355.

[2] 3 Joseph Story, Commentaries on the Constitution of the United States §§ 1786–88 (Da Capo Press 1970) (1833).

[3] Gideon v. Wainwright, 372 U.S. 333 (1963).

[4] 4 William Blackstone, Commentaries *368.

[5] *Id.* at *368–69.

[6] *See, e.g.*, John H. Langbein, *Shaping the Eighteenth-Century Criminal Trial: A View From the Ryder Sources*, 50 U. Chi. L. Rev. 1, 41 (1983):

At common law, judges had discretion to punish misdemeanors (which could be very serious crimes) with prison, whipping, or the pillory.[7] Even in the eighteenth century, some judges exercising this discretion held post-conviction sentencing hearings.[8] The exercise of discretion required information, so a hearing was necessary when a conviction was rendered by default. However, the practice does not appear to have been limited to default judgments.[9]

As discretionary prison terms and guilty pleas became more common, judges vested with sentencing discretion began holding sentencing hearings.[10] The usual evidence rules did not apply, as there was no jury and the offender's character and past conduct were central to the exercise of discretion.[11] The linkage between sentencing discretion and sentencing hearings has been so complete that the Supreme Court has never seen a case where a court imposed sentence without some opportunity to be heard. The constitutional law of sentencing doesn't even begin until the middle of the twentieth century.

In federal cases, the trial judge imposed sentences under the statutory maximum at discretion, including (except for a brief interval during Prohibition) discretion to suspend a sentence and impose probation.[12] Appellate review

> Only a small fraction of eighteenth-century criminal trials were genuinely contested inquiries into guilt or innocence. In most cases the accused had been caught in the act or otherwise possessed no credible defense. To the extent that trial had a function in such cases beyond formalizing the inevitable conclusion of guilt, it was to decide the sanction. These trials were sentencing proceedings.

[7] *See, e.g.*, 1 JOSEPH CHITTY, A PRACTICAL TREATISE ON THE CRIMINAL LAW 710 (J.C. Perkins ed., Springfield, G. & C. Merriam 1841); 4 WILLIAM BLACKSTONE, COMMENTARIES *372–74; 1 JAMES FITZJAMES STEPHEN, A HISTORY OF THE CRIMINAL LAW OF ENGLAND 489–90 (MacMillan & Co., London 1883).

[8] This is pointed out in Anat Horovitz, *The Emergence of Sentencing Hearings*, 9 PUNISHMENT & SOC'Y 271, 279–81 (2007). Horovitz relies on CHITTY, *supra* note 7, at 791–93.

[9] CHITTY, *supra* note 7, at 791–93.

[10] *See, e.g.*, John H. Langbein, *The Historical Origins of the Privilege Against Self-Incrimination at Common Law*, 92 MICH. L. REV. 1047, 1064 (1992) ("The new sanction of imprisonment for a term of years was all but infinitely divisible. It invited the concept of the sentencing range, which effectively transferred from the jury to the judge the power to tailor the sentence to the particular offender."); GEORGE FISHER, PLEA BARGAINING'S TRIUMPH 57 (2003) ("there seems to have been a widespread if not uniform nineteenth-century practice of holding a sentencing hearing, perhaps involving witnesses, even after a defendant pled guilty."); *id.* n.87 (citing examples of sentencing hearings from different jurisdictions).

[11] *See, e.g.*, KATE STITH & JOSE A. CABRANES, FEAR OF JUDGING 15 (1998) ("For the purpose of determining an appropriate sentence, sentencing judges frequently received evidence that was irrelevant or otherwise inadmissible on the issue of guilt or innocence, including testimony about the defendant's reputation and the circumstances that led to the commission of the offense.") (footnote omitted).

[12] See *infra* Chapter 4.

of sentences was unknown.[13] Until the Fourteenth Amendment, the federal Constitution did not require due process in state cases. Even after the Fourteenth Amendment, the Court did not reverse a state conviction for a due process violation until 1923.[14]

C. The Probation Act Cases: Dueling Baselines

In 1916, the Supreme Court held that federal judges had no inherent power to suspend sentences and release offenders on probation.[15] A decade later, Congress adopted a Probation Act that conferred very broad discretion on federal courts to suspend sentences, set conditions of probation, and revoke probation when the offender violated its terms.[16] Federal prisoners soon challenged the procedures used to revoke probation.

In the first case, *Burns v. United States*,[17] Chief Justice Hughes began by characterizing probation "as a privilege" that "cannot be demanded as a right. It is a matter of favor, not of contract."[18] The baseline against which procedural challenges should be measured was not the suspension but the sentence. "The defendant stands convicted; he faces punishment, and cannot insist on terms or strike a bargain."[19] The right-privilege distinction was logical in one way, but disturbing in another. It seemed to suggest that the defendant, once convicted, could not complain of *any* procedure for either granting or revoking probation, coin flips included.

The Justices refused to embrace completely the right-privilege distinction, at least as a statutory matter under the Probation Act. In *Burns*, Chief Justice Hughes conceded that the district court's choice of procedures, like its ultimate decision, was discretionary. Discretion, however, was not unbounded:

[13] Koon v. United States, 518 U.S. 81, 96 (1996) ("Before the Guidelines system, a federal criminal sentence within statutory limits was, for all practical purposes, not reviewable on appeal."); United States v. Colon, 884 F.2d 1550, 1552 (2d Cir. 1989) ("Prior to passage of the Sentencing Reform Act, appellate review of sentences was unavailable unless they exceeded statutory limits, resulted from material misinformation or were based upon constitutionally impermissible considerations.").

[14] Moore v. Dempsey, 261 U.S. 86 (1923).

[15] *Ex parte* United States, 242 U.S. 27 (1916) (discussed *infra* Chapter 4).

[16] *See, e.g.*, Note, *Suspended Sentence for Federal Prisoners—Congress Adopts Probation System for Federal Courts*, 3 Tex. L. Rev. 284, 286 (1925).

[17] 287 U.S. 216 (1932).

[18] *Id.* at 220.

[19] *Id.*

> The question, then, in the case of the revocation of probation, is not one of formal procedure either with respect to notice or specification of charges or a trial upon charges. The question is simply whether there has been an abuse of discretion and is to be determined in accordance with familiar principles governing the exercise of judicial discretion. That exercise implies conscientious judgment, not arbitrary action. It takes account of the law and the particular circumstances of the case and is "directed by the reason and conscience of the judge to a just result."[20]

Appellate review for abuse of discretion presupposed the giving of reasons. The neutrality of the court was taken for granted.

Three years later, in *Escoe v. Zerbst*,[21] Justice Cardozo's opinion for the Court adhered to the *Burns* characterization as a constitutional matter but read the right to be heard into the Probation Act. Escoe had his original sentence suspended on condition of obeying the law and temperance. His father wrote a letter to the probation officer accusing him of drunkenness and forgery. The probation officer reported this to the judge, who issued a warrant for both Escoe's arrest and his commitment to Leavenworth.

The unanimous Court held that this ex parte procedure violated the statute. The statute required that upon arrest, the probationer was "to forthwith be taken before the court." Escoe, "instead of being brought before the court which had imposed the sentence, was taken to a prison beyond the territorial limits of that court and kept there in confinement without the opportunity for a hearing. For this denial of a legal privilege, the commitment may not stand."[22]

The government argued that the judge's decision to order commitment showed the futility of a hearing. The Court, however, responded with a different baseline—the procedural one. "The *non sequitur* is obvious. The judge is without the light whereby his discretion must be guided until a hearing, however summary, has been given the supposed offender."[23] The new baseline, however, did not apply as a matter of constitutional law, because probation "comes as an act of grace . . . and may be coupled with such conditions in respect of its duration as Congress may impose."[24]

20 *Id.* at 222–23.
21 295 U.S. 490 (1935).
22 *Id.* at 492.
23 *Id.* at 494 (citations omitted).
24 *Id.* at 492–93 (citations omitted).

Under the Court's interpretation of the act, revocation was not a sentencing proceeding. The judge might decide that there had been no violation of the conditions or that the violations did not warrant commitment. If, however, the judge committed the probationer, the consequence was the imposition of the original sentence. A subsequent decision expressly forbade increasing the sentence at revocation, but was silent about decreasing it.[25] So while the probation cases accepted the right-privilege distinction as a constitutional matter and rejected it as a statutory matter, these decisions did not purport to apply to the exercise of judicial sentencing discretion immediately following conviction. Ultimately, the sentencing cases would circle back to the revocation cases, with the crucial difference of adopting the procedural baseline for constitutional as well as statutory issues.

D. The First Sentencing Trilogy: *Townsend*, *Gryger*, and *Williams*

In the 1932 Scottsboro case,[26] the Court held that Fourteenth Amendment due process required not just permitting defendants to be heard through counsel, but the appointment of counsel for indigent defendants. The Court quickly made clear that due process did not require appointing counsel in all cases. *Betts v. Brady*,[27] decided in 1942, read the due process right to counsel narrowly, by holding that in noncapital cases, due process required the state court to appoint counsel only when the case presented issues of exceptional difficulty,[28] the so-called special circumstances rule. Soon after *Betts* established a federal constitutional right to counsel at trials involving "special circumstances," the Court heard cases brought by state prisoners complaining that they faced "special circumstances" when they were sentenced, rather than during their trials or guilty pleas.

In 1948, the Court decided two cases in which prisoners in Pennsylvania claimed that their sentences, but not their convictions, violated due process because the sentencing court did not appoint, or at least offer to appoint,

[25] Roberts v. United States, 320 U.S. 264 (1943).
[26] Powell v. Alabama, 287 U.S. 45 (1932).
[27] 316 U.S. 455 (1942).
[28] *Id.* at 473 ("while want of counsel in a particular case may result in a conviction lacking in such fundamental fairness, we cannot say that the amendment embodies an inexorable command that no trial for any offense, or in any court, can be fairly conducted and justice accorded a defendant who is not represented by counsel.").

counsel at sentencing.[29] Frank Townsend pleaded guilty to burglary and robbery and was sentenced to two ten- to twenty-year indeterminate sentences. Francis Gryger had been in prison for receiving stolen goods when the prosecutor filed an information giving notice that Gryger's criminal record made him eligible for a life sentence under the Commonwealth's Habitual Criminal Law. Archibald Cox, who decades later served as special prosecutor in the Watergate crisis, represented both prisoners.

The Court granted relief in *Townsend* and denied it in *Gryger.* The judge who sentenced Townsend had broad sentencing discretion. At the sentencing hearing, the judge based the sentence on prior offenses. The record, however, showed that for three of the offenses the judge mentioned at the hearing, the charges had ended in dismissal or acquittal, not conviction. Justice Jackson wrote for the majority, "while disadvantaged by lack of counsel, this prisoner was sentenced on the basis of assumptions concerning his criminal record which were materially untrue. Such a result, whether caused by carelessness or design, is inconsistent with due process of law, and such a conviction cannot stand."[30]

The Court denied relief to Gryger, who could not point to factual errors like those made by the sentencing judge in *Townsend.* Nonetheless, he had a strong case. The Commonwealth sought to commit him for life after he had been sentenced on his latest offense. He therefore had to prepare a defense in prison, where he had no access to lawbooks, including even a copy of the Habitual Criminal Act.[31] Cox pressed the point, endorsed by four dissenting Justices, that the sentencing judge had treated the Habitual Criminal Act as mandatory when the law said on its face that it was discretionary.[32] Justice Jackson again wrote, but for a different majority.

The *Gryger* majority treated the sentencing judge's denial of discretion as an exercise of discretion, showing that the application of the recidivism statute was a foregone conclusion. The federal courts would not reverse a

[29] Townsend v. Burke, 334 U.S. 736 (1948); Gryger v. Burke, 334 U.S. 728 (1948).

[30] *Townsend*, 334 U.S. at 740–41.

[31] *Gryger*, 334 U.S. at 735 n.6 (Rutledge, J., dissenting). A case after *Gryger* but before *Gideon* substantially adopted Rutledge's dissent. *See* Chewning v. Cunningham, 368 U.S. 443 (1962) (holding that due process required appointment of counsel at post-conviction sentence-enhancement hearing under Virginia habitual felon statute).

[32] Act of April 29, 1929, no. 373, 1929 Pa. Laws 854, § 4 provided that the prosecutor had a duty to file the information, but that if the jury found defendant to be the same person four times convicted, "the court may sentence him to imprisonment for life" and that the "sentence shall be reviewable on appeal by the Supreme or Superior Courts, not only as to alleged legal errors but also as to the justice thereof."

state judgment based on a violation of state law. The federal ground, as Cox and the dissenters argued, was to assistance of counsel who would have pointed out the discretion and made arguments about its exercise.[33] Cardozo had made the same point in *Roberts*. Gryger could not challenge the prosecutor's decision to seek the life sentence on due process grounds because he had taken the position that the filing of the information could not trigger the life sentence without the discretionary approval of the judge.

The next year, in *Williams v. New York*,[34] the Court held that while due process required that sentencing hearings be fair, it did not require the rules of evidence applicable at trials. A New York jury convicted Williams, an African American, of murdering Selma Graff, a white teenager, during the burglary of her home.[35] The jury recommended life imprisonment rather than the death penalty. The judge, however, had discretion to overrule the jury, and did so, after consulting a pre-sentence report that was not introduced at trial. The *Williams* Court affirmed the death sentence, reasoning that, as historical practice showed, the sound exercise of sentencing discretion called for considering hearsay about character and past acts.[36] The opinion closes with this afterthought, tacked on in a footnote: "What we have said is not to be accepted as a holding that the sentencing procedure is immune from scrutiny under the due process clause. See *Townsend*."[37]

In *Gryger*, *Townsend*, and *Williams*, the state law provided a sentencing hearing. The constitutional issue was not the right to be heard, but rather the specific procedures due process requires when the state elects to hold hearings.[38] In US constitutional history, the argument that the

[33] *Gryger*, 334 U.S. at 734 (Rutledge, J., dissenting) ("The denial of the very essence of the judicial process, which is the exercise of discretion where discretion is required, is in itself a denial of due process, not merely an error of state law of no concern to this Court.").

[34] 337 U.S. 241 (1949).

[35] *See, e.g., Supreme Court Upholds Negro Death Verdict*, SARASOTA HERALD-TRIB. (N.Y.), June 6, 1949, at 2. The state's attorney urged Governor Dewey to commute the death sentence, which Dewey did on the day the execution was scheduled. *Dewey Commutes Negro's Death*, ONEONTA STAR (N.Y.), Nov. 17, 1949, at 1.

[36] *Williams*, 337 U.S. at 246–47 ("In addition to the historical basis for different evidentiary rules governing trial and sentencing procedures there are sound practical reasons for the distinction. . . . Highly relevant—if not essential—to [the judge's] selection of an appropriate sentence is the possession of the fullest information possible concerning the defendant's life and characteristics.") (footnote omitted).

[37] *Id.* at 252 n.18.

[38] *See* Sanford Kadish, *Legal Norm and Discretion in the Police and Sentencing Processes*, 75 HARV. L. REV. 904, 917 (1962) ("During judicial sentencing a hearing and counsel are normally available."); *id.* at 917 n.39 (citing *Williams*, 337 U.S. at 251–52, and Thomas v. Teets, 220 F.2d 232, 239 (9th Cir. 1955)) ("It is doubtful that there is any constitutional compulsion upon the sentencing judge to hold any hearing at all on the issue of punishment."). Thomas challenged his death sentence on the grounds that the sentencing judge refused to hear a presentation of mitigating circumstances. The

greater-power-over-substance includes the lesser-power-over-procedure has come, gone, and come again over the years. With respect to judicial sentencing, however, the baseline from the inception of the modern law has not been the maximum liability the legislature authorized.

Townsend's sentence was within the discretionary range provided by statute. He nonetheless had a constitutional right to have that discretion exercised fairly:

> [W]e are not reaching this result because of petitioner's allegation that his sentence was unduly severe. The sentence being with the limits set by the statute, its severity would not be grounds for relief... It is not the duration or severity of this sentence that renders it constitutionally invalid; it is the careless or designed pronouncement of sentence on a foundation so extensively and materially false, which the prisoner had no opportunity to correct by the services which counsel would provide, that renders the proceedings lacking in due process.[39]

Even when a discretionary sentence came in under the statutory maximum, sentencing discretion called for fair procedures.

Neither Townsend nor Gryger complained about *prosecutorial* discretion to file the habitual criminal information. They argued, with the clear support of the statute and Pennsylvania precedents, that the judge had discretion to reject a life sentence even when the offender's record met the statutory criteria. In modern terms, the Pennsylvania habitual criminal term was not a

Ninth Circuit rejected this claim, reasoning that the statutory assignment of discretion to impose death or life "necessarily includes the exercise of discretion as to what, if any, 'matters in mitigation' the trial judge will take into consideration. If, in view of the judge, the circumstances of this crime, in and of themselves, and wholly apart from any other considerations, called for the death penalty, then to impose it was his simple duty. In no respect can his refusal to hear further evidence be deemed a denial of due process." *Thomas*, 220 F.2d at 239. On the facts, the *Thomas* court may have reached the right result under the law of the time, but the quoted language reads too much into *Williams*. *Williams* held that the sentencing judge could consider information outside the trial record and, in addition to the defendant's arguments, not that the judge could refuse to consider defense arguments. *Townsend* held the contrary, that the judge could exercise discretion but only after hearing both sides. *Thomas* recognizes an important limit to the right to be heard—that is, that the right to be heard is not the right to present redundant arguments or cumulative evidence. But the quoted language goes beyond asserting this commonsense limit. It also seems at odds with the Supreme Court's caveat that *Williams* did not hold that "the sentencing procedure is immune from scrutiny under the due-process clause." *Williams*, 337 U.S. at 252 n.18.

[39] *Townsend*, 334 U.S. at 741.

mandatory minimum because the prosecutor's charging decision didn't bind the judge.

Indeed, the Pennsylvania statute, like some of the same vintage in other states, purported to require the prosecutor to file the information.[40] This left much prosecutorial discretion in practice. In a pre-digital age, a prosecutor could always explain not filing based on ignorance of, or doubts about the accuracy of, the record of prior convictions.[41] The prosecutor, however, technically complied with the statute by filing the information rather than failing to file. Those prosecuted could only complain about prosecutorial selection based on arbitrary discrimination from among a pool of others equally eligible but not prosecuted as habitual criminals. That claim would have based on equal protection rather than due process, and neither Townsend nor Gryger raised it.[42]

E. The Second Sentencing Trilogy: *Chewning*, *Oyler*, and *Crabtree*

In 1962, the Court ruled on three *habeas* petitions brought by prisoners challenging their confinement under the recidivism statutes of, respectively, Virginia and West Virginia.[43] In the Virginia case, Morgan Chewning had been serving a prison sentence when he was taken to court to answer an information charging him as a habitual criminal. The court refused to appoint counsel. Chewning was convicted as a recidivist at the same court appearance where he first learned the charge.

[40] *See* Act of April 29, 1929, no. 373, 1929 Pa. Laws 854, § 4 ("it shall be the duty of the district attorney of the county in which the last conviction was had to file an information").

[41] Pennsylvania *ex rel.* Foster v. Ashe, 23 A.2d 245, 248 (Pa. Super. Ct. 1941):

> The district attorney may have notice of a defendant's criminal record but not be prepared to prove it on a jury trial. He must be satisfied of the identity of the defendant with the person convicted in other jurisdictions; of the character of the offenses of which he was convicted and that they fall within the crimes mentioned in section 1, and he must be prepared to satisfy a jury beyond a reasonable doubt of these facts by competent evidence in case the defendant denies the previous convictions as applicable to him, before he is called upon to act by way of filing an information.

[42] *See* Brief for the Petitioner at 5, Townsend v. Burke, 334 U.S. 736 (1948) (No. 542) ("Petitioner was arraigned and sentenced without due process of law."); Brief for the Petitioner at 2, Gryger v. Burke, 334 U.S. 728 (1948) (No. 541) (invoking Due Process, Ex Post Facto, and Double Jeopardy Clauses).

[43] Chewning v. Cunningham, 368 U.S. 443 (1962); Oyler v. Boles, 368 U.S. 448 (1962) (consolidating the cases *Oyler v. Boles*, No. 56, and *Crabtree v. Boles*, No. 57).

In the Supreme Court, Chewning emphasized the judge's discretion under the Virginia statute. The Pennsylvania statute provided that the judge "may" impose a life term, upon proof of the prior convictions, with the decision to do so reviewable for justice in the Pennsylvania Supreme Court. The Virginia statute provided that, on proof of three felony convictions, the trial court might impose such additional sentence as "it may deem proper." The judge in *Townsend* and *Gryger* could choose between imposing life and not increasing a recidivist's sentence at all. The judge in Chewning's case could have added anything from zero up to life. As it happened, the judge imposed ten years.

Chewning also argued that the validity of the prior convictions and the constitutional issues raised by the statute were complex enough to call for appointing counsel under the *Betts* standard for appointing trial counsel. The Court agreed with this latter point and ruled for Chewning without addressing the scope-of-discretion argument. As with the Pennsylvania statute, the Virginia recidivism law was not a mandatory minimum because the judge had discretion to impose no extra time.

The West Virginia statute at issue in the other two cases was not discretionary but doubly mandatory.[44] Like the Pennsylvania statute, it imposed a "duty" on the state's attorney to file the information alleging the prior convictions. Unlike the Pennsylvania statute, it conferred no discretion on the judge. Once the prior convictions and the defendant's identity were proved, a life sentence was mandatory.

The West Virginia prisoners, James Oyler and Paul Crabtree, raised both due process and equal protection arguments. In each case, the defendant was convicted of a felony—Oyler of second-degree murder after a trial, and Crabtree after pleading guilty to forgery. In both cases, the prosecutor filed the recidivism information at the hearing for sentencing on the trial conviction. Unlike Chewning, Oyler and Crabtree were represented by counsel. As a matter of due process, the prisoners argued that they had been called to answer the recidivism information without sufficient notice to prepare a defense.[45]

[44] The relevant statutory provision is set out in Brief for Respondent at 4, Oyler v. Boles, 368 U.S. 448 (1962) (Nos. 56 & 57). *See* W. Va. Code §§ 61-11-18 & -19 (1961).

[45] Brief for Petitioners at 15, Oyler v. Boles, 368 U.S. 448 (1962) (Nos. 56 & 57) ("Without such notice the defendant cannot prepare his defense and the right of counsel accorded him—Oyler and Crabtree, according to the orders which were entered, were both accompanied by counsel at the final hearing before commitment—is wholly frustrated."); *id.* at 16–17 ("Whether Crabtree pleaded guilty in consideration of the Habitual Criminal law not being imposed we do not know. But it is wholly

The equal protection argument exploited the mandatory nature of the West Virginia statute, which facially put a "duty" on prosecutors to file the information and said that the court "shall" impose the life sentence when identity and prior convictions were proved. The petitioners pointed out that, in fact, the recidivism penalty was almost never imposed.[46] Whether they had lost the lottery by chance or by design, an "uneven hand" was enforcing the law.

The Court granted Chewning's petition based on the denial of counsel, applying the *Betts* standard and citing *Townsend*.[47] The Court denied the petitions of Oyler and Crabtree. In the process, the majority opinion gave fresh support to the idea that due process required sentencing hearings, not just that hearings provided by state law be fair ones. Cases addressing due process at sentencing thus far had been "specifically concerned with the right to assistance of counsel . . . but it would have been an idle accomplishment to say that due process requires counsel but not the right to reasonable notice and opportunity to be heard."[48] That said, the majority held that representation by counsel cured whatever notice problem was presented by the West Virginia procedure.[49] Neither the majority nor the dissent spoke to the possibility that the prosecutor had dishonored a plea deal with Crabtree.

As to the equal protection argument, the majority, in a passage not challenged by the dissent, faulted the petitioners for not proving that the cases of nonprosecution were cases in which the state's attorney actually knew about each offender's criminal history.[50] The prisoners, moreover, did not argue that they were selected for prosecution based on some suspect classification such as race:

improbable that Crabtree would have pleaded guilty to this lesser felony if he had known that the mandatory habitual criminal law would be involved against him.") (citation omitted).

[46] *Id.* at 25 ("In 904 of 983 cases informations were not filed. All 983 were similarly situated and yet not all were treated alike.").

[47] *Chewning*, 368 U.S. at 447 (citing, *inter alia*, *Townsend*) ("The issues presented under Virginia's statute so complex, and the potential prejudice resulting from the absence of counsel so great that the rule we have followed concerning the appointment of counsel in other types of criminal trials is equally applicable here.").

[48] *Oyler*, 368 U.S. at 452.

[49] *Id.* at 453 ("petitioners, who were represented by counsel, neither denied they were the persons named nor remained silent. Nor did they object or seek a continuance on the ground that they had not received adequate notice and needed more time to determine how to respond with respect to the issue of their identity.").

[50] *Id.* at 456.

> Moreover, the conscious exercise of some selectivity in enforcement is not in itself a federal constitutional violation. Even though the statistics in this case might imply a policy of selective enforcement, it was not stated that the selection was deliberately based upon an unjustifiable standard such as race, religion, or other arbitrary classification. Therefore grounds supporting a finding of a denial of equal protection were not alleged.[51]

The Court would later cut this "some selectivity" language from the context of an equal protection challenge to departures from a mandatory prosecution policy and paste it into due process jurisprudence as the test of prosecutorial discretion. We shall, however, finish tracing the Court's sentencing cases before turning to the prosecutorial discretion cases in Chapter 4.

F. Sentencing and the Criminal Procedure Revolution

In *Gryger*, *Townsend*, and *Williams*, state law provided a sentencing hearing. The constitutional issue had not been the right to be heard but what specific procedures due process requires when the state elected to hold hearings. The Justices applied to sentencing the same due process standard that governed trial procedure: fundamental fairness, assessed on a case-by-case basis. Three weeks after handing down *Williams*, the Court foreshadowed the incorporation of the specific terms of the Fourth, Fifth, and Sixth amendments into Fourteenth Amendment due process. *Wolf v. Colorado*[52] held that the Fourteenth Amendment incorporates the Fourth Amendment ban on "unreasonable searches."[53] The *Wolf* majority, however, did not read the remedy of the exclusionary rule, applicable in federal courts, to be binding on the states.[54]

A dozen years later, the Warren Court began incorporating the Bill of Rights criminal provisions into the Fourteenth Amendment, a development that came to be known as a "revolution."[55] In 1963, *Gideon v. Wainwright*[56]

[51] *Id.* (citations omitted).
[52] 338 U.S. 25 (1949).
[53] *Id.* at 27–28.
[54] *Id.* at 33.
[55] For a sample of views on the Warren Court revolution, see Craig M. Bradley, The Failure of the Criminal Procedure Revolution (1993); William J. Stuntz, The Collapse of American Criminal Justice (2011); Donald A. Dripps, About Guilt and Innocence (2003).
[56] 372 U.S. 335 (1963).

overruled the *Betts* line of cases by requiring offering appointed counsel to all indigent felony defendants. Gideon had been convicted after a trial, so one open question left after *Gideon* was a temporal one. At what stage of the criminal process did the right to counsel begin and end?

At the front end of the criminal process, the Court settled, after some fits and starts, on recognizing the Sixth Amendment right to counsel when formal adjudication begins, by way of indictment, information, arraignment, or evidentiary hearing.[57] After arrest, but before accusation, the *Miranda* rules, designed to prevent involuntary self-incrimination, regulated police questioning. After an accusation, the Sixth Amendment requires the assistance of counsel, or a waiver, at every "critical stage" in the process, including guilty pleas and trials.[58]

Chewning had established that the due process-based right to counsel in exceptionally grave or complex cases applied at sentencing proceedings, even when a special enhancement procedure was initiated after the offender had begun serving a sentence. After *Gideon*, the question became whether sentencing was part of a "criminal prosecution" so that *Gideon*'s Sixth Amendment holding applied, or whether sentencing was to be governed solely by due process under *Chewning*.

In a pair of cases from Washington State, the Court took the Sixth Amendment route.[59] The Washington sentencing procedure required the trial judge to enter the maximum authorized prison term. The judge, however, could suspend the sentence and impose terms of probation. If the judge committed the defendant to prison, the state Parole Board would consider the case and set the actual length of the sentence. The Board gave substantial weight to the judge's recommendation but ultimately made its own decision.

The two defendants, Jerry Mempa and William Walkling, each advised by counsel, pleaded guilty respectively to auto theft and burglary. Both were sentenced to the statutory maximum, but each sentence was suspended so the Parole Board did not then consider their cases. The state's attorney later moved to revoke probation because Mempa and Walkling were involved in other crimes. The record did not show that either man was offered appointed counsel at the revocation hearings. Both hearings resulted in revocation, and

[57] *See* Kirby v. Illinois, 406 U.S. 682 (1972).

[58] *See, e.g., Gideon*, 372 U.S. 335 (trial); Coleman v. Alabama, 399 U.S. 1 (1970) (preliminary hearing); Arsenault v. Massachusetts, 393 U.S. 5 (1968) (entering guilty plea); Hill v. Lockhart, 474 U.S. 52 (1985) (advising defendant about potential sentence before guilty plea).

[59] Mempa v. Rhay, 389 U.S. 128 (1967) (consolidating *Mempa v. Rhay*, Docket No. 16, and *Walkling v. Washington State Board of Prison Terms and Paroles*, Docket No. 22).

the defendants were committed for the maximum sentence applicable to the offenses of original conviction.

In the Supreme Court, the state argued that the "criminal prosecution" ended with the imposition of the suspended sentence. Revocation was a separate matter, subject to due process but not to the Sixth Amendment.[60] Justice Marshall, for a unanimous court, saw it otherwise. Under the due process "special circumstances" rule, the Court had required the appointment of counsel at preliminary hearings, and in *Townsend* and *Chewning*, at sentencing. Ergo, the pre-*Gideon* cases, once

> the *Betts* requirement of special circumstances is stripped away by *Gideon*, clearly stand for the proposition that appointment of counsel for an indigent is required at every stage of a criminal proceeding where substantial rights of a criminal accused may be affected. In particular, *Townsend v. Burke* [] illustrates the critical nature of sentencing in a criminal case and might well be considered to support by itself a holding that the right to counsel applies at sentencing.[61]

Despite the automatic character of the maximum sentence after revocation, counsel had at least two vital roles at the revocation stage.

First, the revocation hearing was the occasion for the judge to recommend a sentence to the Parole Board, a recommendation that carried significant weight. "Obviously to the extent such recommendations are influential in determining the resulting sentence, the necessity for the aid of counsel in marshaling the facts, introducing evidence of mitigating circumstances and in general aiding and assisting the defendant to present his case as to sentence is apparent."[62] Second, if not noticed at the revocation hearing, the defendant lost the right to appeal and to move to withdraw a guilty plea. These factors assumed "increased significance when . . . as happened in these two cases, the eventual imposition of sentence on the prior plea of guilty is based on the alleged commission of offenses for which the accused is never tried."[63]

[60] Respondents' Brief at 39, Mempa v. Rhay, 389 U.S. 128 (1967) (Nos. 16 & 22) ("If the right to counsel exists, for the aid of convicted persons at probation revocation hearings, it would seem clear that such right is not derived through the Sixth Amendment . . . ").

[61] *Mempa*, 389 U.S. at 134 (footnote omitted).

[62] *Id.* at 135.

[63] *Id.* at 136–37.

Mempa, like the due process cases, could be read as requiring counsel when state law provided a hearing, as distinct from requiring a hearing in the first place. Some loose language in *Specht v. Patterson*,[64] decided the previous term, supported this reading. Specht had been convicted of "indecent liberties" under a Colorado statute that provided a ten-year maximum term. Colorado, however, authorized the sentencing judge to order a psychiatric evaluation and, after considering the medical report, order an indeterminate term of one day to life. Specht complained that he should have had an opportunity to contest the indeterminate sentence with the assistance of counsel.

The Court agreed with Specht on the ground that the indeterminate sentencing was a separate criminal proceeding like the post-conviction resentencing proceedings in *Gryger*, *Chewning*, and *Oyler*. In each of those cases, state law gave the defense full trial rights, excepting only the jury, respecting the validity of the priors and the defendant's identity. Colorado providing no right to be heard, the indeterminate sentence procedure violated due process.

The Court understandably felt the need to reaffirm *Williams*, and began the opinion by stating: "We held in *Williams* [] that the Due Process Clause of the Fourteenth Amendment did not require a judge to have hearings and to give a convicted person an opportunity to participate in those hearings when he came to determine the sentence to be imposed."[65] Justice Douglas then quoted language from *Williams* stating that sentencing courts must rely on probation reports that would not be admissible at trial. *Williams* did (and still does) stand for the proposition that sentencing courts can consider hearsay. It is a very different proposition to say that the court can *refuse* to hear argument or evidence from the defense.

In any event, *Williams* did not "hold" that due process does not require a hearing because New York gave Williams a hearing. The scenario hypothesized by Justice Douglas was not at issue. His unfortunate language was dicta in *Specht* incorrectly describing *Williams*. It nonetheless became the first headnote in the report.

[64] 386 U.S. 605 (1967).
[65] *Id.* at 606 (citation omitted).

G. The Return to Due Process Analysis and the Triumph of the Procedural Baseline

The text of the Sixth Amendment confined its application to protecting the "accused" during "criminal prosecutions." *Mempa* seemed sensible as applied to sentencing in the trial court in the immediate wake of conviction. *Mempa* itself, however, dealt with what the Court characterized as deferred sentencing, as distinct from new proceedings intended to impose a sentence more severe than the maximum authorized by statute for the offense of conviction. Once classified as part of the original "prosecution," the Sixth Amendment required counsel at the probation-revocation-cum-sentencing-hearing.

In the federal probation cases, however, the decisions treated probation revocation as distinct from the original prosecution. Revocation did not lead to a new sentence on the original conviction, but reinstated the sentence that was initially suspended. Under *Burns* and *Escoe*, probationers had hearing rights in revocation proceedings, but only as a matter of statutory "grace." In state cases, revocation of probation or parole was not subject to due process review at all because of the statutory baseline adopted in *Burns* and reaffirmed in *Escoe*. Those statutory hearing rights did not include the Sixth Amendment right to counsel.

The text of the Sixth Amendment blocked any extension of *Mempa* to administrative proceedings remote from the "prosecution." Even if the Court had found a way around the text, the prevailing penology rejected trial-type proceedings for either sentencing or conditional release decisions. Those, *Williams* pointed out, turned on hearsay about character. The rest of the Sixth Amendment—jury trial, public evidence, and confrontation—were out of place, indeed counterproductive.

The path to a coherent and functional law of hearing rights at sentencing and conditional release proceedings opened with the Court's decision in *Goldberg v. Kelly*.[66] *Goldberg* held that due process required notice and an

[66] Goldberg v. Kelly, 397 U.S. 254 (1970). Prior to *Goldberg*, the Court developed the unconstitutional conditions doctrine (UCCD). The UCCD applies when the government conditions a statutory benefit on the surrender of a constitutional right. *See, e.g.*, Sherbert v. Verner, 374 U.S. 398 (1963). By characterizing a sentence below the code and/or statutory maximums as a statutory benefit, the doctrine might apply to trial penalties. *See* Kay L. Levine, Jonathan Remy Nash, and Robert A. Schapiro, *The Unconstitutional Conditions Vacuum in Criminal Procedure*, 133 YALE L.J. 1401, 1451–55 (2024). Parallel to *Goldberg*, in the context of sentencing hearings the right asserted is not some collateral constitutional right, like the right to jury trial, but the right to fair procedure at sentencing itself. To see the difference, suppose the prosecutor elects to bring a charge carrying a mandatory minimum

opportunity to be heard before welfare officials terminated a beneficiary's public assistance benefits. That might seem far afield from criminal justice, but *Goldberg* repudiated the right-privilege distinction that sustained the constitutional doctrine of *Burns* and *Escoe*.[67] With the right-privilege distinction discarded, *Escoe*'s statutory analysis became due process analysis. Fair procedure replaced the statutory maximum as the constitutional baseline.

Two years after *Goldberg*, the Court decided *Morrissey v. Brewer*.[68] The two petitioners had been convicted, incarcerated, released on parole, and then recommitted for parole violations. In both cases, the parole officer directed the offender's arrest for parole violations. After the arrest, the parole officer submitted a written report to the Iowa Board of Parole. The Board then revoked parole, without giving the petitioners an opportunity to be heard. Only after they were returned to the penitentiary did the Board summon them to an informal hearing.

Chief Justice Burger's opinion for the Court began by describing revocation as a two-part decision.

> The first step in a revocation decision thus involves a wholly retrospective factual question: whether the parolee has in fact acted in violation of one or more conditions of his parole. Only if it is determined that the parolee did violate the conditions does the second question arise: should the parolee be recommitted to prison or should other steps be taken to protect society and improve chances of rehabilitation?[69]

in a no-offer case, where the prosecution has no interest in obtaining a guilty plea. That would still violate the due process right to fair sentencing procedures, because the prosecutor, not a judge or a parole board, chose the sentence. Suppose by contrast that a defendant is convicted at trial after declining a good plea offer, and that the offense of conviction carries a thirty-year maximum but no minimum. If the *judge* imposes a thirty-year term as a trial penalty, the sentence might violate the unconstitutional conditions doctrine even though the tribunal is facially neutral.

There is no conflict in pursuing both approaches, and if my argument that due process prohibits prosecutorial sentencing succeeds, it will be time to take a much closer look at trial penalties imposed by judges. The UCCD is notoriously unprincipled. *See, e.g.*, Michael A. Helfand, *There Are No Unconstitutional Conditions on Free Exercise*, 98 Notre Dame L. Rev. Reflections S50, S55–56 (2023). Whether policing judicial trial penalties is worth entangling the criminal process in that Sargasso Sea is a difficult question. There is no similar difficulty in answering whether due process permits prosecutors to control sentences.

[67] *Id.* at 262 ("The constitutional challenge cannot be answered by an argument that public assistance benefits are 'a privilege' and not a 'right.'") (citation omitted).

[68] 408 U.S. 471 (1972).

[69] *Id.* at 479–80.

The first step was a factual finding that the parole had violated applicable conditions. The second step was a discretionary judgment that the violations were serious enough to justify recommitment.

The Chief Justice then set aside the right-privilege distinction. "Implicit in the system's concern with parole violations is the notion that the parolee is entitled to retain his liberty as long as he substantially abides by the conditions of his parole."[70] He continued, "It is hardly useful any longer to try to deal with this problem in terms of whether the parolee's liberty is a 'right' or a 'privilege.' By whatever name, the liberty is valuable and must be seen as within the protection of the Fourteenth Amendment. Its termination calls for some orderly process, however informal."[71] Once granted, parole was an administrative entitlement, like public assistance or public employment. Given *Goldberg*, the only question left was not whether due process required a hearing, but what sort of hearing it required.

The Sixth Amendment dropped from the analysis because "the revocation of parole is not part of a criminal prosecution and thus the full panoply of rights due a defendant in such a proceeding does not apply to parole revocations."[72] That freed the Court to identify the minimum requirements of due process in the revocation context. As other parts of the opinion indicate, the justices had functional as well as formal reservations about extending the Sixth Amendment to revocation proceedings.

Morrissey mandated two different types of hearings. First, following arrest but before recommitment, due process required notice and an opportunity to appear and be heard about whether there was probable cause to believe parole violations had occurred. The hearing officer "need not be a judicial officer" but must be "independent" and "someone not directly involved in the case."[73] The Court explicitly disqualified the offender's supervising officer, who tendered the recommendation for arrest and revocation. The offender must be given notice of the alleged parole violations, and "an opportunity to appear and speak in his own behalf" and to "bring letters, documents, or individuals who can give relevant information to the hearing officer."[74]

Second, if the initial hearing officer decided to commit, due process required a fuller hearing after the return to prison. "This hearing must be the

[70] *Id.* at 479.
[71] *Id.* at 482.
[72] *Id.* at 480.
[73] *Id.* at 485–86.
[74] *Id.* at 487.

basis for more than determining probable cause; it must lead to a final evaluation of any contested relevant facts and consideration of whether the facts as determined warrant revocation."[75] The "minimum requirements of due process" included:

> (a) written notice of the claimed violations of parole; (b) disclosure to the parolee of evidence against him; (c) opportunity to be heard in person and to present witnesses and documentary evidence; (d) the right to confront and cross-examine adverse witnesses (unless the hearing officer specifically finds good cause for not allowing confrontation); (e) a "neutral and detached" hearing body such as a traditional parole board, members of which need not be judicial officers or lawyers; and (f) a written statement by the factfinders as to the evidence relied on and reasons for revoking parole.[76]

Justice Brennan and Justice Douglas wrote separately to advocate for more elaborate procedures. But on the "minimum requirements of due process," the Court was unanimous.

Morrissey left the right to counsel for another day. The year after *Morrissey*, *Gagnon v. Scarpelli*[77] held that probation revocations were subject to the same due process safeguards as the parole revocations at issue in *Morrissey*. *Gagnon*, however, addressed the right to counsel issue. Although "counsel will probably be both undesirable and constitutionally unnecessary in most revocation hearings, there will remain certain cases in which fundamental fairness—the touchstone of due process—will require that the State provide at its expense counsel for indigent probationers or parolees."[78]

The year after *Gagnon*, the Court held that due process requires a sentencing hearing in front of a neutral tribunal. The occasion was a contempt case, *Taylor v. Hayes*,[79] arising out of the trial of accused murderers of two police officers. During the trial, the judge on nine occasions informed Taylor, the counsel for the defense, that counsel was in contempt. Immediately after the jury returned a guilty verdict, Judge Hayes refused the lawyer's request to respond and "declaring that 'I have you' on nine counts, [the judge] proceeded to impose a jail term on each count totaling almost

[75] *Id.* at 488.
[76] *Id.* at 489.
[77] 411 U.S. 778 (1973).
[78] *Id.* at 790.
[79] 418 U.S. 488 (1974).

four and one-half years . . . 'all to run consecutive.' "[80] The Kentucky appellate court reduced the sentence to six months in jail, to square the result with Supreme Court precedent recognizing a "petty offense" exception to the right to jury trial.

In the Supreme Court, Taylor argued that the right to jury trial should be analyzed before, rather than after, conviction and sentencing. The Court rejected this theory.[81] Taylor also argued that the judge had denied him "the opportunity to be heard in defense or mitigation."[82] Even though the trial judge had witnessed firsthand each act of contempt, the Court agreed with Taylor.

Given the judge's knowledge, checked against the trial transcript, "a full-scale trial" was not "appropriate."[83] Nonetheless, "the contemnor might at least urge, for example, that the behavior at issue was not contempt but the acceptable conduct of an attorney representing his client; or, he might present matters in mitigation or otherwise attempt to make amends with the court."[84] The Court went still further, holding that if Taylor was "to be tried again, he should not be tried by respondent [the original trial judge]." The inquiry required by due process "must be not only whether there was actual bias on respondent's part, but also whether there was 'such a likelihood of bias or an appearance of bias that the judge was unable to hold the balance between vindicating the interests of the court and the interests of the accused.' "[85] Only Justice Rehnquist dissented.[86]

Three years later, *Gardner v. Florida* reversed a death sentence imposed by a judge acting on a confidential pre-sentence report that was not requested by or shared with either the prosecution or the defense.[87] The state relied on *Williams v. New York*. The Supreme Court's plurality opinion rejected the state's reliance on *Williams v. New York* for two reasons. First, *Gardner* was a capital case. "In 1949, when the Williams case was decided, no significant

[80] 418 U.S. at 490–91 (footnote omitted).

[81] In a companion case, the petitioners relied solely on the jury trial issue and won because, unlike Taylor, they had received sentences exceeding in aggregate the six-month limit. Codispoti v. Pennsylvania, 418 U.S. 506 (1974).

[82] Brief for Petitioner at 36–41, Taylor v. Hayes, 418 U.S. 488 (1974) (No. 73-473) (arguing that due process requires "the opportunity to be heard in defense or mitigation").

[83] *Taylor*, 418 U.S. at 499.

[84] *Id.* (citation omitted).

[85] *Id.* at 501.

[86] *Id.* at 523 (Rehnquist, J., dissenting). Chief Justice Burger joined Justice Rehnquist on the jury trial issue, but not on the due process issue.

[87] Gardner v. Florida, 430 U.S. 349 (1977) (plurality opinion).

constitutional difference between the death penalty and lesser punishments for crime had been expressly recognized by this Court."[88]

The *Gardner* opinion then dealt with due process at sentencing generally, not just in capital cases:

> Second, it is now clear that the sentencing process, as well as the trial itself, must satisfy the requirements of the Due Process Clause. Even though the defendant has no substantive right to a particular sentence within the range authorized by statute, the sentencing is a critical stage of the criminal proceeding at which he is entitled to the effective assistance of counsel. The defendant has a legitimate interest in the character of the procedure which leads to the imposition of sentence even if he may have no right to object to a particular result of the sentencing process.[89]

Only three Justices—Stevens, Stewart, and Powell—joined this opinion, with its emphatic repudiation of the statutory baseline. Justice Brennan and Justice Marshall agreed, and only Justice Rehnquist would have affirmed the death sentence.[90] The lower courts routinely cite *Gardner* for the principle that the due process clauses apply at sentencing, generally omitting the "plurality opinion" designation.[91] In any event, *Hayes* already had established a constitutional right to be heard about, *inter alia*, "mitigation."

H. Summary of the Sentencing Cases

Convicted offenders have no constitutional right to a sentence under the statutory maximum, or to conditional release. The Supreme Court's cases, however, have thoroughly rejected maximum liability as the baseline. Instead,

[88] *Id.* at 357.

[89] *Id.* at 358 (citations omitted).

[90] *See id.* at 364 (separate opinion of Brennan, J.) ("I agree for the reasons stated in the plurality opinion that the Due Process Clause of the Fourteenth Amendment is violated when a defendant facing a death sentence is not informed of the contents of a presentence investigation report made to the sentencing judge."); *id.* at 365 (Marshall, J., dissenting) (noting the trial judge's reliance on undisclosed portions of the presentence report, and state Supreme Court's failure to discuss the issue, stating that "obviously that alone is enough to deny due process and require that the death sentence be vacated as the Court now holds."); *id.* at 371 (Rehnquist, J., dissenting).

[91] *See, e.g.*, United States v. Smith, 562 Fed. App'x 613, 616 (10th Cir. 2014); United States v. Maroccia, 686 Fed. App'x 138, 146 (3d Cir. 2017) (Krause, J., concurring); State v. Miller, 381 N.W.2d 156, 158 (Neb. 1986); People v. Felix, 446 N.E.2d 757, 761–62 (N.Y. 1983); State v. McCormick, 397 N.E.2d 276, 279 (Ind. 1979).

while offenders have no right to any specific *outcome*, they do have a constitutional right to have discretion exercised according to fair procedures. In the sentencing context, the procedural baseline has prevailed.

A consistent theme in these precedents is the importance of a neutral tribunal to due process.[92] If due process prohibits the supervising parole officer from making the initial revocation decision, is it possible that this decision could be assigned to the police officer who made the arrest leading to the original criminal conviction, or to the prosecutor who filed the original charges? Would *Mempa* be satisfied if sentencing were turned over to the police or prosecutors, provided the police or prosecutors provided an opportunity to be heard through counsel? These questions sound rhetorical, if not absurd altogether. Yet after we have reviewed the Court's prosecutorial discretion cases, the answer to these "rhetorical" questions is not so clear.

[92] *See, e.g.*, Black v. Romano, 471 U.S. 606, 612 (1985) (probationer is entitled to "a neutral hearing body"); Wolff v. McDonnell, 418 U.S. 539, 571 (1974) (holding that prison disciplinary board with power to revoke good-time credits was "not sufficiently impartial to satisfy the Due Process Clause."); Morrissey v. Brewer, 408 U.S. 471, 489 (1972) ("minimum requirements of due process" include "a 'neutral and detached' hearing body"); Gagnon v. Scarpelli, 441 U.S. 778, 786 (1973) (repeating the *Morrissey* formula).

4

The Supreme Court and Prosecutorial Sentencing Discretion

A. Introduction

By the 1920s, in most US jurisdictions, convictions by plea outnumbered convictions by trial by a factor of two or three to one.[1] Despite the frequency of plea bargains, the legitimacy of compromising criminal cases was not established until the Supreme Court decision in *Santobello v. New York*.[2] Chief Justice Burger's opinion for the Court described plea bargaining as "essential" because requiring "full-scale trial[s]" would force the system to "multiply by many times the number of judges and court facilities."[3] Plea bargaining was not just "essential" but "highly desirable" because it minimized pretrial detention and "enhances whatever may be the rehabilitative prospects of the guilty" by "shortening the time between charge and disposition."[4]

Santobello had pleaded guilty in exchange for a lesser included charge and a promise by the prosecutor not to make a sentencing recommendation. The sentencing hearing was delayed, and the new prosecutor who took on the case either was unaware of the deal or deliberately reneged on it by recommending a maximum sentence. Having blessed the plea bargaining process, the *Santobello* Court issued some important caveats.

The accused must either have a lawyer's advice or waive it before pleading guilty. "The plea must, of course, be voluntary and knowing and if it was induced by promises, the essence of those promises must in some way be made known."[5] If promises were made, they had to be disclosed and then fulfilled. The Chief Justice used the term "promise" rather than "threat," but even before *Santobello* the cases had exposed the tension between permitting better

[1] *See* Raymond Moley, *The Vanishing Jury*, 2 S. Calif. L. Rev. 97, 105 (1928).
[2] 404 U.S. 257 (1971).
[3] *Id.* at 260.
[4] *Id.* at 261.
[5] *Id.* at 261–62.

Sentencing Discretion and the Constitution. Donald A. Dripps, Oxford University Press.
 DOI: 10.1093/9780197830390.003.0004

outcomes for defendants who surrendered than for those who chose to put up a fight.

B. The Vindictiveness Doctrine

In 1969, the Court decided two cases in which the petitioners who had successfully challenged their convictions received harsher sentences on remand than the sentences they had challenged.[6] Clifton Pearce was convicted of assault with intent to commit rape, but the conviction was vacated in a state post-conviction proceeding because Pearce's coerced confession was used against him. After remand, Pearce was again convicted. The trial judge imposed an eight-year sentence, which, given the time already served, turned out to be more severe than the original sentence.

The other petitioner, William Rice, pleaded guilty to four burglary charges and was sentenced to ten years. Two and a half years later, a state court vacated the convictions on right-to-counsel grounds. "He was retried upon three of the charges, convicted, and sentenced to prison terms aggregating 25 years. No credit was given for the time he had spent in prison on the original judgments."[7]

The Court, per Justice Stewart, rejected the petitioners' claim that the higher sentences violated the Double Jeopardy Clause. The Court also easily concluded that whatever sentence was imposed after a remand, the defendant should be credited for time already served for the same crimes. The really difficult issue, however, was the appearance of punishing the petitioners not for their crimes but for exercising their legal rights to challenge their convictions.

The Court refused to adopt a per se rule against more severe sentences after remand. It might be that the court had more information about, for example, the defendant's other crimes than it had at the first sentencing. The reasons for a harsher sentence, however, had to be put on the record. Due process, the Court held, forbids "vindictiveness" against the defendant for attacking his conviction. It also forbids deterring others from exercising their legal rights. So if the record at the second sentencing showed no "objective information concerning identifiable

[6] North Carolina v. Pearce, 395 U.S. 711 (1969) (consolidating *North Carolina v. Pearce*, No. 413, and companion case *Simpson v. Rice*, No. 418).

[7] *Id.* at 714 (footnote omitted).

conduct of the defendant" since the first sentence, "vindictiveness against a defendant for having successfully attacked his first conviction" would be presumed.[8]

Subsequent cases established that the appearance of vindictiveness was not present when a subsequent, higher sentence was imposed by a jury or by a different, higher court in a trial de novo.[9] The opinions took *Pearce* as their point of departure and focused on the risk of subjective malice rather than structural neutrality. Juries and higher courts are structurally independent of law enforcement. What, however, about *prosecutors* electing to bring more serious charges against a defendant who exercised his legal right to a trial? That scenario resembles both the vindictiveness condemned in *Pearce* and the plea bargaining celebrated in *Santobello*.

Blackledge v. Perry[10] held that when prosecutors bring more serious charges following a successful challenge to a conviction, they must make the same record showing of changed circumstances required of sentencing judges under *Pearce*. The defendant was a prisoner involved in a fight with another inmate. He was initially charged with a misdemeanor in state district court, convicted, and sentenced to six months to be served consecutively with his ongoing sentence.

Under North Carolina law, a defendant convicted in the district court had an unqualified right to a trial de novo in the superior court. Perry appealed from the district to the superior court, and the prosecution responded by filing a felony charge in that court. Perry took the hint, pleaded guilty, and was sentenced to seven years (this time concurrent with his ongoing sentence but still resulting in extending his period of incarceration relative to the misdemeanor conviction). The Supreme Court held that the more serious charge brought by the prosecutor at the trial de novo stage effectively punished Perry for a lawful appeal, and, absent some explanation such as newly discovered evidence, violated due process.[11]

Pearce adopted the fair-procedure baseline. The Supreme Court knew how the trial court first exercised sentencing discretion. Subsequent departures from that neutral baseline were suspect, even though the offense of conviction carried a higher maximum. *Perry* applied the judicial baseline

[8] *Id.* at 725–26.

[9] *See* Colten v. Kentucky, 407 U.S. 104 (1972) (trial de novo); Chaffin v. Stynchcombe, 412 U.S. 17 (1973) (jury sentencing).

[10] 417 U.S. 21 (1974).

[11] *See id.* at 28–29 & n.7.

to prosecutorial charging decisions. This could have been the first step toward putting charging decisions in neutral actors by requiring active judicial review of charge selection. The subsequent cases, however, established that the code-maximum baseline would test charging decisions. *Perry* had taken a step down a different path—a false step, at least as far as the Court's subsequent cases were concerned.

C. The No-Jury, No-Death Trilogy

In *United States v. Brady*,[12] Brady and an alleged accomplice, Tafoya, were indicted in 1959 for violating the Federal Kidnapping Act. That Act, sometimes referred to as the Lindbergh Act, included 18 U.S.C. §1201(a):

> Whoever knowingly transports in interstate . . . commerce, any person who has been . . . kidnaped . . . and held for ransom . . . or otherwise . . . shall be punished (1) by death if the kidnaped person has not been liberated unharmed, and if the verdict of the jury shall so recommend, or (2) by imprisonment for any term of years or for life, if the death penalty is not imposed.[13]

Since the kidnapping victim had been raped and thus not released unharmed, the defendants were potentially liable to the capital penalty if they pleaded not guilty and elected a jury trial.

After Tafoya turned government witness, Brady pleaded guilty and received a sentence of fifty years' imprisonment. The fifty was later reduced to thirty by executive clemency. In January 1967, about eight years into Brady's thirty-year term, a federal district court in Connecticut dismissed a § 1201(a) count in an indictment against one Charles Jackson, on the ground that exposing only defendants who elect jury trial to the risk of execution was unconstitutional.[14]

Brady then sought habeas corpus relief as a federal prisoner under 28 U.S.C. § 2255, alleging that his guilty plea was involuntary. Subsequently, the

[12] 397 U.S. 742 (1970).

[13] I take the text of the statute from *United States v. Jackson*, 390 U.S. 570, 571 (1968) (holding the authorization of a death sentence only after trial by jury unconstitutional).

[14] United States v. Jackson, 262 F. Supp. 716 (D. Conn. 1967), *aff'd in part, rev'd in part*, 390 U.S. 570 (1968).

Supreme Court upheld the district court's constitutional ruling in *Jackson* but reversed the district court on the severability issue.[15] The district court denied Brady's Section 2255 petition after an evidentiary hearing at which the accomplice and the lawyers for both Brady and the accomplice testified. The district court denied the petition on the ground that Brady chose to plead guilty because of Tafoya's defection, not the risk of capital punishment, and the Tenth Circuit affirmed.[16]

In the companion case of *Parker v. North Carolina*,[17] Parker was charged in 1964 with first-degree burglary as the alleged perpetrator of a home invasion and rape. The North Carolina statute, like the Federal Kidnapping Act, authorized the death penalty for first-degree burglary but only at the discretion of a trial jury; a guilty plea led to an automatic sentence of life imprisonment.[18] Parker pleaded guilty, then three years later challenged his conviction by a petition for habeas in the state courts, which rejected the petition.

The Supreme Court affirmed the lower courts in both *Brady* and *Parker*. Despite the factual finding below that Brady was not motivated by fear of the death penalty when he entered his plea, the Court took the occasion to announce a broad approval of plea bargaining in general.

> [W]e cannot hold that it is unconstitutional for the State to extend a benefit to a defendant who in turn extends a substantial benefit to the State and who demonstrates by his plea that he is ready and willing to admit his crime and to enter the correctional system in a frame of mind that affords hope for success in rehabilitation over a shorter period of time than might otherwise be necessary.[19]

[15] United States v. Jackson, 390 U.S. 570 (1968).

[16] Brady v. United States, 404 F.2d 601 (10th Cir. 1968), *aff'd*, 397 U.S. 742 (1970). It is clear that Brady filed his habeas petition after the district court decision in *Jackson*, and that the Tenth Circuit affirmed the denial of Brady's petition after the Supreme Court decision in *Jackson*. It is not clear from the reports whether the district court decision in *Brady* preceded or followed the Supreme Court's decision in *Jackson*.

[17] 397 U.S. 790 (1970).

[18] "The statute authorizing guilty pleas to capital charges was repealed, effective March 25, 1969. See n. 2, supra. As a result of the repeal, a person who is charged with a capital offense and who is not allowed to plead to a lesser charge must apparently face a jury trial and a death penalty upon a verdict of guilty unless the jury recommends life imprisonment." *Id.* at 795 n.6.

[19] *Brady*, 397 U.S. at 753.

Parker's plea clearly *was* motivated by fear of the death sentence, but given the breadth of the opinion in *Brady*, the Court rejected Parker's coercion claim with little more than a reference to *Brady*.[20]

The *Brady* Court acknowledged both the analogy to police interrogation and the potential risk of plea bargaining to the innocent. With respect to the former, the *Brady* opinion distinguished police interrogation from plea bargaining by invoking *Miranda*.[21] If the presence of counsel dispels coercion, Brady was in fact represented by competent counsel.[22] So too with the innocence problem; the Court declared its trust in the advice of counsel, the skepticism of trial judges receiving pleas, and the option of trial with all its safeguards.[23]

Justices Brennan, Marshall, and Douglas dissented in *Parker* but concurred in *Brady*.[24] Justice Brennan concluded that the North Carolina capital punishment scheme was unconstitutional under *Jackson* (indeed,

[20] *Parker*, 397 U.S. at 795 ("we determined in Brady v. United States [] that an otherwise valid plea is not involuntary because induced by the defendant's desire to limit the possible maximum penalty to less than that authorized if there is a jury trial. In this respect we see nothing to distinguish Parker's case from Brady's.") (citation omitted).

[21] The Court rejected Brady's reliance on Bram v. United States, 168 U.S. 532 (1897) (holding an admission made during police interrogation inadmissible under both the involuntary confession doctrine and the Fifth Amendment self-incrimination privilege) by citing *Miranda*. *See Brady*, 397 U.S. at 754 ("But *Bram* and its progeny did not hold that the possibly coercive impact of a promise of leniency could not be dissipated by the presence and advice of counsel, any more than *Miranda v. Arizona* [] held that the possibly coercive atmosphere of the police station could not be counteracted by the presence of counsel or other safeguards.") (citation omitted).

[22] *See id.* at 754–55:

> Brady's situation bears no resemblance to Bram's. Brady first pleaded not guilty; prior to changing his plea to guilty he was subjected to no threats or promises in face-to-face encounters with the authorities. He had competent counsel and full opportunity to assess the advantages and disadvantages of a trial as compared with those attending a plea of guilty; there was no hazard of an impulsive and improvident response to a seeming but unreal advantage. His plea of guilty was entered in open court and before a judge obviously sensitive to the requirements of the law with respect to guilty pleas. Brady's plea, unlike Bram's confession, was voluntary.

[23] *See id.* at 757–58:

> This is not to say that guilty plea convictions hold no hazards for the innocent or that the methods of taking guilty pleas presently employed in this country are necessarily valid in all respects. This mode of conviction is no more foolproof than full trials to the court or to the jury. Accordingly, we take great precautions against unsound results, and we should continue to do so, whether conviction is by plea or by trial. We would have serious doubts about this case if the encouragement of guilty pleas by offers of leniency substantially increased the likelihood that defendants, advised by competent counsel, would falsely condemn themselves. But our view is to the contrary and is based on our expectations that courts will satisfy themselves that pleas of guilty are voluntarily and intelligently made by competent defendants with adequate advice of counsel and that there is nothing to question the accuracy and reliability of the defendants' admissions that they committed the crimes with which they are charged. In the case before us, nothing in the record impeaches Brady's plea or suggests that his admissions in open court were anything but the truth.

[24] *See Parker*, 397 U.S. at 799 (Brennan, J., concurring in part and dissenting in part).

worse, since under the Federal Kidnapping Act, a defendant could preclude the death penalty by waiving a jury but not a trial). It followed that Parker's case should be remanded, and the conviction set aside if "he can demonstrate that the unconstitutional capital punishment scheme was a significant factor in his decision to plead guilty."[25] Because the lower courts previously determined that the risk of capital punishment had *not* been a "significant factor" in Brady's decision to plead guilty, the *Parker* dissenters concurred in the judgment in *Brady*.

Neither Brady nor Parker had maintained innocence while evincing a willingness to plead guilty. In *North Carolina v. Alford*,[26] Alford was charged with first-degree murder under the same statutory scheme as Parker: a guilty plea precluded the death penalty. Before accepting Alford's guilty plea to second-degree murder and imposing a sentence of thirty years, the trial court judge held a hearing. A police officer's testimony summarized the state's evidence: primarily, the witnesses would testify that Alford had declared his intention to kill the victim, gone to fetch his gun, and later announced that he had killed the deceased.[27]

Unlike Parker or Brady, at the plea colloquy, Alford gave testimony maintaining his innocence and stating that he was pleading guilty only to avoid the gas chamber.[28] Alford challenged his conviction through post-conviction petitions, which were denied until the Supreme Court's 1968 decision in *Jackson* impugned the constitutionality of North Carolina's no-trial, no-death penalty arrangement. After *Jackson*, the Court of Appeals for the Fourth Circuit found the plea involuntary because it was substantially motivated by the threat of the death penalty. The Supreme Court reversed.

Justice White's majority opinion focused on Alford's protestation of innocence, a fact that distinguished his case from Parker's. The claim of innocence did not persuade the Court of a constitutional distinction:

> Here the State had a strong case of first-degree murder against Alford. Whether he realized or disbelieved his guilt, he insisted on his plea because in his view he had absolutely nothing to gain by a trial and much to gain by pleading. Because of the overwhelming evidence against him, a trial was

[25] *Id.* at 813.
[26] 400 U.S. 25 (1970).
[27] *Id.* at 28.
[28] *Id.* at 28 n.2 ("'I pleaded guilty on second degree murder because they said there is too much evidence, but I ain't shot no man, but I take the fault for the other man. We never had an argument in our life and I just pleaded guilty because they said if I didn't they would gas me for it, and that is all.'").

> precisely what neither Alford nor his attorney desired. Confronted with the choice between a trial for first-degree murder, on the one hand, and a plea of guilty to second-degree murder, on the other, Alford quite reasonably chose the latter and thereby limited the maximum penalty to a 30-year term.[29]

In other words, even if Alford's assertion of innocence were *true*, he should still be allowed to accept a deal to his advantage.

It might appear that North Carolina's statute, or the federal kidnapping statute, *required* life rather than death for any defendant willing to plead guilty. In both instances, however, the defendant could not waive jury trial without the consent of the prosecutor.[30] If, as *Brady*, *Parker*, and *Alford* held, a statutory maximum of death set the baseline for prosecutorial charging decisions, setting the baseline in noncapital cases at the maximum prison time authorized by statute would seem to follow.

D. Trial Penalties

A Kentucky grand jury indicted Paul Lewis Hayes for uttering a forged instrument for $88.30. The alleged offense was a felony carrying a two- to ten-year prison term on conviction.[31] Hayes, however, had twice before been found guilty of felony offenses. The prosecutor offered to recommend a five-year sentence if Hayes pleaded guilty, but coupled this proposal with a further, more menacing one. If Hayes refused to plead out, the state would file a superseding indictment adding a recidivism charge carrying a mandatory life sentence on conviction.

Hayes nonetheless elected to face trial, lost at trial, and then challenged the conviction on the Habitual Criminal Act as a violation of due process. Hayes relied heavily on *North Carolina v. Pearce*[32] and *Blackledge v. Perry*.[33] Justice

[29] *Id.* at 37.
[30] Garner v. State, 174 S.E.2d 92, 102 (N.C. Ct. App. 1970) ("The section permitted a defendant in a capital case to tender to the court a written plea of guilty to the charge and if the solicitor for the State agreed to accept the plea, and the presiding judge approved, the acceptance had the effect of a verdict of guilty with a recommendation that the punishment should be imprisonment for life in the State's prison."); United States v. Jackson, 390 U.S.570, 584 ("a defendant has no constitutional right to insist that he be tried by a judge rather than a jury, [] and it is also true 'that a criminal defendant has (no) absolute right to have his guilty plea accepted by the court.'") (citations omitted).
[31] Bordenkircher v. Hayes, 434 U.S. 357 (1978).
[32] 395 U.S. 711 (1969).
[33] 417 U.S. 21 (1974).

Stewart, for the five-Justice majority in *Bordenkircher*, rejected the analogy to post-reversal-of-conviction enhancements that were at issue in *Pearce* and *Perry*: "in the 'give-and-take' of plea bargaining, there is no such element of punishment or retaliation so long as the accused is free to accept or reject the prosecution's offer."[34] Instead, *Bordenkircher* embraced the code-maximum baseline, subject to an exception for invidious discrimination or vindictive retaliation for exercising legal rights:

> Within the limits set by the legislature's constitutionally valid definition of chargeable offenses, "the conscious exercise of some selectivity in enforcement is not in itself a federal constitutional violation" so long as "the selection was [not] deliberately based upon an unjustifiable standard such as race, religion, or other arbitrary classification." [quoting *Oyler v. Boles*]. To hold that the prosecutor's desire to induce a guilty plea is an "unjustifiable standard," which, like race or religion, may play no part in his charging decision, would contradict the very premises that underlie the concept of plea bargaining itself.[35]

As for the innocent, "[d]efendants advised by competent counsel and protected by other procedural safeguards are presumptively capable of intelligent choice in response to prosecutorial persuasion, and unlikely to be driven to false self-condemnation."[36]

Hayes's vindictiveness claim prevailed in the Sixth Circuit and fell one vote short in the Supreme Court. But had it succeeded, it would have altered plea bargaining very little. As all three of the opinions in the Supreme Court decision admitted, prosecutors would have responded by overcharging first and thereby converting the threat into an offer. Neither of the two dissenting opinions proposed to regulate that practice judicially. Four years after *Bordenkircher*, the Court, quite logically, equated adding new charges with dropping old ones.[37]

[34] *Bordenkircher*, 434 U.S. at 363 (citations omitted).
[35] *Id.* at 364–65 (citation omitted).
[36] *Id.* at 363.
[37] United States v. Goodwin, 457 U.S. 368, 380 (1982) ("For just as a prosecutor may forgo legitimate charges already brought in an effort to save the time and expense of trial, a prosecutor may file additional charges if an initial expectation that a defendant would plead guilty to lesser charges proves unfounded.") (footnote omitted).

Bordenkircher has become notorious,[38] but it should be read with an eye on the issue considered and the actual facts. *Bordenkircher* does not hold that the legislature may delegate sentencing discretion to prosecutors. All concerned saw the issue as whether the *Perry* decision should apply to pretrial prosecutorial decisions, not whether the more serious charge carried a mandatory penalty. *Blackledge* and *Goodwin* involved no minimum,[39] and *Bordenkircher* did, but none of the Justices even mentioned this distinction. If the Kentucky habitual criminal law authorized a discretionary term of years up to life, but no minimum, the case would have been briefed, argued, and decided the same way.

It is quite doubtful that the Kentucky statute was, practically speaking, mandatory. In Kentucky, sentences are imposed by the jury, not the court, unless the parties agree otherwise.[40] The early practice was to plead the recidivism count together with the new charge, thus informing the jury both about the defendant's prior record and the life sentence attending a conviction on the recidivism charge. Despite the mandatory language of the statute,[41] juries were instructed that they could avoid the life sentence by not convicting on the recidivism charge, by instead convicting on the current charge alone.[42] It was apparently common for juries to refuse to convict on the habitual criminal charge.[43]

[38] *Compare* Richard L. Lippke, The Ethics of Plea Bargaining 11 (2011) (describing *Bordenkircher* as "infamous"), with Josh Bowers, *Fundamental Fairness and the Path from* Santobello *to* Padilla: *A Response to Professor Bibas*, 2 Cal. L. Rev. Circuit 52, 59 (2011) (describing *Bordenkircher* as "somewhat infamous").

[39] Blackledge v. Perry, 417 U.S. 21, 28–29 (1974) (charges increased "potential" punishment); *Goodwin*, 457 U.S. at 388 (Brennan, J., dissenting) (charges increased "maximum exposure").

[40] Lycans v. Commonwealth, 562 S.W.2d 303, 305 (Ky. 1978) (Commonwealth "had a right to . . . select a jury to fix a penalty for these hideous crimes").

[41] The statute is quoted in the Sixth Circuit's opinion, *Hayes v. Cowan*, 547 F.2d 42, 42 n.1 (6th Cir. 1976) ("Any person convicted a second time of felony shall be confined in the penitentiary not less than double the time of the sentence under the first conviction; if convicted a third time of felony, he shall be confined in the penitentiary during his life.").

[42] Coleman v. Commonwealth, 125 S.W.2d 728, 729 (Ky. 1939) ("Even if former convictions be conclusively established, it is yet within the discretion of the jury whether it will impose a penalty within the statutory limits prescribed for the single crime for which the accused is then being tried, or because of the aggravation and repetition of crime it will augment the punishment by inflicting the severer penalty."); Allen v. Commonwealth, 125 S.W.2d 1013, 1015 (Ky. 1939) ("In this character of prosecution the jury has the right to find the defendant guilty of the particular crime charged and fix his punishment accordingly without being required to find him guilty under the Habitual Criminal Act.").

[43] *Coleman*, 125 S.W.2d at 29:

> As disclosed in many decisions it has not been unusual for juries to disregard former convictions. Perhaps they deemed the principal crime for which the accused was being tried not to merit such severe punishment or that the character of the man himself did not justify it. Hence, in the instant case, we think it error to have omitted from the first

Hayes was convicted at a bifurcated trial, first of the current forgery charge at a trial where his record was inadmissible, and then on the habitual criminal charge. In 1973, when Hayes was tried, jury instructions for the second phase, where the habitual criminal charge was decided, were governed by *Satterly v. Commonwealth*. *Satterly* required instructing the jury of their "option to believe the defendant has been convicted on but one of the previous charges."[44] "Each of the allegations embracing the previous convictions must be so submitted, and no matter how well they have been proved it is still the jury's prerogative to disbelieve any or all of them."[45] *Satterly* was overruled in 1983, but it was good law when Hayes was tried.[46] The trial judge instructed the jury on sentencing as prescribed by *Satterly*, indicating the jury's sentencing options depending on whether they had "reasonable doubt" about any or all of the prior convictions.[47]

Just as the jury had discretion at the front end of the sentence, the parole board had discretion at the back end. Justice Powell's dissenting opinion accepted the premise that Hayes would have been eligible for parole after fifteen years.[48] In fact, Hayes was paroled after nine years.[49]

So Paul Hayes's case would have been a very bad vehicle for testing prosecutorial sentencing, because it was quite unclear just how much control the prosecutor actually had over the sentence. To frame the vindictiveness issue, all that mattered was that the prosecutor had increased the potential maximum dramatically for the admitted purpose of inducing a guilty plea. The Court and the parties understandably barely noticed that the statute was worded as mandatory.

instruction authority for the jury to fix the defendant's punishment within the limits prescribed by the statute for housebreaking, that is, from two to ten years.

[44] Satterly v. Commonwealth, 437 S.W.2d 929, 930 (Ky. 1968).

[45] *Id.*

[46] *See* Payne v. Commonwealth, 656 S.W.2d 719 (Ky. 1983) (reviewing the case law before overruling *Satterly*). Until 1975, when the Kentucky Supreme Court was created, the court of appeals was the Commonwealth's highest court.

[47] Appendix to Petition for Writ of Certiorari at 23–24, Bordenkircher v. Hayes, 434 U.S. 357 (1978) (No. 76-1334).

[48] *Bordenkircher*, 434 U.S. at 370 n.1 (Powell, J., dissenting) ("It is suggested that respondent will be eligible for parole consideration after serving 15 years.").

[49] Dan Canon, Pleading Out: How Plea Bargaining Creates a Permanent Criminal Class 3 (2022). Canon is both a lawyer and a gifted writer, and deserves much credit for shining fresh light on a case that has been written about for almost fifty years. Nonetheless I do not subscribe to everything Canon says. He writes that Hayes's jury "had no choice but to sentence him to life in prison" without discussing the *Satterly* instruction's unsubtle suggestion that the jury might have "reasonable doubts" about Hayes's prior convictions.

E. Lesser Included Offenses and the Selective Prosecution Doctrine

Charge selection is so momentous because legislatures pass multiple statutes providing different penalties for the same conduct. *Borderkircher* adopted the code maximum as the test of pretrial prosecutorial vindictiveness. The sentencing cases adopt the fair-procedure baseline. There is at least one other potential baseline for charge selection, based on the old common-law rule of lenity.

The lenity maxim instructs courts considering two interpretations of a penal statute to prefer the interpretation favorable to the accused, as long as the court is otherwise in equipoise. If applied to lesser and greater included offenses, this principle suggests a *minimum* legally authorized liability baseline. The year after *Bordenkircher*, the Court rejected this minimum liability baseline in *United States v. Batchelder*.[50]

Batchelder was convicted of violating Section 922(h) of U.S. Code Title 18. That section provides that a person with a felony record who possesses a firearm may be punished by up to five years' imprisonment and a $5,000 fine. Batchelder was convicted before the adoption of the Federal Sentencing Guidelines, when the judge had discretion to impose any sentence within the range or even to suspend the sentence. In this case, the judge gave Batchelder the five-year maximum.

Another section of Title 18, 1202(a), *also* made it a crime for felons to possess firearms, but provided only a two-year maximum sentence (but a larger maximum fine of $10,000). Unlike familiar lesser included offenses, such as theft and robbery or murder and manslaughter, the two statutes had precisely the same elements. The unanimous Court saw "no appreciable difference between the discretion a prosecutor exercises when deciding whether to charge under one of two statutes with different elements and the discretion he exercises when choosing one of two statutes with identical elements."[51]

Neither statute specified a *minimum* sentence. The prosecutor's "decision to proceed under § 922(h) does not empower the Government to predetermine ultimate criminal sanctions. Rather, it merely enables the sentencing judge to impose a longer prison sentence than § 1202(a) would permit and precludes him from imposing the greater fine authorized by § 1202(a)."[52]

[50] 442 U.S. 114 (1979).
[51] *Id.* at 125.
[52] *Id.*

There was no conflict between the statutory and procedural baselines because the charging decision only authorized a longer sentence set by Congress. The choice of where within the five-year range to set Batchelder's specific sentence was made entirely by a judge, not by a prosecutor.

Justice Marshall included this important disclaimer: "Selectivity in the enforcement of criminal laws is, of course, subject to constitutional constraints."[53] The supporting footnote adds: "The Equal Protection Clause prohibits selective enforcement 'based upon an unjustifiable standard such as race, religion, or other arbitrary classification.' *Oyler v. Boles* . . . Respondent does not allege that his prosecution was motivated by improper considerations."[54]

The modern "selective prosecution" doctrine is the orphan child of *Bordenkircher* and *Batchelder*. *Batchelder* approves bringing more serious charges because the prosecutor believes those are necessary to authorize proportionate punishment. *Bordenkircher* went further by holding that even if the prosecutor did not believe the higher charge was proportionate, the charge did not violate due process if the motive behind it was to induce a guilty plea to a lesser charge. Adding *Perry* to *Oyler* defined prosecutorial charging discretion by residues. If the subjective motive of the prosecutor was invidious group animus toward a suspect class, the charging decision violated the Equal Protection Clause. If the subject motive was the desire to retaliate against the accused for exercising some constitutional right *other than those waived by pleading guilty*, such as freedom of speech or religion, the charging decision violated the Due Process Clause.

Since *Bordenkircher*, no defendant has presented the Supreme Court with a record of unconstitutional prosecutorial motives for charge selection. In *Wayte v. United States*,[55] the government indicted the defendant for failing to register for the draft. The government's policy only targeted nonregistrants who were affirmatively reported, either by themselves or by others. Each of the identified nonregistrants was notified that they would be prosecuted but could avoid indictment by registering. The Court held that this policy did not select defendants because of their beliefs or statements against the draft, since draft critics who registered were not prosecuted, and reported

[53] *Id.* (citation omitted).
[54] *Batchelder*, 442 U.S. at 125 n.9.
[55] 470 U.S. 598 (1985).

nonregistrants were prosecuted even without a record of opposition to the draft.

Subsequently, in *United States v. Armstrong*,[56] the Court refused even to order discovery for defendants who alleged that federal prosecutors charged only Black defendants with crack cocaine offenses—offenses that were punished much less severely in the state courts. The Los Angeles US Attorney's Office could not identify a single crack case brought against a Caucasian defendant. The defendants, however, "failed to identify individuals who were not black and could have been prosecuted for the offenses for which respondents were charged, but were not so prosecuted."[57]

The opinions in both *Wayte* and *Armstrong* emphasized considerations of institutional competence. Prosecutors are in a better position to evaluate enforcement priorities and the strength of individual cases than judges.[58] The selective prosecution doctrine confirms the Court's commitment to the code-maximum baseline in the charging context. The extremely rare case where a defendant can show selective prosecution proves the general rule of plenary discretion. In the ordinary case, the statutory maximum governed under *Bordenkircher*: "so long as the prosecutor has probable cause to believe that the accused committed an offense defined by statute, the decision whether or not to prosecute, and what charge to file or bring before a grand jury, generally rests entirely in his discretion."[59]

A more robust selective-prosecution doctrine would work little change. The Court has not said just what the remedy for selective prosecution should be, but the only one it has discussed is dismissal of the indictment.[60] If there is strong evidence against the defendant, dismissal of one indictment would leave the government free to assign another prosecutor to the case. The new attorney could bring a new indictment on the same (or perhaps greater) charges, but now acting from such purer motives as the desire to force a guilty plea.

[56] 517 U.S. 456 (1996).

[57] *Id.* at 470.

[58] *Wayte*, 470 U.S. at 607 ("This broad discretion rests largely on the recognition that the decision to prosecute is particularly ill-suited to judicial review."); *Armstrong*, 517 U.S. at 465 ("Judicial deference to the decisions of these executive officers rests in part on an assessment of the relative competence of prosecutors and courts.")

[59] *Armstrong*, 517 U.S. at 464 (quoting *Bordenkircher*) (citation omitted).

[60] *Id.* at 461 n.2.

F. The Nonprosecution Cases

The corollary of discretion to charge is discretion not to charge. In the 1985 decision in *Heckler v. Chaney*,[61] the Court, on somewhat unusual facts, applied the logic of *Wayte* and *Armstrong* to nonenforcement decisions. In *Heckler*, prisoners sentenced to death by lethal injection claimed that the drugs to be used in their executions caused unnecessary pain and therefore were not "safe and effective" as required by the federal drug safety statute. They petitioned the Food and Drug Administration (FDA) to add a warning to the drug labels indicating that they were not approved for human executions, to notify the manufacturers and prison staff that the drugs were not approved for executions, and to "adopt procedures for seizing the drugs from state prisons and to recommend the prosecution of all those in the chain of distribution who knowingly distribute or purchase the drugs with intent to use them for human execution."[62] The FDA declined to act as the inmates requested.

The Administrative Procedure Act (APA) provides that agency actions, including final decisions not to act, are reviewable by the courts, and are held void when they are "arbitrary, capricious, an abuse of discretion, or otherwise not in accordance with law."[63] The APA, however, exempts agency action from judicial review when the decision "is committed to agency discretion by law."[64] The Court agreed with the FDA that the exception applied to executive branch decisions to forgo prosecutions in particular cases.

Justice (not yet Chief Justice) Rehnquist's majority opinion made a strong case for executive discretion over charging decisions. The opinion did not rely on the constitutional doctrine of separation of powers. It explicitly recognized that if the legislature provided clear standards for the exercise of discretion, the courts could review alleged noncompliance with the statutory policy.[65] Instead, precedent based on policy recognized that "an agency's decision not to prosecute or enforce, whether through civil or criminal process, is a decision generally committed to an agency's absolute discretion."[66]

[61] 470 U.S. 821 (1985).
[62] *Id.* at 824.
[63] 5 U.S.C. § 706.
[64] 5 U.S.C. § 701(a)(2).
[65] *Heckler*, 470 U.S. at 833 ("Congress may limit an agency's exercise of enforcement power if it wishes, either by setting substantive priorities, or by otherwise circumscribing an agency's power to discriminate among issues or cases it will pursue.").
[66] *Id.* at 831 (citations omitted). One of the omitted citations is to *Batchelder*.

The precedents reflected pragmatic, functional concerns rather than an executive-branch monopoly on law enforcement. *Heckler*'s exposition of these concerns deserves quotation in full:

> First, an agency decision not to enforce often involves a complicated balancing of a number of factors which are peculiarly within its expertise. Thus, the agency must not only assess whether a violation has occurred, but whether agency resources are best spent on this violation or another, whether the agency is likely to succeed if it acts, whether the particular enforcement action requested best fits the agency's overall policies, and, indeed, whether the agency has enough resources to undertake the action at all. An agency generally cannot act against each technical violation of the statute it is charged with enforcing. The agency is far better equipped than the courts to deal with the many variables involved in the proper ordering of its priorities.[67]

These practical reasons justified judicial refusal to review affirmative decisions *to prosecute* individuals. A decision not to prosecute was an *a fortiori* case of unreviewability, because "when an agency refuses to act it generally does not exercise its *coercive* power over an individual's liberty or property rights, and thus does not infringe upon areas that courts often are called upon to protect."[68]

Heckler blocked private parties from forcing federal authorities to prosecute other private parties. A few years later, the Court protected law enforcement officers from ex post tort liability for injuries they might have prevented. When a child, permanently disabled from beatings by the father, sued officials who had been notified of the abuse for permitting the injury, the Court held that "as a general matter . . . a State's failure to protect an individual against private violence simply does not constitute a violation of the Due Process Clause."[69] The purpose of the Due Process Clauses was "to protect the people from the State, not to ensure that the State protected them from each other."[70] If enforcement officers selected the wrong priorities, the Framers left correction to "the democratic political processes."[71]

[67] *Id.* at 831–32 (citations omitted).
[68] *Id.* at 832 (emphasis in original).
[69] DeShaney v. Winnebago Cnty. Dep't of Soc. Servs., 489 U.S. 189, 197 (1989).
[70] *Id.* at 196.
[71] *Id.*

G. Cases Recognizing the Right to Trial about Facts Triggering Higher Sentences

The Bill of Rights expressly protects various trial rights, including the right to a jury trial, the right to counsel, and the right to confrontation. The Court has interpreted the more general guarantee of due process to include other trial rights, including the requirement that the elements of the charged offense be proved beyond a reasonable doubt. An infinite variety of facts may influence the exercise of sentencing discretion, but the range of sentencing discretion is capped by the maximum penalty provided for the offense of conviction. The Court's opinion in *Booker v. United States* summed the doctrine up in a single sentence: "Any fact (other than a prior conviction) which is necessary to support a sentence exceeding the maximum authorized by the facts established by a plea of guilty or a jury verdict must be admitted by the defendant or proved to a jury beyond a reasonable doubt."[72]

The *Booker* rule has at least one counterintuitive consequence. Juries cannot convict for a crime not charged. If prosecutors, who control the charging function, elect to bring a lesser charge when the evidence establishes a greater one, the jury cannot convict on the higher charge, and the judge, under *Booker*, may only sentence within the range set by the minimum and maximum penalties provided for the charged offense. This gives prosecutors the practical power to define the range of judicial discretion.

Booker itself held that when the amount of illegal drugs possessed by the defendant triggers a mandatory minimum sentence, drug quantity must be established either by guilty plea or by verdict. In Scott Bummer's case, five grams of meth triggered a mandatory minimum of five years, and fifty grams triggered a mandatory minimum of ten years. The prosecution can avoid the "mandatory" minimum by omitting the drug quantity from the indictment.

[72] United States v. Booker, 543 U.S. 220, 244 (2005). Similar pre-*Booker* cases include Blakely v. Washington, 542 U.S. 296 (2004) (holding that when fact that defended acted with "deliberate cruelty" authorized judge to impose a sentence higher than the otherwise applicable maximum, defendant had right to trial on issue of whether he acted with "deliberate cruelty"); Apprendi v. New Jersey, 530 U.S. 466 (2000) (holding that defendant eligible for up to ten years for firearms offense, sentenced to twelve years under a sentencing statute raising the maximum penalty to twenty years when the crime was motivated by racism, violated defendant's right to trial on the issue of whether his motive was racist). For post-*Booker* cases, see Alleyne v. United States, 570 U.S. 99 (2013) (holding that when brandishing a gun during the charged offense triggers a more severe mandatory minimum sentence, issue of whether defendant brandished gun must be established either by guilty plea or jury verdict); Cunningham v. California, 549 U.S. 270 (2007) (holding that statute providing presumptive sentence of twelve years but authorizing sixteen-year sentence if judge found specific aggravating circumstances violated defendant's right to trial with respect to the aggravating circumstances).

The prosecution, however, is free to include the drug quantity in the indictment. The government need not allege any quantity but also may plead a smaller quantity than the evidence proves. The prosecution's last offer to both Amato and Bummer was to plead five grams rather than either fifty grams or no quantity.

H. The Eighth Amendment Cases

The Eighth Amendment prohibits "cruel and unusual punishments." In *Furman v. Georgia*, the Supreme Court held that leaving the decision to impose the death penalty to the unconstrained discretion of juries is "cruel and unusual."[73] In *Gregg v. Georgia*[74] and many subsequent cases, the Court has upheld the death penalty if it is imposed after individualized consideration of aggravating and mitigating facts. The Court has repeatedly held that mandatory capital punishment, for any offense, violates the principles of *Furman* and *Gregg*.[75]

In *Harmelin v. Michigan*, discussed in Chapter 2, Justice Scalia's majority opinion rejected the argument that Harmelin's life sentence was unconstitutional because it was mandatory for the offense of conviction. Justice Scalia relied exclusively on history to support this conclusion. In Chapter 5, we will see that *Harmelin*'s history is at best incomplete. The primary issue in *Harmelin*, however, was not whether the guided-discretion regime should apply in noncapital cases, but whether Harmelin's sentence was unconstitutionally disproportionate to the offense.

The Court's death penalty jurisprudence recognized a proportionality doctrine that prohibits capital punishment for serious but nonhomicidal crimes. The death penalty for rape violates the Eighth Amendment even if the procedure for imposing it complies with the guided-discretion mandate of *Furman* and *Gregg*. How, or even if, the Eighth Amendment's proportionality principle applies to prison sentences has divided the Justices for decades.

In *Harmelin*, Justice Scalia declared that the Eighth Amendment includes no proportionality requirement. Only Chief Justice Rehnquist joined in this conclusion. Justice Kennedy, joined by Justice O'Connor and Justice

73 Furman v. Georgia, 408 U.S. 238 (1972).
74 428 U.S. 153 (1976).
75 Woodson v. North Carolina, 428 U.S. 280 (1976); Sumner v. Shuman, 483 U.S. 66 (1987).

Souter, concluded that the amendment prohibits grossly disproportionate punishments, but that Harmelin's life sentence for a first offense of drug trafficking was not grossly disproportionate. Justice White, joined by Justice Blackmun and Justice Stevens (and supported by Justice Marshall in a separate dissent) would have held Harmelin's sentence unconstitutional. Given that conclusion, the dissent saw "no need" to address Harmelin's argument "that imposition of a life sentence without the possibility of parole necessitates the sort of individualized sentencing determination heretofore reserved for defendants subject to the death penalty."[76]

Subsequently, by a 5–4 vote, the Court rejected a proportionality challenge to a twenty-five-year minimum sentence imposed on a California recidivist whose current conviction was for theft of three golf clubs.[77] Under California law, the sentencing court had discretion to classify some prior convictions as triggering the three-strikes penalty or not—as strikes or balls, to follow the baseball metaphor.[78] In both *Ewing* and a companion case,[79] the sentencing court had declined to exercise discretion to take the sentence out from under the three-strikes law. In neither case was the Supreme Court faced with a prosecutorial charging decision that mandated a minimum sentence.

The most recent noncapital Eighth Amendment decision, *Miller v. Alabama*, again by a vote of 5–4, held that a statute imposing a mandatory life sentence without possibility of parole for a murder committed while the defendant was a juvenile violates *both* the proportionality *and* the guided-discretion doctrines.[80] In the process, however, Justice Kagan's majority opinion took pains to declare that "our ruling thus neither overrules nor undermines nor conflicts with *Harmelin*."[81] The need for this caveat implies that lawyers reading the opinion might very well recognize the tension with *Harmelin*.

[76] *Harmelin*, 501 U.S. at 1027 n.8 (White, J., dissenting).

[77] Ewing v. California, 538 U.S. 11 (2003). Justice O'Connor, joined by Chief Justice Rehnquist and Justice Kennedy, concluded that Ewing's sentence did not violate the gross disproportionality doctrine announced in Justice Kennedy's concurring opinion in *Harmelin*. Justice Scalia read the Eighth Amendment as banning only barbarous types of punishment, and Justice Thomas found no proportionality principle in the amendment at all. Stevens, Souter, Ginsburg, and Breyer dissented.

[78] *See Ewing*, 538 U.S. at 17 (plurality opinion) ("Thus, trial courts may avoid imposing a three strikes sentence in two ways: first, by reducing 'wobblers' to misdemeanors (which do not qualify as triggering offenses), and second, by vacating allegations of prior 'serious' or 'violent' felony convictions.").

[79] Lockyer v. Andrade, 538 U.S. 63, 67–68 (2003) ("The trial court denied Andrade's motion to reduce the offenses to misdemeanors, both before the jury verdict and again in state habeas proceedings.").

[80] Miller v. Alabama, 567 U.S. 460 (2012).

[81] *Id.* at 482.

Yet even if *Miller* portends the end of *Harmelin*, very little would change. The proportionality test, however interpreted, would permit legislatures to impose decades of incarceration for relatively minor crimes. Justice Breyer's dissent in *Ewing* made a point of distinguishing Ewing's sentence as the harshest authorized by any state, noting that four states authorized ten years, four more authorized fifteen, and nine more authorized twenty-five years with the possibility of parole.[82] If proportionality review would permit sentences such as fifteen years for petty theft, as the comparison implies, the common minimums for drug trafficking and firearms offenses are in no jeopardy whatever from the Eighth Amendment.

The extension of the guided-discretion regime to the most serious prison terms likewise would not threaten the most common mandatory minimums. It seems beyond conjecture that any majority of the Court would require the exacting procedures in the capital cases to be followed before imposing any but the lengthiest prison terms. In the usual caught-with-drugs-and-a-gun case, state or federal, the prosecutor would still have plenary discretion to impose one substantial mandatory term for the drugs and another for the gun. The extreme upper bound of sentencing would be capped, but sentences could still be catastrophic, and charging would still be sentencing.

I. Substantive Due Process

The Court has heard and rejected one due process challenge to a mandatory minimum sentence. In *Chapman v. United States*,[83] the Court upheld provisions in the Controlled Substances Act imposing a mandatory minimum for distributing more than one gram of "any mixture or substance containing a detectable amount" of LSD. The defendants argued that the statute should be read to count only the weight of the LSD itself and not the weight of the carrier medium (such as blotter paper or sugar cubes), because the weight of the carrier medium bears no relationship to the harm of the offense or the culpability of the offender. They buttressed their statutory argument by claiming that the contrary interpretation was so irrational as to violate due process.

[82] *Ewing*, 567 U.S. at 53–62 (Breyer, J., dissenting).
[83] 500 U.S. 453 (1991).

This was a substantive, not procedural, due process claim. The Court rejected it by referring to the maximum liability baseline. A defendant duly convicted

> is eligible for, and the court may impose, whatever punishment is authorized by statute for his offense, so long as that penalty is not cruel and unusual, and so long as the penalty is not based on an arbitrary distinction that would violate the Due Process Clause of the Fifth Amendment. In this context, . . . an argument based on equal protection essentially duplicates an argument based on due process.[84]

The Court upheld Chapman's sentence after finding a "rational basis" for counting the carrier medium rather than any "arbitrary distinction" that would violate either substantive due process or equal protection. The defendants did not argue that leaving the decision to charge more or less than a gram to the executive branch was procedurally unfair. *Chapman*, therefore, does not insulate prosecutorial discretion from due process challenge under the sentencing cases.

J. Summary of the Prosecutorial Discretion Cases

The prosecutorial discretion cases establish a broad range of judicially unreviewable decisions to file, or not file, criminal charges. Up to a point, these cases rest on plausible grounds of institutional competence. Judgments about proportionate punishment are notoriously subjective, so courts should defer to legislatures. Selecting cases for prosecution depends on judgments about the offenses that deserve high priority, the limits of the enforcement agency's capabilities, and the prospects of winning convictions in particular cases. As long as officials do not pursue political dissenters or disempowered minorities, these judgments are better left to the executive than to the judicial branch.

When charging decisions determine not just who is to be punished, but *how severely* they are to be punished, the case for unreviewable discretion becomes problematic. We will take up questions of institutional competence shortly. For now, just as a description of the jurisprudence, it suffices to

[84] *Id.* at 465 (citations omitted).

point out that the Supreme Court has never faced a procedural due process challenge to executive selection of charges that have the practical effect of increasing the defendant's sentence. The issue in *Bordenkircher* was whether due process permitted bringing a much more serious charge, whether mandatory or discretionary, solely because the accused refused to plead. In the cases where defendants did challenge mandatory minimums, Harmelin argued only the Eighth Amendment, and Chapman raised only a substantive due process claim.[85]

K. Summary of the Doctrinal Problem

We have two firmly established lines of precedent, both reflecting settled constitutional principles. One line requires neutrality at sentencing, and the other approves executive discretion to select charges. Both lines antedate sentencing guidelines and the routine use of mandatory minimum sentences. *Romano* and *Wayte* were both decided in 1985. Still, even then, both cases applied principles established earlier, in *Brewer*, *Gagnon*, *Taylor*, and *Gardner* on the sentencing side, and *Bordenkircher* and *Batchelder* on the charging side. Today, cases like Scott Bummer's make the conflict between the two lines obvious.

Recall our opening hypotheticals, *Prosecutorial Sentencing* and *229 Degrees*. *Prosecutorial Sentencing* would be unconstitutional, a clear violation of procedural due process, under *Taylor*, *Gardner*, *Gagnon*, and *Romano*. These were all convictions in state courts reversed on federal constitutional grounds. They do not rest on structural separation-of-powers grounds, but on the unfairness of trusting adjudication to a partisan in violation of procedural due process.

What about the formally different, but functionally identical, *229 Degrees*? The Court's prosecutorial discretion cases preclude challenging *229 Degrees* as cruel and unusual punishment, or for enabling grave trial penalties, or as an irrational denial of the liberty protected by substantive due process, or as

[85] Pre-*Furman* cases rejected due process challenges to discretionary capital sentencing. Assuming *arguendo* that these cases remain the law with respect to due process after *Furman*, they do not protect prosecutorial discretion from due process challenge. In these cases, discretion over the death penalty was exercised not by judges but by (equally neutral) juries. *See* Brady v. United States, 397 U.S. 742, 743 (1970); Parker v. North Carolina, 397 U.S. 790, 792 n.1 (1970); North Carolina v. Alford, 400 U.S. 25, 27 n.1 (1970); McGautha v. California, 402 U.S. 183, 185 (1971). In each case, death was discretionary with the jury, not mandatory.

discrimination forbidden by the Equal Protection Clause. The parties in the prosecutorial discretion cases never argued that charging was sentencing, and a close look at their records shows that they could not have raised that claim. The Supreme Court has never heard a procedural due process challenge to prosecutorial control over sentencing outcomes. Only in *Harmelin* and *Chapman* was the mandatory nature of the sentence the focus of the litigation, and in neither case did the defense invoke, or the Court consider, procedural due process.

If factual guilt of all potential charges extinguishes the offender's liberty interest, so that all lesser punishment is lenience, a matter of "grace," a "privilege" rather than a "right," *Mempa, Brewer, Taylor, Gardner, Gagnon*, and *Romano* are wrong. They each recognize constitutional hearing rights regarding the amount of time to be served *under* the statutory maximum. By contrast, if every day behind bars counts as a deprivation of the liberty protected by due process, it is equally wrong to read *Bordenkircher* and *Harmelin* as permitting prosecutors to select, at their pleasure, charges with mandatory sentencing consequences.

Yet it might be that, as Justice Holmes once said, "a page of history is worth a volume of logic."[86] Justice Scalia claimed in *Harmelin* that a long tradition of harsh penalties, discretionary with prosecutors but binding on the courts, foreclosed application of the guided-discretion regime on noncapital sentencing. The next chapter shows that prosecutorial control of lengthy mandatory minimum prison sentences for crimes not otherwise subject to capital punishment is a creature of the late twentieth, not the late eighteenth, century. If the brute force of history confers no constitutional immunity on prosecutorial sentencing, new thinking will be required to settle the border between charging and sentencing.

[86] New York Trust Co. v. Eisner, 256 U.S. 345, 349 (1921).

5
The History of Sentencing Discretion

A. Introduction

In Chapter 2, we saw in the *Harmelin* case that a bare majority of the Justices refused to apply the Eighth Amendment's guided discretion doctrine to non-capital cases. The only reason they gave was the force of history.[1] More recently, a different bare majority of the Court did apply the guided-discretion regime to a juvenile sentence of life without parole.[2] The argument of this book is based on due process, not the Eighth Amendment. Nonetheless, if *Harmelin* is right that mandatory minimum sentences have been normal features of US criminal law since the Founding, history would pose a serious obstacle to any constitutional challenge. The history presented in *Harmelin*, however, is incomplete and potentially misleading.

A statute providing a minimum sentence upon conviction is a necessary, but far from sufficient, condition for prosecutorial sentencing. The necessary and sufficient conditions for prosecutorial sentencing are:

(1) A menu of charges applicable to the same conduct, at least some containing a minimum sentence.
(2) The menu includes minimum penalties that are not *de minimis* but significantly more severe than the sentence that a neutral tribunal would select.
(3) Prosecutors have plenary discretion to select any charge from the menu.

Any one of these features prevailed at different times and in various jurisdictions before the late twentieth century. They occasionally

[1] *See* Harmelin v. Michigan, 501 U.S. 957, 994–95 (1991) ("Severe, mandatory penalties may be cruel, but they are not unusual in the constitutional sense, having been employed in various forms throughout our Nation's history.").

[2] *See* Miller v. Alabama, 567 U.S. 460 (2012). The *Miller* opinion reaffirmed *Harmelin*, apparently believing that the logic of the opinion called *Harmelin* into doubt. *Id.* at 482.

Sentencing Discretion and the Constitution. Donald A. Dripps, Oxford University Press.
 DOI: 10.1093/9780197830390.003.0005

coincided—rarely and briefly. Only late in the nineteenth century did prosecutors gain complete control over which offenses to charge or decline. Only late in the twentieth century did discretion to select different charges become the practical power to choose different sentences. Prosecutorial sentencing has no deep roots in American tradition. An appeal to history cannot counter the logic of due process.

B. Sentencing Discretion and the First Congress

(1) Beccaria's *On Crimes and Punishments*

The Founding Fathers greatly esteemed Cesare Beccaria's *On Crimes and Punishments*. A study of the authors most widely cited by the Founders ranked Beccaria sixth, ahead of Pufendorf, Coke, Rousseau, and Milton.[3] Beccaria was so well-known that in 1770, John Adams opened his jury argument in the Boston Massacre trial by quoting *On Crimes and Punishments*.[4]

Beccaria argued that eighteenth-century punishments were too harsh, so harsh they discouraged enforcement, conferring a lawless impunity on most and arbitrary agony on a few. "Crimes are more effectually prevented by the *certainty*, than the *severity* of punishment. Hence in a magistrate, the necessity of vigilance, and in a judge, of implacability, which . . . should be joined to a mild legislation."[5] Beccaria's insistence on "certainty" went so far as repudiating judicial interpretation of penal laws,[6] claims of situational excuse,[7] and executive clemency.[8] The American Founders did not go that far, but they did base their initial criminal code largely on Beccaria's principles.

[3] *See* Donald S. Lutz, *The Relative Importance of European Writers on Late Eighteenth Century American Political Thought*, 78 Am. Pol. Sci. Rev. 189, 194 (1984).

[4] *See* John Adams, *Adams' Argument for the Defense: 3–4 December 1770*, Nat'l Archives Founders Online, https://founders.archives.gov/documents/Adams/05-03-02-0001-0004-0016 [https://perma.cc/NW6N-2MGG].

[5] Cesare Beccaria, An Essay on Crimes and Punishments 98 (Piccadilly, J. Almon 1767). I have modernized the spelling in the quotations.

[6] *Id.* at 16 ("The disorders, that may arise from a rigorous observance of penal laws, are not to be compared with those produced by the interpretation of them.").

[7] *Id.* at 26–27 ("They err, therefore, who imagine that a crime is greater, or less, according to the intention of the person by whom it is committed . . .").

[8] *Id.* at 176 ("Clemency is a virtue which belongs to the legislator, and not to the executor of the laws; a virtue which ought to shine in the code, and not in private judgment.").

(2) The 1790 Crimes Act

Since Beccaria, jurists and legislatures have recognized the necessity of discretion in sentencing individual offenders. Even Bentham, on so much else, Beccaria's disciple, would have left sentences largely to guided judicial discretion.[9] When the American founders met in the first Congress to establish a federal criminal code, they implemented Beccaria's principles but left precise prison terms, within fairly narrow bounds, to judicial discretion. They made the death penalty, when it applied, the *only* punishment. Their enactment of mandatory death sentences reflects hostility, rather than enthusiasm, for sentencing discretion *qua* discretion. They did not, however, even attempt to write a code with specific, inflexible penalties affixed to distinct and mutually exclusive offenses.

The First Congress adopted An Act for the Punishment of Certain Crimes Against the United States in 1790.[10] Against the backdrop of the common law, which made even larceny a capital crime, the Act applied Beccaria's principles—the death penalty was limited to treason, murder, piracy and robbery, forgery and counterfeiting, and the forcible rescue of a prisoner eligible for capital punishment.[11]

Representative White objected to capital punishment for forgery and counterfeiting, because "punishment ought to be proportioned" and "a capital punishment in this case . . . would tend to prevent convictions."[12] The new nation, however, desperately needed to protect its credit, and the motion to delete capital punishment for counterfeiting and forgery was defeated.[13]

The Act nonetheless sharply reduced the number of capital crimes. Where, however, it provided the death penalty, the death penalty was indeed mandatory. The Act abolished the benefit of clergy, leaving pardons and reprieves as the only officially recognized discretionary checks on executions.[14] The

[9] *See* Jeremy Bentham, *Principles of Penal Law*, in 1 The Works of Jeremy Bentham 365, 515 (John Bowring ed., Edinburgh, William Tait 1843) ("There may, however, often arise, either with regard to offences themselves, or the person of the delinquent, unforeseen and particular circumstances, which would be productive of great inconveniences, if the law were altogether inflexible."); Jeremy Bentham, *Essay on the Promulgation of Laws, and the Reasons Thereof; With Specimen of a Penal Code*, in 1 The Works of Jeremy Bentham at 155, 164 (generally leaving particular sentences to the "option and discretion" of the tribunal, but specifying fifteen factors of aggravation and mitigation to be considered by the tribunal).

[10] Crimes Act of 1790, ch. 9, 1 Stat. 112.

[11] *See id.*, §§ 1 (treason), 3 (murder), 8–10 (robbery and piracy), 14 (forgery and counterfeiting), 23 (rescue).

[12] 2 Annals of Cong. 1521 (1790).

[13] *Id.*

[14] Crimes Act of 1790, § 31.

president's power to commute a sentence from death (required by statute) to a long prison term (*not* authorized by the statute) was not established until *Ex parte Wells* in 1855.[15]

Wells equated the established power to issue conditional pardons with the power to commute a death sentence to life imprisonment. Before *Wells*, it was assumed that the president's constitutional power to "grant Reprieves and Pardons" did not include commutations, and proposals in Congress to authorize commutations failed to pass.[16] Presidents could issue serial reprieves before a pardon, but the president's term limited this.

The 1790 Act imposed a forced choice of death or a relatively short prison term. The First Congress provided mandatory penalties, not a menu of statutory options, some of which carried severe mandatory penalties. The mandatory penalties were expected to be mandatory in the sense of being automatic, not at the discretion of *anyone*.

It didn't work out that way. The first four presidents signed more than three hundred clemency warrants.[17] During that period, from 1790 to 1817, the federal government executed twelve offenders—all for murder.[18] There never were any federal executions for forgery or counterfeiting.

The Act authorized four lesser punishments for other crimes: imprisonment, whipping, fines, and the pillory. It provided *no* minimum quantum for prison, whipping, or fines.[19] An inflexible stand of one hour in the pillory was part of the prescribed penalty for perjury.[20] Like the Act's death penalty

[15] 59 U.S. (18 How.) 307 (1855).

[16] Dwight F. Henderson, Congress, Courts, and Criminals: The Development of Federal Criminal Law, 1801-1829, at 47, 146–47 (1985).

[17] P. S. Ruckman, Jr., Policy as an Indicator of "Original Understanding": Executive Clemency in the Early Republic (1789-1817), paper presented at the Annual Meeting of the Southern Political Science Association, Atlanta, Ga., Sept. 3, 1994, 6 https://web.archive.org/web/20060923034500/http://www.rvc.cc.il.us/faclink/pruckman/pardoncharts/Paper7.pdf (last visited Sept. 30, 2025) ("Washington, Adams, Jefferson, and Madison signed a total of three hundred and fifty-eight clemency warrants."). Many of these were limited to canceling the obligation to pay fines or costs after the prisoner served the sentence. Many others, however, limited the severity of the sentences imposed.

[18] The Federal Death Penalty Project maintains records of each execution with a description of the offenders and their offenses. *List of Federal Executions, 1790-2021*, Federal Death Penalty Project, https://federaldeathpenaltyproject.org/federal-executions-1790-2021/ [https://perma.cc/LKE2-FUSU]. Some of those executed were convicted of piracy, but in each case piracy was accompanied by murder.

[19] Crimes Act of 1790, §§ 13 (punishment for maiming to "be imprisoned not exceeding seven years, and fined not exceeding one thousand dollars."), 16 (larceny to be punished by a fine "not exceeding the fourfold value of the property so stolen . . . and be publicly whipped, not exceeding thirty-nine stripes.").

[20] *Id.*, § 18 (offender shall "be imprisoned not exceeding three years, and fined not exceeding eight hundred dollars; and shall stand in the pillory for one hour . . .").

provisions, however, pillory-for-perjury was not a mandatory minimum but a single, mandatory penalty. The president might pardon the offense, but prosecutors could not add to or subtract from it by bringing a different charge.

The Founders limited judicial discretion by placing strict *upper* bounds on potential sentences. The longest term authorized by the Act was seven years, and most of the maximums were lower still. They rejected mandatory minimum terms, indeterminate sentences, and boundless discretion. Instead, they trusted the judges to act reasonably within the confines of a definite upper limit.

(3) The Original Understanding of Prosecutorial Discretion

The 1790 Crimes Act did provide a mandatory death penalty for the most serious crimes, treason, murder, piracy, and (given the importance of credit to the new government) counterfeiting and forgery. These mandatory death sentences might suggest prosecutorial sentencing. The Founders, however, divided the charging function by giving both grand juries and prosecutors the power to veto an indictment.

In most criminal cases, the suspect would be arrested and taken before a magistrate well before the term of court.[21] The magistrate would examine the witnesses and the prisoner, then commit, bail, or discharge the suspect and put the witnesses under recognizances to appear at the court.[22] At its next term, the court would order the grand jury to consider these cases, clearing the jail as it were. The district attorney's role was to draft indictments in appropriate legal language and ask the grand jury to return true bills.[23]

[21] *See, e.g.*, George J. Edwards, Jr., The Grand Jury 110–15 (1906) (district attorney usually prefers bills against prisoners committed after arrest by magistrate, but may prefer a bill without an arrest or prefer charges not cited by the committing magistrate). Under entries for "arrest," "bail," or "examination," the leading manuals for justices of the peace describe the process in very similar terms. During the Founding era, the leading English JP manual was 1 Richard Burn, The Justice of the Peace, and Parish Officer (London, Strahan & Woodfall, 15th ed. 1785). *See id.* at 109 (procedure after arrest); *id.* at 141 (bail); *id.* at 536 (examination). Early American JP manuals include Samuel Freeman, The Massachusetts Justice (Boston, Thomas & Andrews 1795); Rhodom A. Greene & John W. Lumpkin, The Georgia Justice (Milledgeville, Ga., P.L. & B.H. Robinson 1835); William Waller Hening, The New Virginia Justice (Richmond, Va., T. Nicholson 1795); Henry Hitchcock, The Alabama Justice of the Peace (Cahawba, Ala., W.B. Allen 1822).

[22] *See, e.g.*, Freeman, *supra* note 21, at 164 (form for recognizance of a witness); Hitchcock, *supra* note 21, at 207 (same).

[23] Some federal cases, discussed *infra*, barred the prosecutor from preferring a bill until after the grand jurors presented an accusation in lay terms. When the grand jury presented this, it was usually understood as an instruction to the prosecutor to prepare a bill. 1 Joseph Chitty, A Practical

The district attorney had the important power of filing a writ of *nolle prosequi*, terminating further proceedings. This, however, was a negative power to block prosecution, not a positive power to compel prosecution. What the prosecutor drafted was a bill of indictment. The bill became an indictment only when the grand jury returned "a true bill." If the grand jury thought the case groundless, they would mark the bill "ignoramus" or "not a true bill," thereby ending the prosecution. It was legal, but uncommon and disfavored, for the prosecutor to prefer a similar bill to the same or a later grand jury.[24]

The grand jury had the further power to "present" for prosecution an offender against whom the district attorney had not preferred a bill of indictment. It was then up to the district attorney to draft an indictment in technical language that the grand jury would approve as a true bill. Whether or not the district attorney had a duty to prosecute every person presented by the grand jury, the district attorney could still end the prosecution by filing a *nolle prosequi*.[25] The grand jury could prevent the district attorney from prosecuting by returning a no bill, and the district attorney could prevent the grand jury from launching a prosecution by filing a *nolle prosequi*.

Grand juries had shown their independence on both sides of the Atlantic before 1789. The available evidence shows that late eighteenth-century grand juries rejected a substantial percentage of the cases brought to them.[26]

Treatise on the Criminal Law *163. John Marshall delivered an opinion on circuit holding that the prosecutor was not required to prefer bills whenever the grand jury presented. United States v. Hill, 26 F. Cas. 315 (Cir. Ct. Va. 1809). Like the rule requiring presentment before indictment, this may have reflected a peculiar federal policy against prosecutors inflating their fees by entering more filings than necessary. The prosecutor required to prefer a bill against the evidence could collect one fee for drafting the indictment and then another for filing a *nolle prosequi*. *See infra* (discussing federal fee statutes).

[24] Edwards, *supra* note 21, at 112.

[25] In *United States v. Hill*, 26 F. Cas. 315 (C.C.D. Va. 1809), Chief Justice Marshall on circuit noted that the "usage of this country has been, to pass over, unnoticed, presentments on which the attorney does not think it proper to institute proceedings."). *Id.* at 316. The other view would require the district attorney to file an indictment based on the presentment and then turn about and file a *nolle prosequi*.

[26] *See, e.g.*, J. M. Beattie, Crime and the Courts in England: 1660-1800, at 402 tbl.8.1 (1986) (showing that English grand juries refused in 8.3 percent to 44.4 percent of cases, depending upon offense); Jack D. Marietta & G. S. Rowe, Troubled Experiment: Crime and Justice in Pennsylvania, 1682-1800, at 46 tbl.2.5 (2006) (stating that Pennsylvania grand juries in the 1770s refused to indict in approximately 20 percent of cases). In 1778–1779, Tory supporters of the British occupation of Philadelphia were prosecuted for treason. "Thirty-nine of the forty-one identifiable cases involved charges of treason, and the grand jury issued indictments in twenty-five of these cases. This indictment rate—64.1%—was somewhat lower than the average indictment of 80% for Pennsylvania grand juries in the 1770s." Carlton F. W. Larson, *The Revolutionary American Jury: A Case Study of the 1778-1779 Philadelphia Treason Trials*, 61 S.M.U. L. Rev. 1441, 1456 (2008) (footnotes omitted).

In America, that tradition of independence continued into the nineteenth century.

During the first decade under the Judiciary Act of 1789, federal judges, including Supreme Court Justices riding circuit, delivered well-publicized instructions to grand juries.[27] Different judges gave somewhat different instructions.[28] On three important points, however, there was no expressed disagreement.

The first is that the judges felt the need to charge the jury to enforce even unpopular laws, such as the excise tax.[29] These exhortations were largely unsuccessful. After hearing James Wilson's charge respecting the excise tax, the grand jury in Pennsylvania replied that the need to enforce the revenue laws was "so clearly explained, and so cogently urged" that the jurors would "use our utmost endeavors to support the due execution of those laws . . ." Accordingly, it was "with particular pleasure we offer to the Court our congratulations, that in a District so extensive, and including the first commercial city in the United States, we have found no cause to make even a single presentment."[30] The grand jury in Georgia made a similar in-your-face reply to Justice Iredell by presenting no one for violating the excise law but instead presenting the whiskey tax itself as their first grievance.[31]

Second, there was nothing irregular about informing grand juries about possible sentences. Wilson and Iredell read many sections of the *Crimes Act*, including penalties, in their instructions.[32] Chase took care to distinguish the Act's capital crimes from the rest.[33]

[27] Many of these are collected in THE DOCUMENTARY HISTORY OF THE SUPREME COURT OF THE UNITED STATES, 1789-1900 (Maeva Marcus et al. eds., 1985–2004) [hereinafter DHSC].

[28] Compare James Wilson's Charge to the Grand Jury for the District of Pennsylvania, 2 DHSC 33, 35–36 (Apr. 12, 1790) (the standard of proof for indictment should be "moral certainty," not "probable cause"), with James Iredell's Charge to the Grand Jury for the District of Georgia, 2 DHSC 216, 223 (Oct. 17, 1791) ("a high probability, and that alone, of a person having committed an offence . . . can justify their presenting the bill as a true one.").

[29] *See, e.g., Wilson's Charge*, 2 DHSC at 44–45; *Iredell's Charge*, 2 DHSC at 221–22; John Jay's Charge to the Grand Jury for the Circuit Court of the District of Vermont, 2 DHSC 282, 283 (June 25, 1792).

[30] *Wilson's Charge*, 2 DHSC at 45.

[31] *Iredell's Charge*, 2 DHSC at 224.

[32] James Wilson's Charge to the Grand Jury of a Special Session of the Circuit Court for the District of Pennsylvania, 2 DHSC 142, 145–52 (Feb. 21, 1971); James Iredell's Charge to the Grand Jury of the Circuit Court for the District of Georgia, 2 DHSC 263, 267–68 (Apr. 26, 1792); James Iredell's Charge to the Grand Jury of the Circuit Court for the District of Virginia, 3 DHSC 74, 79–80 (Nov. 23, 1795).

[33] Samuel Chase's Charge to the Grand Jury of the Circuit Court for the District of Pennsylvania, 3 DHSC 408, 414 (Apr. 12, 1800).

The third common feature of the various grand jury charges delivered in the 1790s is the conspicuous absence of any significant role for the district attorney. Most of the charges don't mention the attorney for the United States at all. Two that do, both delivered by Chief Justice Oliver Elsworth, say that the US attorney is available to advise the grand jurors should they ask for assistance.[34] District attorneys today routinely not only attend the grand jury's sessions, but summon and question the witnesses. During the Founding era, however, Ellsworth's trivialization of the district attorney was orthodox.[35]

Aaron Burr's expedition down the Mississippi led to a dramatic illustration of the respective roles of the grand jury and the district attorney. The federal district attorney for Kentucky, Joseph Hamilton Daveiss, suspected that Burr was planning an illegal military expedition.[36] After sending warnings to President Jefferson, without a satisfactory reply, Daveiss tried to prosecute Burr for violating the federal statute that prohibited preparing a military invasion of the territory of any government at peace with the United States.[37]

The law offered Daveiss two familiar ways to initiate a prosecution. He might have gone to a judge and sought an arrest warrant. He might also prefer a bill of indictment to the grand jury. The law, however, did not permit either an arrest warrant or an indictment based on hearsay.[38]

Daveiss frankly admitted that he lacked admissible evidence sufficient to justify Burr's conviction at trial.[39] He moved the court to adopt a novel

[34] Oliver Ellsworth's Charge to the Grand Jury of the Circuit Court for the District of Georgia, 3 DHSC 119, 120 (Apr. 25, 1796) (grand jurors "may expect . . . such assistance from Mr. Attorney, and also from the Court, and you may have occasion, for it shall be proper for them respectively to give."); Oliver Ellsworth's Charge to the Grand Jury of the Circuit Court for the District of New York, 3 DHSC 158, 159 (Apr. 1, 1797) ("Should it be necessary, Mr. Attorney will assist you with forms, or the court with further directions.").

[35] Edwards, *supra* note 21, at 129–30 (at common law, the public prosecutor had no right "to be present to examine the witnesses and conduct the case for the government.") (footnote omitted).

[36] Mary K. Bonsteel Tachau, Federal Courts in the Early Republic: Kentucky, 1789-1816, at 138–39 (1978).

[37] *Id.* at 139–40.

[38] Laurent Sacharoff, *The Broken Fourth Amendment Oath*, 74 Stan. L. Rev. 603, 663–64 (2022); Chitty, *supra* note 23, at *319 ("evidence of what third persons said will not be good in order to support a bill before the grand inquest" and the grand jury "ought not to find an indictment upon the testimony of incompetent witnesses."); Francis Wharton, A Treatise on the Criminal Law of the United States 126 (Philadelphia, Kay, Jun. & Bro. 1846) ("A grand jury, it has been said, is bound to take the best legal proof of which the case admits; and it is the duty of the prosecuting officer of the state to take care that no evidence is received by them which would not be admissible at trial.").

[39] United States v. Burr, 25 F. Cas. 1 (C.C.D. Ky. 1806) (Daveiss's affidavit swears that he "is informed, and verily believes" that Burr planned an illegal expedition); W. E. Beard, *Colonel Burr's First Brush with the Law: An Account of the Proceedings Against Him in Kentucky*, 1 Tenn. Hist. Mag. 3, 6 (1915) (Daveiss argued that information and belief are the only possible evidence to support a prosecution for preparatory offenses, and so should suffice to initiate process).

procedure, whereby the court would order the appearance of Burr and other witnesses. Daveiss proposed to question Burr in open court, as at a post-arrest examination, and to question the witnesses inside the grand jury room.

As pointed out by a young Henry Clay, on behalf of Burr, this proposed procedure was unprecedented. *After* an arrest, the magistrate could question the witnesses (under oath) and the prisoner (unsworn). The district attorney could prefer a bill of indictment to the grand jury, but the prosecutor's role stopped there. The bill included the names of the witnesses who testified in secret in the grand jury room from which the prosecutor was excluded. Likening Daveiss's proposal to the "screws and tortures made use of in the dens of despotism," Clay challenged Daveiss "to produce a single instance where the public attorney has been accustomed to examine the witnesses before the grand jury; to sound the jurors and enter into all their secrets."[40] Daveiss produced no such instance, and the judge denied the motion as unprecedented.[41]

The death sentences required by the 1790 act in practice were rarely inflicted. Between 1790 and 1825, when Congress adopted a comprehensive reform of the criminal code, the federal government executed only thirty offenders.[42] Two were for robbery of the mail,[43] and six were for piracy that did not result in immediate loss of life.[44] The other twenty-four were either for murder at sea or for piracy involving murder.

There is direct evidence that federal grand juries blocked many capital cases from prosecution. In the 1795 whiskey rebellion cases, the district attorney preferred thirty-five bills of indictment for treason.[45] "The grand jury

[40] TACHAU, *supra* note 36, at 143.

[41] *Burr*, 25 F. Cas. at 2 ("No instance has occurred (within my recollection, since I have become acquainted with judicial proceedings, when a crime or misdemeanor has been committed) of a motion being made to a court to award process to arrest the offender in the first instance; neither have I knowledge of the existence of a law to authorize it."). English practice was different. *See* CHITTY, *supra* note 23, at *317 ("It is not unusual, except in the King's Bench, where the clerk of the grand juries attends them, to permit the prosecutor to be present during the sitting of the grand jury to conduct the evidence on the part of the crown."). In England, however, there was no public prosecutor analogous to the US district attorneys until the twentieth century. The "prosecutor" in English parlance was not a government lawyer but "some one, as often as not a police-constable, [who] is bound over by the magistrate to prosecute." 1 JAMES FITZJAMES STEPHEN, A HISTORY OF THE CRIMINAL LAW OF ENGLAND 273 (1883).

[42] FEDERAL DEATH PENALTY PROJECT, *supra* note 18.

[43] *Id.* (cases of Joseph T. Hare and John Alexander).

[44] *Id.* (cases of John F. Ferguson, Israel Denny, George Clark, Henry Roberts, John Desfarges, and Robert Johnson).

[45] HENDERSON, *supra* note 16, at 13.

returned twenty-five as true bills."[46] In the Fries Rebellion cases, after the indictment of three ringleaders, the grand jury rejected six of the twenty-two bills put before them.[47] For the period 1801–1829, Professor Henderson found ninety-eight indictments for murder (with a mandatory death penalty) and thirteen for the lesser included offense of manslaughter (with a three-year maximum sentence and no minimum).[48]

The discretion of grand juries, however, is far from a complete explanation for the rarity of executions under the 1790 Crimes Act. Two other factors were nullification by trial juries and executive clemency. Both played substantial roles.

(4) Nullification and Clemency in the Early Republic

Henderson's sample of cases from 1801 to 1829 includes sixty-six cases where the accused was convicted and sentenced to death.[49] He also reports seventy-seven indictments for counterfeiting, punishable, under the 1790 act, by death and only death.[50] That suggests nullification, either by the judges or more likely by juries.

Of the sixty-six defendants sentenced to death, "only thirty-two were actually executed."[51] In one of the piracy cases, the entire crew of eighteen was sentenced to death, but executive clemency spared sixteen.[52]

Clemency became a routine part of the federal criminal process. Under a procedure initiated by Jefferson and followed subsequently, when the president, upon receipt of a pardon petition, would solicit the views of the district attorney and the trial judge.[53] "The pardon archives indicate that if both judge and prosecutor recommended mercy, a pardon would generally issue."[54]

[46] *Id.*
[47] *Id.* at 15.
[48] *Id.* at 215, app. III.
[49] *Id.* at 216, app. IV.
[50] *Id.* at 215, app. III.
[51] *Id.* at 47.
[52] Federal Death Penalty Project, *supra* note 18 (cases of John Desfarges and Robert Johnson).
[53] Henderson, *supra* note 16, at 47.
[54] George Lardner, Jr. & Margaret Colgate Love, *Mandatory Sentences and Presidential Mercy: The Role of Judges in Pardon Cases, 1790-1850*, 16 Fed. Sent'g Rep. 212, 213 (2004).

(5) The Limited Role of District Attorneys

If the grand jurors played a larger part than their modern counterparts, Founding-era US Attorneys played a smaller one. "District Attorney" was an office, but not an institution, not even a job.[55] The US Attorney was a lawyer for whom the government was one client among many.

The 1789 Judiciary Act compensated district attorneys for fees, based on the going rate for similar services in the state in which the district was located.[56] US Attorneys were not put on annual salaries until 1896.[57] A 1799 statute included mileage and a per diem for attending court, but continued to borrow the local rates for other fees.[58] The fee sheets show charges for "attending examination and motion to adjourn same," "drawing indictment," and "counsel perusing and amending."[59]

Early US Attorneys had no interest in obtaining guilty pleas. Quite the opposite. In support of an 1853 reform statute, the House Judiciary Committee began its list of "prominent abuses" with the "prosecution of several suits or indictments, which . . . should be consolidated into one."[60] The statute provided that whenever "two or more indictments, suits or proceedings, are or shall be prosecuted, which should be joined, the district attorney prosecuting them shall be paid but one bill of costs for all of them. . . ."[61]

The 1853 statute set a "docket fee" for criminal jury trials of $20 and added a contingency fee. The district attorney who tried an indictment by jury and obtained a conviction was due "a counsel fee in proportion to the importance and difficulty of the cause, not exceeding thirty dollars."[62] From the perspective of the US Attorney, guilty pleas were bad for business.

In the social hierarchy, grand jurors typically outranked upwardly striving lawyers.[63] While procedures for selecting grand jurors varied, the available

[55] *See* Exec. Off. For U.S. Att'ys, U.S. Dep't of Just., Bicentennial Celebration of the United States Attorneys 3 (1989).

[56] Judiciary Act of 1789, ch. 20, § 35, 1 Stat. 73, 92 (providing US Attorneys the same fees as would be assessed in the supreme court of the state where the federal district was located).

[57] Nicholas R. Parrillo, Against the Profit Motive: The Salary Revolution in American Government, 1780-1940, at 286–89 (2013). Even then, "[m]ost U.S. Attorneys were still part-time in 1896, and it remained permissible for them to engage in part-time private practice for nearly sixty years afterward." *Id.* at 289 (footnotes omitted).

[58] Act of Feb. 28, 1799, ch. 19, § 4, 1 Stat. 624, 625–26.

[59] *See* H.R. Rep. No. 32-50, at 9 (1852) (reproducing sample fee claims).

[60] *Id.* at 4.

[61] Act of Feb. 26, 1853, ch. 80, 10 Stat. 161, at 162.

[62] *Id.*

[63] Thanks to George Fisher for mentioning this point.

evidence indicates that the grand jurors would have more wealth, more political experience, and possibly more legal knowledge than the prosecuting attorney.[64] From 1789 to 1809, every federal grand jury in Virginia included several members "who were or recently had been members of Virginia's General Assembly or of Congress, and more than a few served prominently in one or the other legislative body or as governor after they were on the grand jury."[65]

(6) Summary of Founding-Era Federal Practice

The sentences approved by the First Congress differed from modern mandatory minimum prison terms in key respects. First, in general, the Founders replaced most of the common law's formally mandatory death sentences with prison terms. The terms they provided included no minimums, set the maximums no higher than seven years, and delegated discretion over particular prison terms to judges, not prosecutors. Second, even when the Founders provided mandatory death sentences, they limited prosecutorial discretion by limiting the menu of charges and penalties, and by vesting charging discretion in grand juries rather than public prosecutors. The system they set up included mandatory sentences, not prosecutorial sentencing power.

C. Federal Sentencing from the Founding to the Civil War

(1) Ad Hoc Sentencing Statutes from 1790 to 1825

According to a comprehensive government report,[66] the earliest minimum prison terms approved by Congress appeared in the Sedition Act of 1798[67] and the Logan Act of 1799.[68] These provisions have some common

[64] Larson, *supra* note 26, at 1457 & n.125.

[65] Brent Tyler & Wythe Holt, *The Apparent Political Selection of Federal Grand Juries in Virginia, 1789-1809*, 49 AM. J. LEG. HIST. 257, 263 (2007).

[66] U.S. SENT'G COMM'N, 2011 REPORT TO THE CONGRESS: MANDATORY MINIMUM PENALTIES IN THE FEDERAL CRIMINAL JUSTICE SYSTEM 9 (2011) [hereinafter USSC REPORT].

[67] Act of July 14, 1798, ch. 74, § 1, 1 Stat. 596 (providing six months to five years for conspiracy or solicitation with the object of impeding "the operation of any law").

[68] Act of Jan. 30, 1799, ch. 1, 1 Stat. 613 (providing six months to three years for private correspondence with a foreign government).

features. First, they established only a six-month minimum, which by today's standards might be viewed as *de minimis.* In few, if any, cases would judicial discretion dictate a shorter sentence for any serious crime. Second, both were partisan measures of dubious constitutionality. Third, both fell into oblivion (regarding the Sedition Act, odium might be a better word) almost immediately.

Some of those prosecuted for participating in the Fries Rebellion did receive the prescribed minimum under Section 1.[69] However, the "Sedition Act contained a sunset provision and automatically expired on March 3, 1801, on the last day of President John Adams's term in office."[70] Jefferson nullified the prosecutions upon taking office:

> As one of his first official acts of office, Jefferson pardoned all those who had been convicted under the Sedition Act and freed those who were still in jail, noting that he considered the act "to be nullity as absolute and as palpable as if Congress had ordered us to fall down and worship a golden image."[71]

In 1840, Congress "repaid all the fines levied under the Sedition Act, with interest" and declared that the Act's unconstitutionality had been "conclusively settled."[72]

History records only one indictment for violating the Logan Act, an accusation dropped before trial in 1803.[73] Congress deleted the mandatory minimum, although the date of the revision is not clear.[74] The six-month minimum vanished at least before Charles Warren's 1917 report on the Logan Act.[75]

[69] Dwight F. Henderson, *Treason, Sedition, and Fries' Rebellion*, 14 AM. J. LEG. HIST. 308, 318 (1970).

[70] USSC REPORT, *supra* note 66, at 9–10 (footnote omitted).

[71] Geoffrey Stone, *The Story of the Sedition Act of 1798: "The Reign of Witches," in* FIRST AMENDMENT STORIES 14, 35 (Richard W. Garnett & Andrew Koppelman eds., 2012) (footnote omitted).

[72] *Id.* at 36 (footnote omitted).

[73] MICHAEL V. SEITZINGER, CONG. RSCH. SERV., RL33265, CONDUCTING FOREIGN RELATIONS WITHOUT AUTHORITY: THE LOGAN ACT 3 (2015).

[74] USSC REPORT, *supra* note 66, at 10.

[75] CHARLES WARREN, HISTORY OF LAWS PROHIBITING CORRESPONDENCE WITH A FOREIGN GOVERNMENT AND ACCEPTANCE OF A COMMISSION, S. Doc. No. 64-696, at 3 (1917).

(2) The Non-Importation Laws

In 1807, Congress prohibited the importation of slaves. Two of the specific offenses carried mandatory minimum prison terms, one for two years and the other for five.[76] New importation offenses were added in 1818, carrying three-year minimums.[77] These provisions were mild in theory and hortatory in practice.

From 1807 on, opponents of the slave trade demanded the death penalty.[78] In 1820, Congress added a mandatory death penalty for sailors serving on slave ships.[79] Unlike modern minimum sentences, the "mandatory" minimums for the importation of slaves appear to have gone entirely uninflicted.[80] According to W. E. B. Du Bois, "voluminous" testimony supported the view that "the act of 1807 came very near to being a dead letter."[81]

Professor Henderson agreed that the "enforcement pattern for the twenty-year period is bleak. The government initiated approximately six cases per year or 169 for the period 1801-1829."[82] There were only "twenty criminal charges brought into the courts resulting in nineteen indictments but only three convictions."[83]

Prosecutors can neither threaten nor impose minimum sentences unless they can credibly threaten and practically obtain convictions at trial. The nonenforcement of the slave trade laws is one of the worst disgraces in American legal history. The disgrace, however, was that offenders were not sentenced at all, not that prosecutors controlled their sentences.

[76] Act of Mar. 2, 1807, ch. 22, §§ 5 (bringing slaves to the United States; five-to-ten-year sentence) and 7 (serving on vessels holding slaves; two-to-four-year sentence), 2 Stat. 426, 427–28.

[77] Act of Apr. 20, 1818, ch. 91, §§ 3 (outfitting vessels for the slave trade), 4 (citizens transporting slaves), and 6 (importing slaves to the United States), 3 Stat. 450, 451–52.

[78] *See* USSC Report, *supra* note 66, at 10 ("the mandatory minimum penalties were much less severe than the mandatory death penalty many in the House of Representatives wanted to attach to these offenses"); W. E. B. Du Bois, The Suppression of the African Slave-Trade to the United States of America 1638-1870, at 102 (1896) ("Advocates of the severer punishment [*i.e.*, death] dwelt on the enormity of the offence.").

[79] Act of May 15, 1820, ch. 113, §§ 4 (serving on foreign vessel seizing persons for the slave trade) and 5 (forcibly confining individuals destined for the slave trade), 3 Stat. 600, 600–1.

[80] *See* Hugh Thomas, The Slave Trade 774 (1997) (prior to the hanging of Captain Gordon in 1862, "[m]any slave captains had been captured, but none had been severely punished, much less hanged, even though the offense of slave trading had been a capital one since 1820. Between 1837 and 1860 seventy-four cases had been brought by the United States on charges related to slaving, but few captains had been convicted, and those had received trifling sentences, which they had usually been able to avoid.").

[81] Du Bois, *supra* note 78, at 109.

[82] Henderson, *supra* note 16, at 199.

[83] Federal Death Penalty Project, *supra* note 18.

(3) The 1825 Post Office Act

The 1792 Post Office Act provided a mandatory death penalty for robbing the mail.[84] In 1810, Congress replaced the mandatory death penalty for the first offense of robbing the mail with a zero-to-ten-year prison term (provided that life was not threatened nor wounds inflicted, in which case death was the only punishment).[85] In 1818, Joseph T. Hare and John Alexander were executed for a mail robbery in which the letter carrier was wounded.[86] Hare's younger brother, Lewis, was convicted but pardoned.

In 1825, Congress added a five-year minimum for the first offense, again provided that life was not threatened nor wounds inflicted.[87] For second convictions, and for first convictions involving endangering the postal worker, death was the only authorized punishment. In theory, the prosecutor *could* charge a recidivist, or a violent first offender, with mail robbery *simpliciter*. In the legal system of the time, however, prosecutors could not in fact select the higher or lower sentence, because they didn't control charge selection, they couldn't count on a conviction, and even a capital conviction was a likely candidate for executive clemency.

The grand jury might refuse to indict, the trial jury might refuse to convict, and the president might pardon. The executive paid close attention to judicial recommendations for pardons of offenders facing the mandatory minimum.[88] The severe prison terms for mail offenses were a common subject of executive clemency.[89]

The death penalty for violent or repeat offenders was even less "mandatory" than the minimum prison terms. Hare and Alexander were the last federal convicts to be executed for mail robbery.

(4) The 1825 Crimes Act

The same Congress that adopted the Postal Service Act of 1825 also adopted a new general crimes act.[90] The new code required the death penalty for

[84] Postal Service Act of 1792, ch. 7, § 17, 1 Stat. 232, 237.
[85] Act of Apr. 30, 1810, ch. 37, § 19, 2 Stat. 592, 598.
[86] Federal Death Penalty Project, *supra* note 18.
[87] Act of Mar. 3, 1825, ch. 64, § 22, 4 Stat. 102, 108.
[88] *See* Lardner & Love, *supra* note 54, at 216–17.
[89] *Id.* at 5–6.
[90] Crimes Act of 1825, ch. 65, 4 Stat. 115.

arson, murder, and rape. The only minimum prison term was a one-year minimum for debasing specie currency; the maximum was ten years.[91] For many offenses, the act increased the maximum prison term, but on the whole reduced severity for pragmatic reasons that echoed Beccaria.[92] The act deleted the pillory provision from the penalty for perjury in 1825.[93] The same Act replaced the death penalty for forgery and counterfeiting with a prison term "not exceeding ten years."[94]

Like the original 1790 Crimes Act, the 1825 code had none of the features of prosecutorial sentencing. There was no minimum menu, because there was only one trivial minimum prison term and the capital crimes carried death-only penalties. Even if the prosecutor brought a capital charge, the grand jury might refuse to indict, the trial jury might acquit, and the president might pardon.

(5) The 1831 Code for the District of Columbia

In 1831, Congress adopted An Act for the Punishment of Crimes in the District of Columbia.[95] The Act "included 18 offenses with punishments for conduct occurring in the District of Columbia, fifteen of which carried mandatory minimum penalties."[96] As with the sentences adopted for participating in the slave trade, some qualifications are in order.

Congress had adopted the organic act creating the District in 1801.[97] Section 1 of the organic act provided that the laws of Virginia and Maryland, respectively, "shall be and continue in force" in the parts of the district composed of territory ceded by those states. Congress promptly passed a supplementary act.[98] Section 3 of the supplementary act provided that "all felonies committed within the county of Alexandria shall be punished in the same

[91] *Id.*, § 24.
[92] USSC Report, *supra* note 66, at 11.
[93] Crimes Act of 1825 § 13.
[94] *Id.*, §§ 17, 18, & 20.
[95] Act of Mar. 2, 1831, ch. 37, 4 Stat. 448 [hereinafter D.C. Crimes Act].
[96] USSC Report, *supra* note 66, at 12. *See, e.g.*, D.C. Crimes Act § 6 ("every person duly convicted of burglary, or as accessary thereto before the fact, or of robbery, or as accessary thereto before the fact, shall be sentenced to suffer imprisonment and labour, for the first offence for a period not less than three nor more than seven years, and for the second offence for a period not less than five nor more than fifteen years.").
[97] An Act Concerning the District of Columbia, ch. 15, 2 Stat. 103 (1801).
[98] Act of Mar. 3, 1801, ch. 24, 2 Stat. 115.

manner as such crimes were punishable by the laws of Virginia, as they existed prior to the year one thousand seven hundred and ninety-six. . . ."

I have found no direct evidence of the purpose behind this provision, but there is strong circumstantial evidence. In 1796, Virginia adopted the penitentiary system and limited the death penalty to first-degree murder. "In this code, enacted twenty years after the state's first constitution, Virginia's legislature replaced capital punishment for most felony offenses with terms of imprisonment in the new penitentiary."[99] Congress, however, did not give final approval for a federal penitentiary in the District until 1831.[100]

Before the completion of the D.C. penitentiary in 1831, the D.C. courts had only the common law's old instruments of punishment—hanging, whipping, pillory, fines, and prison (a dreadful jail, really). Without the new institution of the penitentiary, the district courts could not have implemented the laws of Virginia post-1796. Maryland's penitentiary opened in 1811.[101] The organic act, however, froze the law of Maryland in 1801.

As a result, under the organic act, the D.C. courts had to apply the anachronistically sanguinary eighteenth-century laws even after Virginia and Maryland had adopted humane reforms. The legislative history of the 1831 D.C. Crimes Act makes clear that Congress intended to *reduce* the severity of punishments. In 1830, the Board of Inspectors of the penitentiary, which was then nearing the end of construction, filed its first report to the president and Congress.[102] The inspectors pleaded for a new criminal code to accompany the new penitentiary:

> The criminal law here remains almost unchanged, as it existed upon the cession of this District by the States of Maryland and Virginia, and partakes of the sanguinary character of the statute and common law punishments of England . . .
>
> Severe and cruel punishments, unsustained by public opinion, cannot be executed with certainty, and, when inflicted, beget a sympathy unfriendly to virtue and good morals.[103]

[99] Nancy J. King, *The Origins of Felony Jury Sentencing in the United States*, 78 Chi.-Kent L. Rev. 937, 937 (2003).

[100] *See* Act of Feb. 25, 1831, ch. 31, 4 Stat. 445.

[101] *See* H. B. Latrobe, Jr., Picture of Baltimore 86–89 (1832).

[102] *See* Message from the President of the United States, Transmitting the Annual Report of the Inspectors of the Penitentiary in the District of Columbia, H.R. Doc. No. 21-46 (1830).

[103] *Id.* at 3.

On March 3, the House Committee for the District of Columbia presented a report deploring the criminal law of the District as frozen as it stood in Virginia and Maryland "nearly thirty years ago" full of "sanctions only suited to barbarous ages, and which have long since been wisely abrogated by the respective states, but are still in force in this District."[104] The report then catalogued the Maryland capital crimes still in effect in the district, including "horse stealing," "breaking into a shop . . . and stealing goods to the value of five shillings," and "stealing a boat or a negro."[105] The old Virginia code governing Alexandria had "about the same sanguinary character . . . in consequence, many offences are suffered to go either unpunished, or punished in such manner as amounts, in effect, to no punishment."[106]

The committee had solicited comments from the D.C. legal community and attached those comments to the report. Many responded, but of these, the most notable is James Dunlop, a lawyer who would later serve for decades as a judge in the District.[107] His views deserve study because he authored a proposed bill that is tracked nearly verbatim by the 1831 D.C. Crimes Act.[108] Congress tweaked Section 1's definition of gaming to include keeping a faro table specifically, and divided Dunlop's proposed Section 4 on assault with intent to commit rape to differentiate offenses by slaves and by free persons, which alters the section numbers by one thereafter. Otherwise, the actual statute is virtually identical to that proposed by Dunlop, until Sections 17 and 18, relating to abduction of free Negros and crimes by slaves not resident in the district. These provisions are absent in Dunlop's proposal.

In his letter to the committee, Dunlop stated:

> The criminal law is bad, and the system of administering it worse . . . The law is too sanguinary, and cannot be enforced, because unsupported by public opinion. We have not less than 18 capital felonies . . . [J]uries will not convict, or, if they do, the Executive is importuned to pardon, and pardons, and the offender goes free of punishment. Larceny is the crime which largely swells the criminal calendar. For this, public whipping is the punishment.

[104] Gershom Powers, Laws for the District of Columbia, H.R. Rep. No. 21-269, at 7 (1830).
[105] *Id.* at 8
[106] *Id.*
[107] *See Dunlop, James*, Fed. Jud. Ctr., https://www.fjc.gov/history/judges/dunlop-james [https://perma.cc/3AXH-PLFL].
[108] H.R. Rep. No. 21-269 at 79–81.

> It produces no other effect than to degrade and disgrace the offender, and sends him out upon the public, only to renew his depredations.[109]

The overall effect of the D.C. Crimes Act was to reduce the potential severity of sentences. The mandatory minimums for arson, robbery, burglary, horse theft, and so on eliminated the death penalty for those offenses. Section 8, the perjury provision, omitted the pillory. Section 9's theft provision's minimum sentence of one year eliminated whipping.

Prior to the 1831 act, the D.C. judges faced a dilemma between hanging and taking no action against offenders. They did not have the discretionary power to impose prison terms, even if they did have the discretionary power under Virginia or Maryland law to spare minor offenders from the noose. Recalling how short the minimum terms were (one year for theft, three for robbery or burglary), the effect of the 1831 act was to give the judges more, rather than less, discretion than they had exercised before.

The 1831 penalties did not replace those in the 1825 Crimes Act, which included only one, one-year minimum prison term. They replaced the "sanguinary" punishments, "only suitable to barbarous ages," that applied in the District under the organic act long after Maryland and Virginia had left those penalties behind. In 1839, Congress completely abolished whipping and the pillory as punishments for crimes.[110] The abolition of corporal punishment, however, was not accompanied by minimum prison sentences.

The 1831 D.C. Crimes Act adopted minimum prison terms not to replace discretionary prison terms, but to replace the noose, the whipping post, and the pillory. If Congress had objected to judicial sentencing discretion, Congress would have added minimums to the 1825 Crimes Act. The D.C. judges were not given as much sentencing discretion as judges enjoyed under the 1825 act, but in reality, far more than they had exercised under the organic act.

To the extent that the D.C. Crimes Act gave charging decisions mandatory sentencing consequences, it is clear from the legislative history that grand juries, not the district attorney, were making charging decisions. Some commentators complained about private accusations causing the

[109] *Id.* at 71.

[110] Act of Feb. 28, 1839, ch. 36, § 5, 5 Stat. 321, 322 ("the punishment of whipping and the punishment of standing in the pillory, so far as they now are provided for by the laws of the United States, be, and they are hereby, abolished.").

jailing of people ultimately not charged by the grand jury.[111] Another commentator referred to one term's three murder cases, "of which one was acquitted, one returned ignoramus, and in one case a nolle prosequi."[112] The same writer pointed to a criminal underclass, who became "frequent subjects for our grand jury and courts."[113] Other than the one mention of a *nolle prosequi* in a murder case, none of the comments reference the district attorney.

The grand jury continued to exercise the charging power after the adoption of the 1831 act. In 1845, a D.C. grand jury presented William R. Elliott, "for causing the death of W.Z. Kendall, by shooting him with a pistol in self-defence, when he was attacked by and was retreating from the said Kendall."[114] Elliott understandably moved to be discharged. "The district attorney resisted the motion."[115] The court, however, treated the presentment as precluding prosecution and ordered Elliott released.

The *Elliott* court noted a 1722 Maryland statute that *prohibited* the attorney general or JP from submitting a bill of indictment to a grand jury without an order from the court to consider the case or a previous finding of a presentment by the grand jurors on their knowledge.

> Under this law, a practice has grown up to precede indictments by presentment. This I understand to be the uniform practice at this day, and it has been followed in this instance, the witnesses having been all summoned by the district attorney at the request of the defendant's counsel, so that the investigation might be made without delay by the grand jury, he having no further or otherwise interfered.[116]

[111] *See, e.g.*, H.R. Rep. No. 21-269 at 50 (letter from Francis Key) ("Instances of accused persons . . . suffering imprisonment for months in a most loathsome jail, and then discharged, either without any bill found against them by the grand jury, or tried and acquitted, have been numerous."); *id.* at 56 (letter from Thomas Carbery) ("Many cases of hardship occur, by the confinement of persons in the jail, during the recess of the court, six months, charged with petty offences, and against whom no presentments are made by the grand jury."); *id.* at 85 (letter from Joseph Gales) ("upon any frivolous accusation, made, upon oath, by a person however unprincipled, individuals may, and often do, lie within four naked stone walls for five months before the *ignoramus* of a grand jury can discharge them.").

[112] *Id.* at 30 (letter from Henry Morfit).

[113] *Id.* at 33.

[114] United States v. Elliott, 25 F. Cas. 1003 (D.C. Crim. Ct. 1845).

[115] *Id.*

[116] *Id.*

The court could summon the witnesses to testify before the grand jury, and would do so if the grand jury requested it.[117] The grand jury could not call, on its own, for witnesses to testify about defenses such as insanity.[118] In *Elliott*, the district attorney had agreed to summon witnesses who could testify about self-defense, but the grand jury itself could not have done so. Nonetheless, presentments preceded indictments. The decision to charge rested with the grand jury.

While I have found no record of D.C. judges suspending sentences under the Act,[119] even before the Act, the judges actively solicited pardons when they thought the legal sentence excessive.[120] This practice continued under the Act.[121] On the one hand, this practice shows that the judges felt compelled to impose some sentences they thought excessive. On the other hand, it shows that while the president controlled the pardon power, the judges had substantial influence over its exercise. There was, in short, a realistic escape hatch from the Act's minimum terms.

(6) Summary of Sentencing Discretion in the Federal System from the Founding to the Civil War

Like the mandatory death penalty provisions in the 1790 act, subsequent mandatory penalties were attached to a limited statutory menu controlled more by grand juries than by prosecutors. They were rarely enforced, and typically repealed in relatively short order. When charges carrying

[117] *See* United States v. Lloyd, 26 F. Cas. 986 (D.C. Crim. Ct. 1834) (holding that indictment not endorsed by a prosecutor was valid if either the court had ordered the witnesses to the grand jury or the grand jury had asked for them).

[118] United States v. Lawrence, 26 F. Cas. 886 (C.C.D.C. 1835) (rejecting grand jury's request to hear medical experts on the issue of the suspect's sanity). The grand jury's foreperson in *Lawrence* was Thomas Carberry, who had been foreperson as of his submission to the house committee five years before. This suggests a grand jury with experience across many terms of court, one more likely to act independently than modern counterparts.

[119] As discussed *infra*, some courts expressly disclaimed the power to suspended sentences indefinitely, but I have found no such case from the District under the Act.

[120] *See* Lardner & Love, *supra* note 54, at 213–16.

[121] *See* United States v. McCarthy, 26 F. Cas. 1046, 1048 (C.C.D.C. 1833) (defendant, convicted of forgery, "was pardoned, upon the recommendation of the court."); United States v. Pearl, 27 F. Cas. 484, 485 (C.C.D.C. 1838 (defendant was convicted of under D.C. Crimes Act § 9, larceny of property worth more than five dollars, carrying a one-year minimum sentence: "Verdict, 'Guilty.' There was a motion in arrest of judgment; but before it was argued, the president pardoned the defendant, and he died."); United States v. McDaniel, 26 F. Cas. 1073 (C.C.D.C. 1836); United States v. Kurtz, 26 F. Cas. 826 (C.C.D.C. 1836) (defendant charged with larceny of property worth more than five dollars: "Verdict: Guilty. Sentenced to the penitentiary. Pardoned.").

mandatory penalties were brought, there was a realistic chance of jury nullification and a systematic reliance on executive clemency.

D. Sentencing Discretion in the States before the Civil War

A comprehensive treatment of sentencing in the United States in the last two centuries is beyond the scope of this book. The modest treatment here nonetheless shows no evidence of prosecutorial sentencing as we see it today. Given the multiplicity of jurisdictions and the passage of time, any broad assertion would outrun the evidence I have seen. Considerable caution is warranted.

The evidence I have seen suggests that when there were mandatory prison terms, grand juries, not prosecutors, exercised discretion over charging. After public prosecutors gained practical control of grand juries, judges suspended sentences and legislatures adopted statutory systems of probation and parole.

The overview here does not exclude the possibility that something like modern prosecutorial sentencing operated in some states at some times before the late twentieth century. That said, the evidence—on a topic thus far without any definitive and comprehensive study—amply suffices to shift the burden of historical proof. Any claim that mandatory sentences in the states set a precedent for the system we have now needs to be proved, not just asserted.

(1) First-Generation Statutes: Curtailing the Death Penalty

The D.C. Crimes Act generally followed prior developments in the states, where the creation of penitentiaries was coupled with minimum prison terms for previously capital crimes. New York and Pennsylvania were leaders in the penitentiary movement. In 1790, Pennsylvania abolished the death penalty for robbery, burglary, and sodomy, replacing it with forfeiture of land and goods and "servitude of any term or time, at the discretion of the court passing the sentence, not exceeding ten years, in the public gaol or house of correction . . . ."[122] In 1794, there followed the famous limitation of the

[122] An Act to Reform the Penal Laws of this State, ch. 565, § 2, 1789–1790 Pa. Laws 801, 802.

death penalty to first-degree murder.[123] Benefit of clergy was abolished, and all felonies hitherto clergyable were to be punished from six months to two years in the house of corrections.[124] The specific sentences of up to ten years were retained for robbery, burglary, and sodomy.

The 1794 Act provided life imprisonment for second offenders.[125] The life term applied only to the commission of two offenses that were either capital or subject to death without benefit of clergy, as of 1786. At common law, larceny and other minor felonies were capital but clergyable. Clergy was only available once, so the second-offense provision functioned as a substitute for the death penalty.

In New York, a 1796 statute established a new prison system.[126] It also retained the death penalty for murder, but for "any other felony now punishable with death for the first offence except the crime of stealing from a church shall instead of being punished with death, be punished with imprisonment for life in one of the State prisons herein aftermentioned"; the law conferred judicial discretion to determine "imprisonment only" or further punishments of hard labor, solitude, or both.[127] An 1801 statute made it explicit that the mandatory life term applied to rape, sodomy, burglary, and robbery.[128]

For any other felony worse than petty larceny, the act provided prison terms to be set by the judges "on a consideration of all the circumstances of the case to imprisonment in the said prison . . . for any term not more than fourteen years." Second offenders were subject to life, but as in Pennsylvania, this was just another substitution of mandatory life for the death penalty for felons who had lost the benefit of clergy.[129]

Virginia and Maryland provide another telling example. Before Congress established a penitentiary for the District of Columbia, both states adopted penitentiary laws that curtailed the death penalty. As we have seen, without a

[123] An Act for the Better Preventing of Crimes, and for Abolishing the Punishment of Death in Certain Cases, ch. 257, 1793 Pa. Laws 599.
[124] *Id.*, § 9, 1793 Pa. Laws at 604.
[125] *Id.*, § 13, 1793 Pa. Laws at 605.
[126] An Act Making Alterations in the Criminal Law of this State and for Erecting State Prisons, ch. 30, 1796 N.Y. Laws 669.
[127] *Id.*
[128] An Act Declaring the Crimes Punishable with Death or with Imprisonment in the State Prison, ch. 58, 1801 N.Y. Laws 97.
[129] The analogy between clergy and the second-offense provision was noted in *People v. Youngs*, 1 Cai. 37 (N.Y. Sup. Ct. 1803). The court refused to permit proof of the first offense by the same procedure as used in England for showing prior benefit of clergy. The effect of the ruling was to subject the second-time thief to the fourteen-year maximum rather than life.

penitentiary, the District suffered under the common-law penalty structure that Virginia and Maryland had left behind.

Virginia adopted An Act to Amend the Penal Laws of this Commonwealth on December 15, 1796.[130] Section 1 provided "no crime whatsoever committed by any free person against this commonwealth (except murder in the first degree) shall be punished by death within the same." Section 4 punished second-degree murder by imprisonment for "not less than five, nor more than eighteen years." Similar minimum prison terms applied to other previous capital crimes. For example, Section 6 punished horse stealing by "not less than three, nor more than ten years." Section 24 provided a mandatory life term for "any person convicted of any crime, which now is capital, or a felony of death without benefit of clergy, shall commit any such offence a second time, and be thereof legally convicted, he or she shall be sentenced to undergo an imprisonment.... during life." As in Pennsylvania and New York, the mandatory life term applied to offenders who were ineligible for the benefit of clergy under the prior law.

Virginia's treatment of arson illustrates the linkage between minimum terms and the death penalty. In 1803, Virginia raised the penalty for arson from five to twelve years to a term "not less than ten years, nor more than twenty-one years."[131] The following year, the legislature once again made arson punishable by death.[132]

In 1793, Maryland adopted a law that gave judges the discretion to punish "[a]ny felony, with or without benefit of clergy" either with "such judgment as the law requires for such crimes" (in other words, death), or to "labour for any time, in their discretion, not exceeding seven years for the same crime on the public roads."[133] Discretion to impose forced labor instead of death extended even to murder.[134] On the other hand, under the 1793 Act, the judges retained discretion to hang offenders for lesser felonies such as burglary.

In 1809, Maryland established a penitentiary.[135] The new institution enabled the sweeping curtailment of capital punishment, which Maryland retained only as discretionary for treason and mandatory for first-degree

[130] An Act to Amend the Penal Laws of This Commonwealth, ch. 2, 1796 Va. Acts 4.

[131] An Act to Amend the Act, Intituled, An Act to Amend the Penal Laws of This Commonwealth, and for Other Purposes, ch. 117, 1803 Va. Acts 82.

[132] An Act Further to Amend the Penal Laws of This Commonwealth, ch. 5, 1803 Va. Acts 6.

[133] An Act Respecting the Punishment of Criminals, ch. 57, § 10, 1793 Md. Laws 38, 39.

[134] State v. Ben, 1 H.& J. 99, 1800 WL 234 (Md. Gen. Ct. 1800).

[135] An Act Concerning Crimes and Punishments, ch. 138, 1809 Md. Laws 88.

murder.[136] Section 5, for example, punished burglary by confinement for "not less than three nor more than ten years."

The early reform statutes created penitentiaries and discarded the gallows for any but the most serious crimes. It would be fair to say that early American lawmakers approved of minimum prison terms for any offense otherwise punishable by death. That is a far cry from saying that they approved, for any particular crime, prosecutorial discretion over a menu of charges, each carrying a different minimum sentence.

(2) The Early History of Prosecutorial Discretion in the States

Just as in the federal system, grand juries, not professional prosecutors, exercised the charging power under these early state penal codes. The new American states generally followed common-law criminal procedure, including the requirement that serious crimes be charged by indictment. Charge selection had sentencing consequences, but at least initially, professional prosecutors did not control charge selection. Private prosecution remained common well into the nineteenth century.[137]

In the states, the role of the district attorney was at least as modest as in the federal practice. According to Professor Steinberg, "[b]efore the twentieth century the District Attorney was a secondary figure in American criminal justice."[138] In general, state district attorneys, like their federal counterparts, were compensated by fees rather than by salary, with similar incentives to maximize court appearances and trial convictions.[139]

[136] *Id.*, §§ 2 (treason) & 4 (murder).

[137] *See, e.g.*, Mike McConville & Chester Mirsky, *The Rise of Guilty Pleas: New York, 1800-1865*, 22 J. L. & Soc'y 443, 452–53 (1995) ("Until mid-century, lawyers, similar to the barrister class then in existence in England, frequently represented the private prosecutor in one case and the defendant in another, whilst being bound by the attorney-client privilege."); *id.* at 453 ("During this period, the District Attorney did not resemble a state agent concerned with orchestrating case outcomes to further social control objectives. Rather, the District Attorney's principal function was to receive the case file assembled by the magistrate and to guide the case to conclusion often representing the private prosecutor at trial, when the prosecutor was not represented by privately retained lawyers."); *id.* ("Should a private lawyer represent the prosecutor at trial, as was common in the first half of the nineteenth century, the District Attorney might prepare briefing notes for private counsel . . . "); Mary E. Vogel, Coercion to Compromise: Plea Bargaining, the Court and the Making of Political Authority 185 (2007) ("Cases in the lower courts were usually handled swiftly by a judge alone with public prosecutors rarely involved before 1850 . . . the plea bargain appeared in the lower court long before the district attorney did . . .").

[138] Allen Steinberg, *The "Lawman" in New York: William Travers Jerome and the Origins of the Modern District Attorney in Turn-of-the-Century New York*, 34 U. Tol. L. Rev. 753, 753 (2003).

[139] Parrillo, *supra* note 57, at 267–68.

As in Virginia, in Pennsylvania, the grand jurors came from the same demographic as the justices of the peace. In Philadelphia in 1778, among the eighteen grand jurors, only two "had an assessed wealth below the 80th percentile and ten were in the 90th percentile or higher."[140] Six held commissions as justices of the peace.[141] To the typical district attorney, the grand jurors would have looked more like potential clients and patrons than like manipulable dullards.

As for the division of labor between grand juries and the attorney for the state (whether paid by public or private funds), Founding-era grand juries had as much independence in the states as in the federal practice. Recall that the Maryland rule applicable in the District of Columbia, requiring presentment before the district attorney was permitted to prefer a bill of indictment. As late as 1827, the New York Supreme Court resolved a conflict in the lower courts by opining that the "district attorney ought not to attend the grand jury for the purpose of examining witnesses, nor for any other purpose, except to advise them upon any question which they may put to him in relation to their duty."[142]

Professor Fisher found early plea bargaining emerging in Massachusetts liquor prosecutions.[143] These cases required public prosecution because they involved no victims. The applicable statute provided mandatory penalties without judicial discretion.[144] The penalty structure paralleled our hypothetical *229 Degrees.* What bears emphasis here is that early in the nineteenth century, this arrangement was the exception, not the rule.[145]

Statistical evidence of the grand jury's independence can be found in a series of reports prepared by the Massachusetts Attorney General, beginning in 1833.[146] The reports show that grand juries rejected a significant percentage of the bills preferred to them. For example, in 1834, the attorney

[140] Larson, *supra* note 26, at 1459.
[141] *Id.* at 1461.
[142] Anonymous, 7 Cow. 563 (N.Y. Sup. Ct. 1827) (per curiam). Until the creation of the Court of Appeals in 1847, the Supreme Court was the highest court in New York.
[143] George Fisher, *Plea Bargaining's Triumph*, 109 YALE L.J. 857, 868–84 (2000).
[144] *Id.* at 874 ("By depriving judges of almost all sentencing discretion in liquor-law cases, the legislature had assured that prosecutors could—by over-charging, selectively nol prossing, and manipulating the amount of costs—dictate the defendant's sentence.").
[145] *Id.* ("Excepting only those very serious crimes that carried mandatory life or death sentences, none of the typical common-law offenses called for a minimum sentence.").
[146] For these reports and their limitations, see *id.* at 935 n.287.

general reported, for the whole Commonwealth, 1,031 bills and 286 no bills—20 percent of all the bills preferred.[147]

Although subsequent reports require summing the numbers reported for the several districts, the ratio is consistent over time at one no bill to every three or four bills.[148] The last Report before the war shows a slightly smaller ratio, although there is some uncertainty because of the way the statistics were reported.[149]

After the war, the rate of no bills declined, but the grand jury still exercised the power to nullify. For the year ending September 30, 1867, there were 5,995 indictments and 789 no bills (11.5 percent of the bills preferred).[150] As of September 30, 1868, there were 3,449 indictments and 1,168 no bills (25 percent of the bills preferred).[151] What happened to cause the surge in no bills?

"The two years 1866 and 1867 were the high point of the attempt to enforce prohibition in Massachusetts."[152] If we subtract from the 1,168 no-bills the 900 returned in liquor cases, there were 268 no bills, compared to the 1,845 non-liquor indictments (a rate of 12.7 percent of all non-liquor bills preferred). Grand juries were rejecting fewer bills in general, but were still nullifying many prosecutions they regarded as misguided.

147 1834 MASS. ATT'Y GEN. ANN. REP. 54. The category of "bills" means true bills found, because the "total cases" matches the sum of cases continued from the previous report, bills, appeals from the sessions courts, and no bills. The figures don't match if "no bills" is a subset of "bills."

148 For example, the data from the 1839 MASS. ATT'Y GEN. ANN. REP. record 196 bills and 67 no bills from the Northern District, 389 bills and 79 no bills from Suffolk County, 156 bills and 100 no bills from the Southern District, 98 bills and 29 no bills from the Western District, and 140 bills and 93 no bills from the Middle District. The totals come to 979 bills and 368 no bills. The no bills are 27 percent of the 1,347 total bills preferred.

149 1856 MASS. ATT'Y GEN. ANN. REP. 57 tbl.XVII lists 635 no bills but does not report a number for true bills. The number of true bills must be at least 3,131 (the sum of 1,950 convictions, 403 acquittals, and 778 dismissals by *nolle prosequi*). Adding the no bills yields 3,766 bills preferred, and 635, 17 percent, rejected. The Report, however, also lists 1,032 cases as pending. If those were persons arrested but not yet indicted, the ratio of bills to no bills wouldn't change. That explanation is plausible because Massachusetts prosecutors developed a system of "informal probation" whereby the case was left "on file," prosecuted no further unless the accused offended again. THEODORE FERDINAND, BOSTON'S LOWER CRIMINAL COURTS, 1814-1850, at 68–69 (1991). But if many were indicted defendants with cases awaiting trial, the no bills would be a smaller percentage of all bills preferred.

150 1868 MASS. ATT'Y GEN. ANN. REP. 104–5.

151 1869 MASS. ATT'Y GEN. ANN. REP. 77–78.

152 ROGER LANE, POLICING THE CITY: BOSTON, 1822–1885, at 138 (1967).

(3) Executive Clemency in the States

In many states, statutorily mandatory death penalties or minimum prison terms were subject to serious review via the pardon power. At least in some jurisdictions, pardons accounted for a significant percentage of discharges from state prisons.[153] Pardons were common enough to provoke harsh criticism for undermining the certainty of punishment.[154] The strident tenor of the soft-on-crime critique suggests that, like their federal counterparts, state mandatory sentences were not mandatory in practice.

E. Sentencing Discretion in the States after the Civil War

Before the war, prosecutors shared discretion over charges with grand juries. Both could initiate a prosecution, and both could veto one. Late in the nineteenth century, prosecutors acquired a practical monopoly on discretion to prosecute and what charges to bring. We begin with this well-known increase in prosecutorial power before turning to developments in sentencing law that generally denied prosecutors control over sentences, even after they monopolized discretion over charges.

[153] For discussion of statistics on pardons, see GUSTAVE DE BEAUMONT & ALEXIS DE TOCQUEVILLE, ON THE PENITENTIARY SYSTEM IN THE UNITED STATES, AND ITS APPLICATION IN FRANCE app. at 258–59 (Francis Lieber, trans., Philadelphia, Carey, Lea & Blanchard 1833). They give figures of the annual ratio of prisoners pardoned to total prisoners, ranging from a high of one in four (New York's Newgate Prison) to Connecticut's one in fifty-seven. These statistics are somewhat misleading, because a prisoner might be pardoned in any year of a long sentence. The Report notes that In Ohio, two-thirds of prisoners discharged were released by pardons. Haines reports in 1822 that, in New York, since 1796, there were 5,069 commitments, of whom 2,819—more than half—were discharged early by pardons. CHARLES GLIDDEN HAINES, REPORT ON THE PENITENTIARY SYSTEM IN THE UNITED STATES 91 (New York, Mahlon Day 1822). Judge Kuntz's study found that in antebellum Massachusetts, approximately 20 percent of prisoners released were freed by pardons. *See* WILLIAM FRANCIS KUNTZ, CRIMINAL SENTENCING IN THREE NINETEENTH-CENTURY CITIES: SOCIAL HISTORY OF PUNISHMENT IN NEW YORK, BOSTON, AND PHILADELPHIA, 1830-1880, at 124–25 (1988). New York's reliance on clemency was likewise substantial. *Id.* at 177 (between 1817 and 1847, "nearly two-thirds of those sentenced to life terms at Sing-Sing prison had been released by gubernatorial action. Furthermore, any inmate sentenced to more than three years was shown to have no worse than a one in three chance of being pardoned.").

[154] HAINES, *supra* note 153, at 33 ("evil" of frequent pardons "although most deeply felt in all the states, has been endured with the most fatal consequences" in states with penitentiary systems, "pernicious" "to the last degree" in Pennsylvania, New York and Massachusetts); BEAUMONT & TOCQUEVILLE, *supra* note 153, at 236 (describing professional pardon-petitioners in New York). The reliance on pardons reflected the pragmatics of prison overcrowding and incentivizing good behavior rather than the merciful impulses of elected officials. KUNTZ, *supra* note 153, at 162 & 191.

(1) The Changing Relationship between the Grand Jury and the Prosecutor

Prosecutorial sentencing depends on prosecutorial control over charges carrying different penalties for the same conduct. Grand juries provided a significant check on public prosecutors until after the Civil War. In the late nineteenth century, about half the states authorized felony prosecutions by information. Where the grand jury remained, it became an appendage of the prosecutor. In antebellum Massachusetts, grand juries rejected about 20 percent of the bills preferred to them. The modern figure is less than 1 percent.[155]

Felony informations, somewhat loosely described as abolition of the grand jury, were the most dramatic and conclusive shift of power from grand juries to prosecutors: "[a] search of 12,000 newspapers—including half a billion pages of content—from 1700 to 2019 for the phrase 'abolish grand jury' reveals over 2,800 returns. In that database, the phrase first crops up in 1842, but does not pick up real steam until the 1870s."[156] Abolition required first a constitutional amendment and then implementing legislation.

The first authorizing amendments were passed into law in Indiana and Michigan in 1850.[157] Michigan was the first state to enact legislation authorizing felony informations in 1859.[158]

The approval of felony informations did not abolish grand juries entirely; those might be retained for particular investigations. It did abolish the grand jury's power to overrule prosecutorial charging decisions. Prosecutors, however, control charging decisions today even in jurisdictions that require indictments. Prosecutorial capture was the premise, not the product, of authorizing informations.

The primary cause of prosecutorial capture was epistemic. Antebellum law enforcement was reactive and private. Citizens who knew of a crime had a duty to report it to the JP, who would issue an arrest warrant, and, after examination, release or bind over the suspect. The district attorney would prefer indictments against those bound over.

[155] Andrew D. Leipold, *Why Grand Juries Do Not (and Cannot) Protect the Accused*, 80 Cornell L. Rev. 260, 274 (1995).

[156] Nino C. Monea, *The Fall of Grand Juries*, 12 Ne. U. L. Rev. 411, 430–31 (2020).

[157] Richard D. Younger, *The Grand Jury Under Attack—Part I*, 46 J. Crim. L., Criminology & Police Sci. 26, 33–37 (1955) (these were followed by Oregon in 1857).

[158] Act of Feb. 12, 1859, ch. 138, 1859 Mich. Pub. Acts 391; *see, e.g.*, Thomas M. Cooley, Michigan: A History of Governments 301 (Boston, Houghton, Mifflin & Co. 1885).

The grand jurors, however, were supposed to bring their own information with them. The district attorney didn't have a police force (or the Federal Bureau of Investigation or the Drug Enforcement Administration) bringing information in from ongoing investigations. Like the JPs, the jurors were expected to act as "watchmen." They might know about crimes that had not been reported to a JP. They might also have reasons, unknown to the district attorney, to doubt the testimony of some witnesses and trust the testimony of others. The system evolved in an overwhelmingly rural society, and worked tolerably well in that context.

The context, however, changed rapidly. In 1790, 95 percent of the US population was rural and 5 percent urban.[159] In 1840, 89 percent was rural and 11 percent urban. The distribution continued to shift, with the urban population being 26 percent in 1870 and 40 percent in 1900.

With urbanization came the perception, and probably the reality, of increasing crime.[160] Institutions that had once functioned adequately in "small and homogenous" communities became dysfunctional as those communities "grew larger and more anonymous."[161] In 1873, an association of Philadelphia reformers (unsuccessfully) proposed abolition, noting that while in "the country districts" the grand jury functions well, "[i]n a city of three-quarters of a million souls it is simply an anachronism, powerless for good yet powerful for evil."[162]

In the usual case of a suspect bound over for trial after arrest and examination, the grand jury inevitably approved the bills preferred by the district attorney. When, however, grand juries began to act on their own, either considering bills preferred by private prosecutors or independently investigating supposed offenses, they did far more harm than good.

Abolitionists advanced this can't-help-but-can-hurt critique from the start of their movement. Speaking at the Indiana constitutional convention in 1850, John Pettit, who had served as a federal district attorney and

[159] Campbell Gibson, *Fig. 2-2: Percent Distribution of the Population by Urban-Rural and Farm Residence for the United States: 1790 to 2010*, Am. Demographic Hist. Chartbook (May 6, 2013), https://demographicchartbook.com/index.php/chapter-2-urban-rural-and-farm-population-and-large-cities/2-2-percent-distribution-of-the-population-by-urban-rural-and-farm-residence-for-the-united-states-1790-to-2010/ [https://perma.cc/QC8T-9H42].

[160] David R. Johnson, Policing the Urban Underworld 16 (1979) ("the rhetoric indicates a widespread belief that crime had become a major problem, and in the absence of any contrary evidence, that attitude became an important justification for changing the existing law enforcement machinery.") (footnote omitted).

[161] Samuel Walker, Popular Justice 27 (2d ed. 1998).

[162] 1 Debates of the Convention to Amend the Constitution of Pennsylvania 212, 215 (Harrisburg, Benjamin Singerly 1873) (Memorial of Citizens' Municipal Reform Association).

who would later serve on the Indiana Supreme Court, made both points. In the cases that came in after arrest, examination, and commitment or bail, the grand jurors, "guided entirely" by the prosecutor, are merely the "machinery" that "the prosecuting attorney sets in motion."[163] By contrast, of the indictments that originated with the grand jury itself, only one in twenty led to a conviction.[164]

Worse than wasting time on unpromising cases was the abuse of the grand jury for personal advantage. Allen Steinberg's classic study of private prosecution in nineteenth-century Philadelphia documents the rampant abuse of grand juries for, *inter alia*, debt collection, extortion, and revenge.[165] The concern with abuse of (or by) the grand jury figured prominently in the rhetoric of abolitionists.[166]

The authorization of felony informations closely tracked urbanization.[167] Yet the grand jury survived in New York, in Pennsylvania, and in the federal practice. What explains the institution's persistence?

Grand jury abolition ran out of gas because prosecutors captured the grand jury. The difference between the information system and the grand jury system, practically speaking, had become trivial. What were grand jurors supposed to do when summoned to serve in a big city or a federal district?

If they had the theoretical power to initiate presentments, they would have little if any firsthand knowledge about actual cases. Even if the district attorney had a duty to draft an indictment, the same district attorney could file a nolle prosequi. The district attorney, by contrast, had information from

[163] 1 REPORT OF THE DEBATES AND PROCEEDINGS OF THE CONVENTION FOR THE REVISION OF THE CONSTITUTION OF THE STATE OF INDIANA 154 (Indianapolis, H. Fowler 1850) (statement of John Pettit). For Pettit's biography, see *John Pettit*, BIOGRAPHICAL DIRECTORY OF THE U.S. CONG., https://bioguide.congress.gov/search/bio/p000277. For a similar view in the 1850 Michigan convention, see REPORT OF THE PROCEEDINGS AND DEBATES IN THE CONVENTION TO REVISE THE CONSTITUTION OF THE STATE OF MICHIGAN 203 (Lansing, R.W. Ingals 1850) (statement of Andrew S. Robertson) (after probable-cause finding by the examining magistrate, followed by a one-sided presentation by the prosecuting attorney, grand jury is "almost certain to find a bill").

[164] INDIANA CONVENTION REPORT, *supra* note 163, at 148.

[165] ALLEN STEINBERG, THE TRANSFORMATION OF CRIMINAL JUSTICE: PHILADELPHIA, 1800-1880, at 56–57, 78 (1989). In theory, the prosecutor for the commonwealth could file a *nolle prosequi*, but "[t]he fee system effectively negated the district attorney's ability to assume any real discretion over criminal cases." *Id.* at 83.

[166] MICHIGAN CONVENTION REPORT, *supra* note 163, at 198 (statement of William S. McCleod) (describing use of grand jury to defame political rivals); the legislative report on the Michigan bill to authorize informations reported that a "grand jury of this State once indicted a man for being simply mean." MICH. H. JUDICIARY COMM., MICH. H.R. DOC. NO. 20-4, at 15 (1859) (on recommending the passage of the Bill to Provide for the Trial of Offences upon Information).

[167] Monea, *supra* note 156, at 456–58.

the police or federal agents. The district attorney could not only draft bills to match the jail delivery cases, but could also call witnesses to advance ongoing police investigations.

Could the grand jurors prevent the DA from taking weak cases to trial? There would be no cross-examination of the witnesses, and no presentation of exculpatory evidence. No matter what the standard of proof to justify an indictment, the jurors were in no position to second-guess the DA.

The one function grand juries still served, into the twentieth century, is nullification of prosecutions for violations of unpopular laws. Grand juries contributed to the nullification of liquor prohibition.[168] They also played a role in nullifying murder prosecutions for lynchings.[169]

In information states, however, politically motivated prosecutors and trial juries could nullify any prosecution a grand jury might have stopped. According to Judge Campbell, the practical effects of adopting the information procedure in Michigan were negligible.[170] For example, Michigan's information procedure did not enable effective enforcement of Prohibition.[171]

Either by authority to file ex parte informations or by practical control of the information heard by grand juries, public prosecutors gained control of charge selection. This development made prosecutorial sentencing possible, but not inevitable. The information procedure did not enable Michigan prosecutors to control sentences, because Michigan's penal code provided only three mandatory penalties for serious crimes—death for treason and

[168] *See, e.g.*, Henry Moskowitz, Alfred E. Smith: An American Career 253 (1924) (quoting message from then-Governor of New York Alfred E. Smith) ("The burden imposed on the State to prosecute traffickers in liquor as violators of the State statute is a wasteful and futile one because of the refusal of grand juries to indict and of petit juries to convict."); *The Prohibition Amendment: Hearings on H.R.J. Res. 11, 38, 99, 114, 219, and 246 before the H. Comm. on the Judiciary*, 71st Cong. pt. 1 at 183 (1930) (statement of Hon. George H. Williams, former Senator from the State of Missouri) ("the foreman of the grand [federal] grand jury [in St. Louis] advised the . . . court that his jury would not indict.").

[169] Grand juries, of course, were not the only institutions protecting racist violence. *See, e.g.*, Clay S. Conrad, *Scapegoating the Jury*, 7 Cornell J.L. & Pub. Pol'y 7, 29 (1997). The grand jury could be counted on, however, to block prosecution should the prosecuting attorney attempt one. *See* Gunnar Myrdal, An American Dilemma: The Negro Problem and Modern Democracy 562 (1944) ("The lynchers are seldom indicted by a grand jury."). Myrdal, like Conrad, noted the pervasiveness of the tolerance for lynching. He cites, for example, one study of 100 lynchings in which it was estimated that police officers took an active part in the killing in half the cases. For another grim statistic, see James R. McGovern, Anatomy of a Lynching: The Killing of Claude Neal 11 (1982) (less than 1 percent of lynchings in the period 1900–1930 resulted in the conviction of any responsible individuals).

[170] *See* James V. Campbell, Outlines of the Political History of Michigan 562–63 (Detroit, Schober & Co. 1876).

[171] *See* Karen Dybis, The Witch of Delray 16 (2017) ("Despite Prohibition, drinking and importing alcohol was so rampant Detroit became known as Whiskeytown.").

life for first-degree murder or arson of an occupied dwelling at night.[172] For other, even very grave offenses or repeat offenders, Michigan law did not impose minimum sentences.[173]

A new generation of penal codes, written to punish different degrees of familiar offenses with different prison terms, had the potential to transform the prosecutor's power over charge selection into power to set sentences. That potential, however, was not immediately realized because this period saw the emergence of suspended sentences and parole boards.

(2) Second-Generation Statutes and Suspended Sentences

To the extent these first-generation penal codes provided minimum prison terms, those terms stood in for the death penalty that had previously applied. The D.C. Crimes Act was a late example of these first-generation criminal codes. Two years before the D.C. Crimes Act, in 1829, New York adopted a second-generation statute that replaced the crude scheme of life for robbery and burglary and a range of zero to fourteen years for most other common-law felonies. The new code, for example, defined three degrees of burglary, with the first degree punishable by "not less than ten years," the second degree by "not more than ten years, nor less than five," and the third degree by a term "not exceeding five years."[174]

This arrangement takes a long step toward prosecutorial sentencing because the selection of one charge from a menu covering the same conduct determined the minimum sentence. Guilty pleas became progressively more common in the succeeding years. Prosecutors circumvented grand juries by bringing multicount indictments, then dismissing some counts by *nolle prosequi* in exchange for a guilty plea.[175]

The New York minimum sentences, however, were never as mandatory as their modern counterparts. New York judges, without suspending sentence

[172] 2 MICH. COMP. LAWS 1871, ch. 243, § 1, at 2069 (James S. Dewey comp., W.S. George & Co. 1872) (treason); *id.*, ch. 244, § 1, at 2070 (first-degree murder); *id.*, ch. 245, § 1, at 2078 (arson of occupied dwelling at night).

[173] *Id.*, ch. 244, § 2, at 2070 (all other murder punished by life "or any term of years, in the discretion of the court"); *id.*, ch. 245, § 10 at 2080 (armed burglary at night of occupied dwelling punished by "not more than twenty years"); *id.*, ch. 245, § 19, at 2082 (larceny recidivists punished by "not more than twenty years").

[174] 2 REVISED STATUTES OF NEW YORK 1828-1835, pt. IV, ch. 1, tit. 3, art. 2, §§ 10–21, at 556–58 (Albany, Packard & van Benthuysen 1836).

[175] Fisher, *supra* note 143, at 1034–35.

altogether, in fact imposed some prison terms lower than the minimum authorized by statute.[176] The extent of this bold practice can only be guessed. It is clear, however, that if a judge imposed a sentence below the minimum, there was no practical way to enforce conformity with the statute.

A defendant could appeal a conviction by writ of error, but prosecutors could not.[177] The only avenue for a challenge was mandamus, an unlikely option for a fee-motivated, part-time district attorney. In antebellum New York, where the judge appointed the prosecutor,[178] that option was all the more improbable.

Unreviewable defiance of statutory minimums is hard to measure. The routine use of suspended sentences is easier to document. Blackstone paraphrased Lord Hale's earlier discussion of a common-law power to reprieve "where the judge is not satisfied with the verdict, . . . or sometimes if it be a small felony, or any favorable circumstances appear in the criminal's character, in order to give room to apply to the crown for either an absolute or conditional pardon."[179] Whatever its common-law origins, some judges in New York were suspending sentences by 1860.[180]

In 1894, the Court of Appeals, New York's highest court, denied a prosecutor's petition for mandamus to compel imposition of a sentence the trial-level court had suspended.[181] By the time the case reached the New York Court of Appeals, the legislature had adopted a statute expressly approving discretionary judicial power to suspend any sentence less than ten years. The prosecutor, however, challenged the statute as an unconstitutional infringement of the executive's pardon power.

The court of appeals unanimously rejected this argument. Indeed, the court went beyond upholding the statute to announce inherent judicial power to suspend sentence. The statute was only declaratory of "a power

[176] *See* KUNTZ, *supra* note 156, at 187–89 (noting a sentence of forty-nine months to five years for rape despite the statute's ten-year minimum, *see id.* at 42–43 tbl. 1.3).

[177] People v. Corning, 2 N.Y. 9 (1848).

[178] KUNTZ, *supra* note 153, at 161.

[179] 4 WILLIAM BLACKSTONE, COMMENTARIES *387; 2 MATTHEW HALE, HISTORIA PLACITORUM CORONAE: THE HISTORY OF THE PLEAS OF THE CROWN 412 (Sollom Emlyn ed., [London] in the Savoy, E. and R. Nutt, and R. Gosling for F. Gyles 1736).

[180] In *People v. Morrisette*, 20 How. Pr. 118 (N.Y.O.&T. 1860), the prisoner was indicted for first-degree arson, but in an apparent plea bargain, the district attorney expressed doubt about proving any degree higher than the fourth. The defendant pleaded guilty to the fourth-degree charge and asked the court to suspend the sentence. Judge Balcom disclaimed any judicial power to suspend sentence indefinitely, but noted that some New York courts were exercising this power, and some newspaper stories had referred to its exercise.

[181] People *ex rel.* Forsyth v. Court of Sessions of Monroe Cnty., 36 N.E. 386 (N.Y. 1894).

inherent in such courts at common law, which was understood when the constitution was adopted to be an ordinary judicial function, and which, ever since its adoption, has been exercised by the courts[.]"[182] The minimum sentences in the New York statutes were mandatory—except when they were suspended, in the discretion of the judges.

The US Supreme Court later came to the opposite result, holding, in 1916, that federal district courts did not have inherent power to suspend sentence indefinitely.[183] The Supreme Court cited cases from New Jersey, Illinois, Massachusetts, Florida, North Carolina, New York, Ohio, New Hampshire, and Pennsylvania as upholding the inherent power to suspend sentence. That was a minority position, but a substantial one.[184] Moreover, by 1910, thirty-four states had created probation systems by statute.[185]

In jurisdictions that denied inherent judicial power to suspend sentence, probation statutes were upheld against separation-of-powers challenges. These same statutes also limited the availability of probation to certain offenses or offenders. Since statutes control the common law, the statutory limits were followed by courts even in jurisdictions with inherent powers.

In some cases, then, prosecutorial charge selection had the effect of making the defendant ineligible for a suspended sentence. This power went unchallenged, but in light of the development of the constitutional law of *judicial* sentencing, this is unsurprising. If defendants had no constitutional right to notice and a hearing before judges exercised sentencing discretion, there would be no obvious conflict with having prosecutors set sentences.

The courts rejected due process challenges to state statutes that authorized executive branch officials to revoke probation or parole without notice and hearing.[186] These decisions, like the Supreme Court's decision in *Escoe*, viewed conditional release through the lens of the distinction between "vested rights" and matters of "grace" or "forbearance." Once convicted, the offender had no residual right to any sentence less than the statutory

[182] *Id.* at 388.

[183] *Ex parte* United States, 242 U.S. 27 (1916). This decision is discussed in detail in the next section.

[184] *Id.* at 48 n.2.

[185] Charles A. De Courcy, *The Probation System in Massachusetts*, 19 YALE L.J. 187, 191 (1910). De Courcy did not list the individual states. New York was one state that recognized inherent judicial power and also had a probation act. There may, or may not, have been additional overlap among the inherent-power and probation-act states. A clear majority, however, authorized suspended sentences by inherent power, by statute, or by both.

[186] *See, e.g.*, Pagano v. Bechly, 232 N.W. 798 (Iowa 1930); *Ex parte* Patterson, 146 P. 1009 (Kan. 1915); State v. Collins, 125 S.W. 465 (Mo. 1910).

maximum. On that view, a prosecutor selecting a charge with a minimum sentence no more called for a hearing than a judge deciding to impose the same punishment. The conflict in the jurisprudence between sentencing and charging arose only after the Supreme Court firmly established hearing rights at sentencing in the 1970s.[187]

(3) The Rise of Indeterminate Sentencing

During the second half of the nineteenth century, the pattern of discretionary but definite sentences set by judges gave way to a new regime based on rehabilitation. Probation remained an option for the sentencing court, but sentences themselves became discretionary with correctional officers: "[t]he twin foundations of the new dispensation were, first, that inmates should be provided and incentive for betterment, and, second, that experts—not judges—should determine when sufficient improvement had taken place."[188] The courts imposed either sentences without any fixed duration or superficially long terms that were subject to review by the parole board.[189]

By 1926, forty-six states had parole systems, and by 1937, thirty-nine jurisdictions had indeterminate sentencing laws.[190] "Parole and the indeterminate sentence were deeply discretionary; but they were also powerful instruments of control."[191] The indeterminate sentence regime took some, but by no means all, sentencing discretion away from judges and vested it, not in prosecutors, but in professional corrections administrators.[192]

[187] In People v. Cummings, 50 N.W. 310 (Mich. 1891), the Michigan Supreme Court struck down the state's indeterminate sentencing law. The opinion includes rhetoric suggestive of due process. *See, e.g., id.* at 313 ("The governor has the undoubted right to pardon. He may pardon on conditions, but neither he nor any other person can have, under our laws, the sole right to determine whether or not such conditions have been violated. This must be determined by the courts by the usual and proper proceedings."). The decision, however, rested on the statute's encroachment on the governor's pardon power. *Cummings* was undone by a constitutional amendment adopted in 1902. Manaca v. Ionia Cir. Judge, 110 N.W. 75 (Mich. 1906).

[188] Kate Stith & Jose A. Cabranes, Fear of Judging 17 (1998).

[189] On the two types of statutes, and a review of their origins, see Edward Lindsey, *Historical Sketch of the Indeterminate Sentence and Parole System*, 16 J. Am. Inst. Crim. L. & Criminology 9 (1925).

[190] Note, *Indeterminate Sentence Laws—The Adolescence of Peno-Correctional Legislation*, 50 Harv. L. Rev. 677, 678 (1937) (these jurisdictions included the District of Columbia and pre-statehood Territory of Hawaii).

[191] Friedman, *supra* note 190, at 305.

[192] Note, *Due Process and Legislative Standards in Sentencing*, 101 U. Pa. L. Rev. 257, 258 (1952):

> Parole or sentence fixing boards exercise a large slice of this power, for the majority of state court sentences are indeterminate; and even where the sentence is determinate the

F. Suspended Sentences in Federal Court in the Nineteenth and Twentieth Centuries

After the adoption of the D.C. Crimes Act, Congress adopted various *ad hoc* minimum prison terms.[193] When federal legislation was collected in the Revised Statutes in 1878, dozens of offenses carried mandatory minimum terms, most for one year or less, but several for terms up to five years.[194] Congress knew, however, that these "mandatory" terms were subject to a practical power to suspend sentence.

During the nineteenth century, the practice of suspending sentences entirely, conditioned on good behavior, became widespread in the federal courts. The Supreme Court disapproved this practice in a mandamus action that the government brought against District Judge John M. Killits.[195] The case, however, makes clear just how common the practice was.

James J. Henahan pleaded guilty to an indictment for embezzling the funds of a national bank. The statute provided a minimum sentence of five years and a maximum of ten. Killits suspended the sentence, and at the behest of the government expressly stated that the suspension was not to permit proceedings for legal relief but because, given Henahan's clean record and the request of the victimized employer for mercy, the interests of justice were thereby served, all things considered.[196] The government moved the Supreme Court for a writ of mandamus compelling the district judge to order Henahan's commitment to Leavenworth. The Supreme Court unanimously ruled for the government.

effect is the same, because parole is usually available after a stated proportion of the sentence has been served. But the trial judge's discretion is still very broad. It is he who makes the choice between probation and imprisonment, and he still has an effective voice in the duration of imprisonment through his control over the base sentence which must be served before parole eligibility is reached. (footnotes omitted).

[193] USSC Report, *supra* note 66, at 13–14.

[194] *See id.*, app. C, tbl.C-1 ("Mandatory Minimum Penalties in the 1878 Revised Statutes").

[195] *Ex parte* United States (Killits), 242 U.S. 27 (1916). The issue went unresolved so long because the Supreme Court, following the weight of state decisions, denied the government the right to bring a writ of error unless the statute conferring jurisdiction explicitly authorized it to do so. United States v. Sanges, 144 U.S. 310 (1892). The only avenue for the government to challenge a suspended sentence was mandamus, and district attorneys had practical incentives not to sue the judges they appeared before. The petition for mandamus in *Killits* was filed by the attorney general, not by the US Attorney for Northern Ohio. *See* Petition for Writ of Mandamus, *Ex parte United States*, 242 U.S. 27 (1916) (No. 11), ProQuest ID 11-ORIG_1916_PWM_0002.

[196] *See id.* at 16 & 42–44 (reproducing the district court's ruling of Apr. 9, 1915).

Chief Justice White rejected the claim of inherent judicial power "since it must rest upon the proposition that the power to enforce begets inherently a discretion to permanently refuse to do so." That power "to relieve from the punishment fixed by law and ascertained according to the methods by it provided, belongs to the executive department."[197]

White's invocation of the pardon power made sense against the background of contemporary federal crimes. The embezzlement statute created an isolated offense with a single penalty range, not a menu of charges with distinct but mandatory minimum sentences. Federal deposit insurance and expansive interpretations of the Commerce Clause were decades away. Henahan stole the property of the Second National Bank of Toledo, not government property, and didn't use the mails to do so. The sole basis of federal jurisdiction was the bank's national character.

The only federal crime available to the prosecution was the embezzlement charge with a five-year minimum.[198] Prosecutors could charge multiple counts, but because the judges had discretion to run sentences concurrently or consecutively, this meant only prosecutorial discretion to increase the potential maximum, not the mandatory minimum. On each count, Congress delegated discretion within the range of five to ten years. This discretion, however, went to judges, not prosecutors. Nothing in *Killits* intimates that the president's pardon power allows Congress to delegate sentencing discretion to US Attorneys.

When Congress delegates sentencing discretion to the court, the pardon power permits the executive to reduce the sentence that is, or might be, imposed by the court. It does not give the executive power to compel imposition of a sentence more severe than the judge believes is justified. Where this latter power exists, it comes from a legislative delegation of sentencing discretion to prosecutors via a menu of overlapping charges, some carrying mandatory minimum sentences. The constitutionality of these delegations cannot be established by reference to the pardon power.

Chief Justice White admitted that many district judges had suspended sentences for good behavior, often with the acquiescence or even request of the government. Other judges had refused, with Chief Justice White concluding that "we think it may be said that the exertion of the power

[197] *Id.* at 42.

[198] Comp. Stat. ch. 3 § 9772 (1913) (R. S. § 5209). Section 9771 created an offense with a five-year maximum and no minimum, but applied only to falsely certifying checks, not to the abstraction of funds.

under the circumstances stated was intermittent, and was not universal, but partial."[199]

"Intermittent" is not an entirely fair description, given the immediately following admission that more than two thousand persons "are now at large who otherwise would be imprisoned . . . ."[200] In 1915, the average daily population of institutions administered by the federal Bureau of Prisons was 2,265.[201] In other words, for every federal convict serving time when *Killits* was decided, there was another federal convict out on a suspended sentence.

If suspended sentences were "intermittent," they were certainly not exceptional. Rather than swamp the prison system, "President Wilson did the unprecedented thing of issuing a blanket pardon to these men and women. Had he not done so, all these persons, many of whom had reformed and were entirely rehabilitated in society, would have had to be returned to court for sentence."[202]

The precise point at which federal judges began suspending prison sentences is unknown, but it appears to have been an option before the Civil War.[203] Professor Henderson's study of federal criminal prosecutions for the years 1801–1829 found that the court imposed no sentence in 5.2 percent of all convictions.[204] His statistics account for arrested judgments and escapes, so while it is possible that some of the never-sentenced cases were due to accidents such as an early pardon or the death of the prisoner, Henderson's findings do not suggest that early federal courts felt an obligation to impose sentence.

Ten years after the Supreme Court's *Killits* decision, the federal prison population had grown to 6,403 persons.[205] Reform efforts that had been underway since *Killits* succeeded when Congress adopted the Probation Act in 1925. The act "authorized [district judges] to suspend sentence and place

199 *See Killits* at 51.

200 *Id.* at 52.

201 Bureau of Just. Stat., U.S. Dep't of Just., BJS Rep. NCJ 102529, Historical Corrections Statistics in the United States, 1840-1984, at 143 tbl.6.2 (Dec. 1986), https://bjs.ojp.gov/content/pub/pdf/ushcs5084.pdf [https://perma.cc/BL3F-4G68].

202 Note, *Suspended Sentence for Federal Prisoners—Congress Adopts Probation System for Federal Courts*, 3 Tex. L. Rev. 284, 285–86 (1925).

203 *See* Answer of Respondent at 4, *Ex parte* United States, 242 U.S. 27 (1916) (No. 11), ProQuest ID 11-ORIG_1916_ANS_0009 ("the power to suspend sentence in one form or another, has been exercised by judges of the District Court of the United States for time out of mind").

204 *See* Henderson, *supra* note 16, at 216, app. IV.

205 Bureau of Just. Stat., U.S. Dep't of Just., ICPSR 8912, Historical Statistics on Prisoners in State and Federal Institutions, Yearend 1925-1986, at 5 tbl.1 (May 1988), https://bjs.ojp.gov/content/pub/pdf/hspsfiy2586.pdf [https://perma.cc/XT4N-8MJR].

offenders on probation 'after conviction or after a plea of guilty or *nolo contendere* for any crime or offense not punishable by death or life imprisonment.' . . . The courts may fix any terms and conditions of probation and may revoke or modify these at pleasure."[206] Judge Killits lost the battle, but won the war.

Even when judges imposed, rather than suspended, a minimum prison term, from 1910 on, Congress provided that prisoners would be eligible for parole after serving one-third of the nominal sentence or fifteen years of a life sentence.[207] Under the 1910 legislation, each federal penitentiary had its own parole board, composed of the superintendent of prisons in the Justice Department together with the warden and physician of the particular institution. Legislation passed in 1930 created a single national parole board of three members appointed for indefinite terms by the attorney general.[208]

Until 1984, when Congress eliminated parole and instituted the sentencing guidelines, a facially mandatory minimum prison term was presumptively subject to judicial discretion to suspend sentence under the Probation Act, and the parole board's discretion to order an early release. In a few instances before the 1980s, Congress specifically excluded certain offenses from probation or parole. We turn now to those exceptions.

G. Mandatory Minimum Sentences under the Boggs Act

Drug abuse in the United States increased sharply after World War II.[209] The genuine problem was magnified by a scare campaign orchestrated by Harry Anslinger, the chief of the Treasury Department's narcotics bureau.[210] Congress responded.

[206] *Suspended Sentence for Federal Prisoners*, *supra* note 203, at 284–86 (footnote omitted).

[207] *See* U.S. PAROLE COMM'N, NCJ 202937, HISTORY OF THE FEDERAL PAROLE SYSTEM 6 (2003).

[208] *Id.* at 7.

[209] *See* Richard J. Bonnie & Charles Whitebread II, *The Forbidden Fruit and the Tree of Knowledge: An Inquiry into the Legal History of American Marijuana Prohibition*, 56 VA. L. REV. 971, 1064 (1970) ("The hearings before the Subcommittee of the House Ways and Means Committee and the floor debate show that the primary reason for passage of the Boggs Act was the increase in narcotic use in the period 1948-1951. Testimony and evidence from a wide variety of sources indicated an abrupt and substantial increase in addiction, especially among teenagers, between 1947 and 1951.") (footnote omitted).

[210] *See, e.g.*, RUFUS KING, THE DRUG HANG UP: AMERICA'S FIFTY-YEAR FOLLY chs. 13 & 14 (1972).

The 1951 Boggs Act established mandatory minimum sentences for various narcotics offenses.[211] In its initial form, the act permitted suspension of sentence and probation for first-time drug offenders. The 1956 Narcotic Control Act prohibited probation or parole for even a first distribution offense or a second possession offense.[212] Many states followed Congress by adopting "little Boggs Acts."[213]

In form, the mandatory minimum sentences in the amended Boggs Act were no different than their modern counterparts. The prescribed minimums applied after conviction, but conviction was contingent on prosecutorial charging decisions. Federal prosecutors could leave a case to the state authorities, charge possession rather than sale even when the facts showed a sale, charge multiple counts arising from the same conduct, and file an information triggering the higher minimum sentences for drug recidivists. Control of sentencing, in large measure, passed to the executive rather than the judicial branch.

The Supreme Court rejected a constitutional challenge to charging, convicting, and sentencing the defendant under three different statutes for the same drug sale.[214] Why was the substitution of prosecutorial for judicial discretion not challenged as a due process violation? One reason is that in many cases brought by federal prosecutors, the judges ended up imposing more than the required minimum, which would make any constitutional error harmless as to the particular defendant. There are, moreover, two more general and more powerful reasons why due process challenges were not brought.

First, under the constitutional law of sentencing that prevailed into the 1960s, once convicted, offenders had no constitutional hearing rights respecting the denial or revocation of probation or parole. It was not even clear, under the 1949 *Williams* case, whether defendants had a right to be heard before the judge pronounced sentence.[215] If a defendant had claimed that the Boggs Act transferred sentencing discretion to prosecutors, the response

[211] Boggs Act of 1951, Pub. L. No. 82-255, ch. 666, 65 Stat. 767 (1951).

[212] Narcotic Control Act of 1956, Pub. L. No. 84-728, ch. 629, 70 Stat. 567 (1956); *see also* Moore v. United States, 334 F.2d 25, 25 (5th Cir. 1964) (per curiam) (under amended Boggs Act, "probation and parole are all denied to the Defendant.").

[213] Bonnie & Whitebread, *supra* note 210, at 1074 ("Seventeen states (including Virginia) and the Territory of Alaska responded by passing 'little Boggs Acts' by 1953, and eleven other states increased their penalties by 1956.").

[214] Gore v. United States, 357 U.S. 386 (1958).

[215] *See* Williams v. New York, 337 U.S. 241 (1949).

would have been: "So what? Any sentence you get below the code maximum is a matter of legislative grace, entitling you to no hearing whatsoever."

Second, it would have been impossible to challenge prosecutorial control of sentencing outcomes without acknowledging plea bargaining. Doubts about the voluntariness of guilty pleas obtained by promises of lenience were not put to rest until *Santobello* in 1970.[216] As the Court said in a 1977 case, *Blackledge v. Allison*, plea bargaining before *Santobello* "was a sub rosa process shrouded in secrecy and deliberately concealed by participating defendants, defense lawyers, prosecutors, and even judges."[217] At the plea colloquy the defendant would deny receiving any promise or threat.[218] A defendant challenging a prosecutorial decision to charge high would have had to confront the official story that prosecutors never went low.

By the time the Supreme Court recognized both plea bargaining and hearing rights in the sentencing process, Congress repealed the mandatory minimum sentences in the Boggs Act. Presidential commissions called for restoring some degree of discretion in 1963 and again in 1967.[219] The Comprehensive Drug Abuse Prevention and Control Act of 1970, with bipartisan support, repealed all the mandatory minimums for drug offenses, excepting only the "kingpin" statute punishing "continuing criminal enterprises."[220]

[216] *See, e.g.*, Motley v. United States, 230 F.2d 110 (5th Cir. 1966) (holding that district court should have held hearing on defendant's claim that guilty plea was induced by promise of lenience allegedly transmitted from prosecutor by defense counsel).

[217] Blackledge v. Allison, 431 U.S. 63, 76 (1977).

[218] In *Allison*, the defendant alleged that the prosecution had broken a promise and that, on advice of counsel, he had relied on the promise but denied the existence of any such promise in court. This practice of disclaiming the deal in court was common enough for the *Allison* Court to require a hearing on the factual issue of just what promise, if any, had been made. *See generally* Robert L. Segar, *Plea Bargaining Tactics*, 25 AM. JUR. TRIALS 69 § 2 (1978):

> In the past when a defendant entered a guilty plea, everyone in the courtroom, including the judge, knew that the plea was very likely the result of an agreement with the prosecutor whereby certain charges were reduced or some charges dismissed. Nevertheless, the usual litany of questions and answers were asked and answered.
>
> The judge would first inquire whether the defendant was pleading guilty freely and voluntarily. To this, the response would be in the affirmative, and the court would then ask whether the defendant had been promised leniency, or whether any other promises had been made in return for the plea of guilty. The generally untruthful answer to these questions was, of course, that no such promises had been made. (footnotes omitted).

[219] *See* PRESIDENT'S ADVISORY COMM'N ON NARCOTIC AND DRUG ABUSE, FINAL REPORT 39–42 (1963), https://archive.org/details/presidentsadviso00pres; PRESIDENT'S COMM'N ON L. ENF'T & ADMIN. OF JUST., THE CHALLENGE OF CRIME IN A FREE SOCIETY 223 (1967).

[220] On the history of the repeal, see Molly M. Gill, *Correcting Course: Lessons From the 1970 Repeal of Mandatory Minimums*, 21 FED. SENT'G REP. 55 (2008).

H. The Eclipse of Executive Clemency

Executive clemency is, of course, still available today. Today, however, clemency, once an essential feature of the system, has become a trace element.[221] Two developments explain this transformation. First, the creation of parole systems obviated the need for systematic reliance on pardons.[222] Then, the politics of crime that led to the abolition of federal parole in 1984 also led to a stingier review of pardon applications within the Justice Department.[223]

The vigor of executive clemency, leaving aside patently political cases, is unlikely to increase. Even if it did, the prospect of regulating prosecutorial sentencing by standardless review by more remote prosecutors seems unpromising. In the words of a former US pardon attorney, "the president cannot be well-served in the exercise of his pardon power as long as responsibility for pardon policy and practice remains in an agency responsible for criminal prosecutions and under the control of federal prosecutors."[224]

The same political incentives bear on state governors as on presidents. Gavin Newsom, a liberal governor in a liberal state, has issued 207 pardons during his five years in office.[225] There are more than ninety thousand inmates serving time in California prisons.[226]

[221] President Biden, like his predecessors, granted few pardons but issued a comparatively large number of commutations. Jon Gramlich, *Biden Granted More Acts of Clemency Than Any Prior President*, Pew Rsch. Ctr. (Feb. 7, 2025), https://www.pewresearch.org/short-reads/2025/02/07/biden-granted-more-acts-of-clemency-than-any-prior-president/ [https://perma.cc/328S-9NZW]. Biden's total of 4,165 commutations compares to a current federal prison population of more than 150,000. *BOP: Population Statistics*, Fed. Bureau of Prisons (last updated June 5, 2025), https://www.bop.gov/about/statistics/population_statistics.jsp [https://perma.cc/UYM3-5JSA].

[222] Margaret Colgate Love, *The Twilight of the Pardon Power*, 100 J. Crim. L. & Criminology 1169, 1187–88 (2010).

[223] Margaret Colgate Love, *Reinventing the President's Pardon Power*, 20 Fed. Sent'g Rep. 5, 6–7 (2007).

[224] Margaret Colgate Love, *Justice Department Administration of the President's Pardon Power: A Case Study in Institutional Conflict of Interest*, 47 U. Tol. L. Rev. 89, 103 (2015).

[225] Press Release, Gov. of Cal., Governor Newsom Grants Executive Clemency (Nov. 27, 2024), https://www.gov.ca.gov/2024/11/27/governor-newsom-grants-executive-clemency-11-27-24/ [https://perma.cc/5AYX-JYCT].

[226] Heather Harris & Sean Cremin, *California's Prison Population*, Pub. Pol'y Inst. Cal. (Sept. 2024), https://www.ppic.org/wp-content/uploads/jtf-prison-population-jtf.pdf [https://perma.cc/9559-MBZ3].

I. Modern "Mandatory" Minimums

As explained by the Supreme Court's opinion in *Simpson v. United States*,[227] Congress adopted a new mandatory minimum in the Gun Control Act of 1968, which included the first version of Section 924(c).[228] The 1968 law created a separate offense of using a gun "to commit" any federal felony, and of carrying a gun "during the commission" of any federal felony. A first offense was punishable by one to ten years, and the second by two to twenty-five years. The sentence for a second or subsequent offense could not be suspended and was required to be served consecutively rather than concurrently.

The original 924(c) carried a mandatory minimum barely worthy of the name. The first offense triggered a one-year minimum that might be suspended during probation. The minimum for the second offense was indeed mandatory, but for two years rather than the latter twenty-five. It would be an extremely rare case where judicial discretion would impose anything less for offenses of armed violence. For example, the defendants in *Simpson* were convicted of two bank robberies using guns. The district court imposed twenty-five-year sentences, the statutory maximum, on the bank robbery charges. As a matter of principle, the 1968 statute did shift a measure of sentencing authority to prosecutors, but it was a very small measure.

In the next decade, both crime and public concern about sentencing disparities increased.[229] Michigan's 650-lifer law, discussed in Chapter 2, is one example of state responses to these concerns. The Michigan law exemplified a national trend. "By the late 1970's and early 1980's, States began developing sentencing guidelines, enacting mandatory minimum sentences and adopting other sentencing reforms to reduce disparity in sentencing and to toughen penalties for certain offenses, specifically drug

[227] Simpson v. United States, 435 U.S. 6 (1978).

[228] *See* Gun Control Act of 1968, Pub. L. No. 90-618, § 102, 82 Stat. 1213, 1214 (amending 18 U.S.C. §§ 921–28).

[229] On rising crime rates, see, e.g., Bureau of Just. Stat., U.S. Dep't of Just., BJS Rep. NCJ 236018, Homicide Trends in the United States, 1980-2008, at 2 (Nov. 2011), https://bjs.ojp.gov/content/pub/pdf/htus8008.pdf [https://perma.cc/AXE4-5PT4]. On concern with disparities, see, e.g., Stith & Cabranes, *supra* note 188, at 40 (between 1977 and 1984, the Senate Judiciary Committee reported a sentencing guidelines bill five times; each bill "had the stated objectives of 'avoiding unwarranted sentencing disparity' . . . and providing 'honesty in sentencing' (by providing for the elimination of parole).") (footnote omitted; parenthetical in original).

offenses (as part of the 'war on drugs'), offenses with weapons, and offenses committed by repeat or habitual criminals."[230]

At the federal level, the Comprehensive Crime Control Act of 1984 created the Sentencing Commission with the power to promulgate mandatory guidelines.[231] It upped the mandatory minimum for 924(c) violations to five years for a first offense and ten years for subsequent offenses and barred probation or concurrent sentences for first as well as subsequent offenses.[232] It also created the Armed Career Criminal Act, providing a mandatory, consecutive fifteen-year term for anyone possessing a firearm after a third conviction for robbery or burglary.[233] "Every two years thereafter, from 1986 through 1990, Congress enacted additional mandatories and stiffened some of those already on the books."[234]

The social and political causes of this punitive turn in US policy are the subject of a substantial literature. Rising crime rates clearly played some role.[235] Other factors, including racism,[236] a moral panic over drug abuse,[237] and the difficulty of adopting alternative policies in the US political system,[238]

[230] Bureau of Just. Stat., U.S. Dep't of Just., BJS Special Rep. NCJ 170032, Truth in Sentencing in State Prisons 2 (Jan. 1999), https://bjs.ojp.gov/content/pub/pdf/tssp.pdf [https://perma.cc/T448-3FV4].

[231] Comprehensive Crime Control Act of 1984, Pub. L. No. 98-473, tit. II, 98 Stat. 1837, 1976–2194.

[232] *Id.*, § 1005, 98 Stat. at 2138–39.

[233] *Id.*, §§ 1801–3, 98 Stat. at 2185.

[234] Stephen J. Schulhofer, *Rethinking Mandatory Minimums*, 28 Wake Forest L. Rev. 199, 201 (1993) (footnote omitted).

[235] *See, e.g.*, Lisa L. Miller, The Myth of Mob Rule 121 (2016) ("Serious violence grew suddenly and dramatically and was sustained for a long period of time beginning in the 1960s. Public and political attention to crime waxed and waned in rough parallel with this violence, even after the 1980s.").

[236] *See* Michelle Alexander, The New Jim Crow: Mass Incarceration in the Age of Colorblindness 2 (2012) ("Rather than rely on race, we use our criminal justice system to label people of color 'criminals' and then engage in all the practices we supposedly left behind."); *id.* at 223 ("Few Americans today recognize mass incarceration for what it is: a new caste system thinly veiled by the cloak of colorblindness."); Michael H. Tonry, Malign Neglect: Race, Crime, and Punishment in America 32 (1995) ("By analogy with the criminal law, the responsibility of the architects of contemporary crime control policies is the same as if their primary goal had been to lock up disproportionate numbers of young blacks."); Naomi Murakawa & Katherine Beckett, *The Penology of Racial Innocence: The Erasure of Racism in the Study and Practice of Punishment*, 44 Law & Soc'y Rev. 695, 696 (2010) (arguing that "the penology of racial innocence begins with presumptions of race-neutrality and adopts narrow definitions of racism, as well as data and methods often ill-suited to its analysis, even as the policies and practices of criminal justice expand in evermore race-laden ways.").

[237] *See* Michael Tonry, Thinking About Crime: Sense and Sensibility in American Penal Culture 60–61 (2006) (discussing how mass media coverage of, for example, the crimes of Willie Horton and the overdose death of Len Bias "produced moral panics" that produced calls for "unprecedentedly repressive policies," and how "American governmental institutions and political culture provided many fewer buffers to the force of that emotionalism than do the governmental institutions and political culture of other countries").

[238] Miller, *supra* note 236, at 158–60.

have been suggested. Wherever the truth lies in these debates, powerful political forces led to a turn to more punitive policies, including mandatory minimums.

When those political forces ebbed, a modest reaction set in. In 1994, Congress adopted the so-called safety valve statute, providing for sentencing less culpable drug-trafficking offenders under the sentencing guidelines, without regard to the otherwise applicable mandatory minimum.[239] The 2010 Fair Sentencing Act changed the crack/powder ratio from 100:1 to 18:1.[240] The 2018 First Step Act significantly expanded eligibility for the 1994 Safety Valve.[241]

The reaction had a judicial dimension. In 2005, the Supreme Court in the *Booker* case held the mandatory minimums in the sentencing guidelines unconstitutional because they required more severe penalties triggered by facts not triable by jury.[242] *Booker*'s remedy for the violation was to make the guidelines advisory, subject to discretionary deviations by the sentencing judge.[243]

This reduced the severity of federal sentences, but it also magnified prosecutorial power over sentences. Hitherto, legislatures could create penalties that were mandatory with respect to prosecutors, by specifying facts that could be found by the sentencing court independently and that trigger a mandatory minimum. After *Booker*, prosecutors can control the application of mandatory minimum's by omitting the triggering facts from the indictment.[244]

After *Killits*, and then again after the Boggs Act, Congress adopted sweeping substitutions of judicial discretion for mandatory minimums. The reaction against modern mandatory minimums has been nowhere near as thorough. The safety valve is available only to offenders with minimal criminal history and to offenses without gun involvement. Even after the First Step Act, only about a quarter of those convicted of offenses carrying a mandatory minimum are eligible for the safety valve.[245] The statistics

[239] Violent Crime Control and Law Enforcement Act of 1994, Pub. L. No. 103-322, § 80001, 108 Stat. 1796, 1985–86 (codified as amended at 18 U.S. § 3553(f)).

[240] Fair Sentencing Act of 2010, Pub. L. No. 111-220, 124 Stat. 2372; for discussion of the crack/powder ratio and its significance, see, e.g., Harvey Gee, *Striving for Equal Justice: Applying the Fair Sentencing Act of 2010 Retroactively*, 49 Wake Forest L. Rev. 207, 213–16 (2014).

[241] First Step Act of 2018, Pub. L. No. 115-391, 132 Stat. 5194.

[242] United States v. Booker, 543 U.S. 220 (2005).

[243] *Id.* at 258–60.

[244] *See, e.g.*, State v. Franklin, 878 A.2d 757 (N.J. 2005).

[245] The latest statistics show that 26.6 percent of federal convictions carried a mandatory minimum, but only 19.5 percent were relieved from the mandatory minimum by the safety valve.

on sentences actually imposed omit the many cases where the US Attorney's Office threatened to add charges carrying mandatory minimums but ultimately did not execute the threat.

The safety valve applies only to minimum sentences under the Controlled Substances Act, and not to 924(c) firearms offenses or the Armed Career Criminal Act. Even when the safety valve applies, the offender who avoids the mandatory minimum presumptively receives the guidelines sentence. The Sentencing Commission has had to ratchet up the guidelines range to reflect the mandatory minimums, and these inflated guidelines apply even when no statutory minimum sentence applies.[246] *Booker* had no effect on statutory mandatory minimums, as distinct from the guidelines, because the defendant, by electing to stand trial rather than plead guilty, can have a jury decide whether there is reasonable doubt about triggering facts, like presence of a firearm or the quantity of illegal drugs.

J. Conclusion

Justice Scalia's statement in *Harmelin* that mandatory penalties *in one form or another* were known throughout our history is not incorrect. In their modern form, where, as in *Harmelin* itself, they bind the courts but not the prosecutor, without possibility of probation or parole, they were unknown at the Founding. Grand juries, not prosecutors, controlled the charging function then. The First Congress adopted no minimum prison terms. Early state minimum terms replaced capital punishment, and the decision to file the triggering charges rested with grand juries.

During the nineteenth century, in both the federal and the state systems, prosecutors captured the charging function, and penal codes established menus of overlapping offenses carrying minimum penalties. In jurisdictions that rejected probation statutes, indeterminate sentences, and inherent judicial power to suspend, something like modern prosecutorial sentencing existed. Jurisdictions that rejected all three checks on prosecutorial sentencing, however, were exceptional.

Another 14.4 percent avoided the mandatory minimum by providing substantial cooperation, and 7.1 percent had the benefit of both the safety valve and substantial assistance.

[246] For a discussion of the dilemmas faced by the Commission, see Keven Bennardo, *Decoupling Federal Offense Guidelines from Statutory Limits on Sentencing*, 78 Mo. L. Rev. 683 (2013).

One general indication that prosecutors induced guilty pleas by promising reductions, rather than threatening increases, in the sentences expected from judges or parole boards comes from the early critics of negotiated guilty pleas. Until late in the twentieth century, plea bargaining was criticized as unduly lenient, rather than as coercive or draconian.[247] Indeed, this concern about undue lenience persisted into the 1960s, and only then did the objection to plea bargaining as coercive become prominent.[248]

Prosecutorial sentencing, where it prevailed, escaped constitutional scrutiny in the era of the right-privilege doctrine. Outside the context of prosecutorial discretion, the Supreme Court has repudiated the right-privilege distinction for half a century now. If modern "mandatory" minimums survive due process challenge in the context of modern constitutional law, it will be for reasons that have little to do with history.

[247] William Ortman, *When Plea Bargaining Became Normal*, 100 B.U. L. Rev. 1435, 1459–63 (2020). For examples, see Roscoe Pound, Criminal Justice in America 184 (1998) (1930); Raymond Moley, Politics and Criminal Prosecution 190 (1929).

[248] Ortman, *supra* note 248, at 1488–98.

PART II

THE THEORETICAL PROBLEMS

6

The Baseline Problem in Criminal Procedure

A. The Code-Maximum Baseline

Guilty pleas accounted for most convictions long before 1971,[1] when the Supreme Court first acknowledged this reality. *Santobello v. New York*[2] held that defendants who pleaded guilty as part of a deal have a due process right to enforcement of the agreement. After *Santobello*, the Court confronted the issue of whether guilty pleas entered to avert catastrophic trial penalties were voluntary or coerced.

Suppose, for example, the defendant was guilty of forgery and subject to a five-year maximum, but also liable to a recidivism charge punishable by twenty-five years to life. May the prosecutor represent that the recidivism charge will be brought if—and only if—the defendant insists on trial? The Court faced this issue in *Bordenkircher v. Hayes*[3] and resolved it by reference to the statutory baseline.

The *Bordenkircher* Court anticipated Alan Werthheimer's normative model of coercion.[4] The Wertheimer model characterizes inducements as either offers or threats. Offers give the recipient an option likely to make them better off than they otherwise would be. Threats give the recipient an option to avoid being made worse off than they otherwise would be.

The comparison required by "otherwise would be" depends on a pre-inducement prediction of the recipient's future—a baseline.[5] Baselines can be purely descriptive (what *will* happen if the recipient declines the inducement) or normative (what *should* happen if the recipient declines the inducement).

[1] Raymond Moley, *The Vanishing Jury*, 2 S. Calif. L. Rev. 97 (1928).
[2] 404 U.S. 257 (1971).
[3] 434 U.S. 357 (1978).
[4] Alan Wertheimer, Coercion (1987).
[5] *Id.* at 204, 222 ("coerciveness of proposals is all in the baseline. And relative to that baseline, only threats are coercive.").

Sentencing Discretion and the Constitution. Donald A. Dripps, Oxford University Press.
 DOI: 10.1093/9780197830390.003.0006

Justice Stewart, for the Court in *Hayes*, adopted a normative baseline based on the code maximum:

> Within the limits set by the legislature's constitutionally valid definition of chargeable offenses, "the conscious exercise of some selectivity in enforcement is not, in itself, a federal constitutional violation" so long as "the selection was [not] deliberately based upon an unjustifiable standard such as race, religion, or other arbitrary classification." To hold that the prosecutor's desire to induce a guilty plea is an "unjustifiable standard," which, like race or religion, may play no part in his charging decision, would contradict the very premises that underlie the concept of plea bargaining itself.[6]

I bracket important controversies over Wertheimer's model.[7] Even on Wertheimer's account, the statutory maximum seems implausible as a normative baseline.

The statutory baseline is normative, not statistical, because practically no offender receives a code-maximum sentence. But the code maximum is arbitrary, normatively irrelevant. Legislatures don't intend the actual imposition of the paper code. The code maximum is not a directive but a delegation.

The legislature provides a minimum penalty, too. Indeed, the code minimum is *zero*, because prosecutors can enter into nonprosecution agreements by which the defendant is never charged for anything.[8] The statutory maximum applicable after conviction has no greater claim to being either normal or desirable than the minimum. If the legislature believes the minimum penalty suffices for justice in at least some cases, why not use the minimum as the normative baseline? From that baseline, the prosecutor's representation that the recidivism charge would be brought only if Hayes insisted on trial is coercive.

To be clear, I am not suggesting the least serious possible charge as the baseline for coercion analysis. That would be morally arbitrary, too. The legislature *permits* the minimum and the maximum but does not *require* either. Illustratively, the Federal Sentencing Guidelines direct the judge to use a "base offense level" well below the statutory maximum, and then adjust

[6] *Bordenkircher*, 434 U.S. at 364–65 (citation omitted).

[7] *Cf.* Scott A. Anderson, *The Enforcement Approach to Coercion*, 5 J. Ethics & Soc. Phil. 1 (2010).

[8] *E.g.*, U.S. Dep't of Just. Off. Pro. Resp., Executive Summary of Report—Investigation into the U.S. Attorney's Office for the Southern District of Florida's Resolutions of Its 2006-2008 Federal Criminal Investigation of Jeffrey Epstein and Its Interactions With Victims During the Investigation (Nov. 2020).

the sentence up or down depending on facts specific to the case.[9] The flaw in *Bordenkircher*'s logic is the premise that the maximum liability permitted by the penal code is normatively desirable in every case. That's a normative baseline without any normative justification.

B. The Statistical Baseline

If the statutory baseline is arbitrary, what alternative should we use to decide whether the trial penalty is, or is not, coercive? One alternative is "the going rate": that is, what, as a descriptive, statistical matter, we would expect to happen in this case, compared to prior similar cases. Like the code-maximum baseline, the going-rate baseline is normatively arbitrary. It cribs the standard of proportionality from prior charging decisions by prosecutors.

One challenge to relying on prior practice is that prior practice won't yield clear guidance in very many cases. What if, as Professor Stuntz suggested, courts required prosecutors to prove a record of consistent charging decisions in similar cases?[10] Prosecutors could (almost) always show that prior charging decisions were consistent with the charges in the present case. They could (almost) always distinguish apparently similar cases by understandably opaque references to the strength of the case or the value of cooperation in cases of lenience, or to the offender's involvement in serious but uncharged crimes in cases of severity.

Let's assume, however, that prior practice could be juiced for concrete guidance in future cases. This gives prosecutors an incentive to bring charges carrying high sentences across the board. That's the baseline that enables catastrophic penalties for going to trial and catastrophic rewards for cooperation. Standardizing current charging decisions honestly would require standardizing the prevailing breaks for cooperation and penalties for going to trial. We would have the same sentences we see now, plus an unhelpful addition to the cost of sentencing hearings.

9 U.S. Sent'g Comm'n, Guidelines Manual ch. 2 (2024) ("Offense Conduct").

10 *E.g.*, William J. Stuntz, The Collapse of American Criminal Justice 297 (2011) ("For all sentences of incarceration over some minimal level . . . prosecutors should be required to show that sentences at least as severe have been imposed some minimum number of times for the same crime in the same state on similar facts."); Annie R. Traum, *Using Outcomes to Reframe Guilty Plea Adjudication*, 66 Fla. L. Rev. 823, 874 (2014) ("Trial courts should focus their energies on monitoring plea outcomes that are above market rates or contain mandatory minimum sentences.").

C. The Mysterious Baseline Requiring Fair Sentencing Hearings

Bordenkircher's statutory baseline harkens back to the days of the right-privilege distinction. The distinction permitted governments to condition benefits on the surrender of constitutional rights. Holmes expressed the distinction in a canonical epigram. Rejecting the constitutional claim of a police officer fired for political fundraising, Holmes wrote that the petitioner "may have a constitutional right to talk politics, but he has no constitutional right to be a policeman."[11] Transposed to plea bargaining, *Bordenkircher* says that the defendant may have a constitutional right to a trial, but he has no constitutional right to a sentence below the statutory maximum.

For many years the Court relied on the distinction to deny due process review of the procedures used by judges at sentencing, absent special circumstances that made the sentencing fundamentally unfair.[12] That changed after the Court's decision in *Goldberg v. Kelly*.[13] *Goldberg* repudiated the right-privilege distinction that justified the prior cases on sentencing and revocation.[14] Ever since *Goldberg*, the Court—outside the context of prosecutorial discretion—has honored the principle that legislatures may delegate sentencing discretion only to neutral tribunals.

The Court's modern sentencing cases reject the statutory maximum as the constitutional baseline for assessing the abuse of discretion. They hold, in effect, that the baseline for challenges to judicial sentences is the sentence within the statutory range that would be imposed after an adversary process. Legislatures may delegate sentencing discretion to judges, but only if the judges comply with standards of procedural fairness set by the Court rather than by legislatures. Clearly, these cases reject the statutory-maximum baseline. Arguably, as in *Goldberg*, official custom gives rise to justifiable expectations. On that reading, the defendant in *Bordenkircher* had a "new property" right in the five-year sentence. The new-property approach would lead to the statistical baseline discussed in Section (2) and face the same objections.

[11] McAuliffe v. Mayor of New Bedford, 29 N.E. 517, 517 (Mass. 1892).

[12] The cases, reviewed in Chapter 3, followed a long and winding road but are aptly summarized by Sanford Kadish, *Legal Norm and Discretion in the Police and Sentencing Processes*, 75 HARV. L. REV. 904, 917 & n.39 (1962) ("During Judicial sentencing a hearing and counsel are normally available." The footnote adds: "It is doubtful that there is any constitutional compulsion upon the sentencing judge to hold any hearing at all on the issue of punishment.").

[13] 397 U.S. 254 (1970).

[14] *Id.* at 262 ("The constitutional challenge cannot be answered by an argument that public assistance benefits are 'a privilege' and not a 'right.'") (citation omitted).

Rights to sentencing hearings, however, don't fit the new-property model very well. It might make sense to say that after the judge selects the nominal sentence and the defendant is released early on probation or parole, release is an administrative entitlement, forfeitable only for cause. That might make the constitutional case for fair hearings before revocation of probation or parole,[15] but it doesn't fit the judge's initial selection of the nominal sentence from within the statutory range. One might say that modern sentencing guidelines indeed resemble criteria for revocation of conditional release, but the Court required sentencing hearings long before the guidelines. Something else is going on in the cases, leaving aside that the guidelines have been only advisory since the *Booker* decision in 2005.

By holding sentencing hearings required by due process, the Court has rejected the statutory baseline. But it is not at all clear just what baseline has replaced it. If we could articulate the implicit baseline, we would have a plausible alternative to the code maximum the Court clings to in the context of prosecutorial discretion. That challenge, however, has thus far not been met.

D. A Substantive Proportionality Baseline?

One response to the baseline problem is to say that the statutory baseline is right, but the statutes themselves are wrong. Legislatures should curtail the egregious severity of American sentences. That's unlikely in the extreme, so the substance-is-the-problem argument turns to substantive constitutional limits on sentence severity.[16] The aptest constitutional provision is the Eighth Amendment's "cruel and unusual punishments" clause.[17]

The Court's decisions notoriously reject Eighth Amendment challenges to lengthy prison sentences for nonviolent crimes. Even the dissents in these cases say that long prison terms for minor crimes normally survive judicial scrutiny. New Justices have joined the Court many times since the *Rummel*

[15] As required by *Morrissey v. Brewer*, 408 U.S. 471 (1972) (parole revocation), and *Gagnon v. Scarpelli*, 411 U.S. 778 (1973) (probation revocation).

[16] William J. Stuntz, *The Uneasy Relationship between Criminal Procedure and Criminal Justice*, 107 Yale L.J. 1, 76 (1997) ("Defendants' interests might best be protected by less procedure, coupled with a much more activist judicial posture toward funding, the definition of crime, and sentencing—all areas where judges have been loath to take dramatic stands.").

[17] *Id.* at 72 ("The prohibition of cruel and unusual punishments could plausibly be read to imply a proportionality principle for sentencing, capital and noncapital alike.").

case in 1980.[18] In the forty years since, the Court held only one prison term imposed on an adult offender to be unconstitutionally disproportionate—a life-without-parole sentence for a habitual but nonviolent offender convicted of writing a "no account" check for $100.[19] In *Ewing v. California*,[20] the Court upheld a twenty-five-year sentence for theft by a recidivist. Even *the dissent* accepted the laws of thirty-three other jurisdictions that capped the punishment of a recidivist convicted for shoplifting at ten years.[21]

Perhaps this extraordinary record of futility makes the case for a more robust constitutional proportionality doctrine. If criminal law theorists agreed on a proportionality metric, courts might read the constitution to prohibit gross departures from that metric even if disproportionate sentences reflected the going rate. There is, however, no agreement on a proportionality metric. In fact, there is a growing consensus that the quest for one is hopeless.

[18] Rummel v. Estelle, 445 U.S. 263 (1980) (rejecting Eighth Amendment challenge to a life sentence for a third conviction for minor fraud offenses).
[19] Solem v. Helm, 463 U.S. 277 (1983).
[20] 538 U.S. 11 (2003).
[21] *Id.* at 53 (Breyer, J., dissenting).

7
The Proportionality Problem in Criminal Law

A. Proportionality's Functions

Begin with the familiar distinction between cardinal and ordinal proportionality judgments. Ordinal judgments compare different wrongs with one another. We might say, for example, that robbery is worse than burglary and burglary worse than theft. Cardinal judgments prescribe the proportionate penalty for an offense without reference to others. We might say, for instance, that eight months in jail is too light a sentence for sexual assault, even if eight months is a jurisdiction's typical sentence for that offense.

Just assessments of cardinal proportionality for every offense logically entail a just ordinal ranking as well. The reverse, however, is not true. Just assessments of ordinal proportionality might yield disproportionately severe or disproportionately lenient penalties across the board. Many criticize sentences in the United States as generally too severe. That criticism is quite independent of arguments about ordinal rankings of, say, drug trafficking, perjury, and Medicare fraud.

Legislatures make ordinal judgments to distinguish tort from crime, misdemeanor from felony, lesser included offenses from greater offenses, and capital from noncapital murder. Sentencing guidelines identify factors that aggravate or mitigate individual cases that arise within particular statutory ranges. When judges exercise sentencing discretion, their decisions reflect ordinal proportionality judgments—within the range prescribed by the legislature, a particular case belongs near the maximum, near the minimum, or near the median.

Indeed, we have no record of *any* legal system that prescribed a single penalty for all offenses. While the methods of punishment have varied over the centuries, they have at least one common feature—namely, they are scalar rather than binary. Prison and pillory are different types of punishment, but

Sentencing Discretion and the Constitution. Donald A. Dripps, Oxford University Press.
 DOI: 10.1093/9780197830390.003.0007

both can be graduated infinitely over time.[1] Lashes were numbered too, with the nice touch that a flogging that would be fatal if inflicted on a single occasion could be distributed over several days.[2] Historically, there were even "degrees of death."[3] The details belong in a footnote, which is not for the squeamish.[4]

Modern theories of criminal law—retributive, utilitarian, or expressivist—disagree about the ultimate justification of state-sanctioned punishment—the "general justifying aim" of the criminal justice system. They agree, however, that the gravity of offenses and the severity of punishment are scalar and that more severe punishments should be inflicted for graver crimes. Proportionality, however, is under formidable theoretical attack. To understand contemporary critiques of proportionality, we must first look at least to the recent history of the concept.

B. The Revival of Retributivism in the Twentieth Century

Modern criminal law theory begins in the late eighteenth and early nineteenth centuries, with the writings of Beccaria, Bentham, and Kant. Beccaria and Bentham reasoned from utilitarian premises to criticize draconian punishments as needlessly cruel and indeed self-defeating.[5] Harsh penalties encouraged discretionary mercy, which in turn undermined deterrence. Better, they said, to threaten certain but mild punishments than unlikely but terrible ones.

[1] *See, e.g.*, An Act for the Punishment of Certain Crimes Against the United States, ch. IX, 1 Stat. 112 § 18 (1790) (perjurers shall "be imprisoned not exceeding three years, and fined not exceeding eight hundred dollars; and shall stand in the pillory for one hour . . . ").

[2] *See, e.g., id.*, § 16 (larceny to be punished by a fine "not exceeding the fourfold value of the property so stolen . . . and be publicly whipped, not exceeding thirty-nine stripes.").

[3] *See* Stuart Banner, The Death Penalty: An American History 53 (2022).

[4] *See, e.g.*, Ken Armstrong, *Broken on the Wheel*, Paris Rev. (Mar. 13, 2015), https://www.theparisreview.org/blog/2015/03/13/broken-on-the-wheel/ (describing use of rack during questioning and execution on the wheel); Sabine Baring-Gould, Curiosities of Olden Times 99 (New York, Whittaker 1896) (describing execution of Balthasar Gérard for assassinating William the Silent); Michel Foucault, Discipline and Punish 1–6 (Alan Sheridan trans., Vintage Books 2d ed., 1995) (1978) (describing the execution of Robert-Francois Damiens for the attempted assassination of Louis XV).

[5] *See* Cesare Beccaria, An Essay on Crimes and Punishments 43 (Piccadilly, J. Almon 1767) (punishments should be chosen "as will make the strongest and most lasting impressions on the minds of others, with the least torment to the body of the criminal."); Jeremy Bentham, *Principles of Penal Law*, *in* 1 The Works of Jeremy Bentham 365, 397 (J. Bowring ed., Edinburgh, William Tait 1843) ("All punishment being in itself evil, upon the principle of utility, if it ought at all to be admitted, it ought only to be admitted in as far as it promises to exclude some greater evil.").

Kant parted company with the utilitarians. Kant argued that justice requires the community to punish criminals according to their desert.[6] Whereas the utilitarians recommended punishment up to but no further than the point where the pain inflicted exceeded the pain prevented via deterrence, Kant endorsed the *jus talonis* as the test of the punishment society must impose.[7]

The difficulties with the *jus talonis* are well-known. The offender may be judgment-proof; there are some penalties society is unwilling to inflict, even when condign, and many serious offenses inflict no material injury on specific victims.[8] The last serious attempt to proportion punishments according to the *jus talonis* was Thomas Jefferson's draft penal code for the newly independent Commonwealth of Virginia.[9] The proposal did not pass, and the *jus talonis* has fallen into disrepute. Today, it is more an object of disgust and ridicule than a serious policy alternative.

What, however, did proportionality mean, once the *jus talonis* was rejected? In the United States, the nineteenth century saw the development of the penitentiary system and a reliance on unregulated judicial discretion to select the length of prison terms from within statutory ranges.[10] In the late nineteenth and early twentieth centuries, the rehabilitative model of punishment led to widespread reliance on indeterminate sentences based on the offender's predicted future behavior rather than the crime committed in the past.[11]

Indeed, indeterminate sentences turned the old utilitarian critique of arbitrary severity on its head.[12] "Parole and the indeterminate sentence were

[6] Immanuel Kant, The Metaphysics of Morals 332–33 (Mary Gregor trans., 1996).

[7] *Id.* ("But only the law of retribution (jus talonis) . . . can specify definitely the quantity and quality of punishment.").

[8] As reflected in the title of Michael Tonry, Of One-Eyed and Toothless Miscreants: Making the Punishment Fit the Crime? (2020).

[9] Thomas Jefferson, *A Bill for Proportioning Crimes and Punishments*, in 2 The Writings of Thomas Jefferson 203 (Paul Leicester Ford ed.) (New York, G.P. Putnam's Sons, 1904).

[10] *See, e.g.*, Kate Stjth & José A. Cabranes, Fear of Judging 10–11 (1998).

[11] The statutes either authorized a prison term that was literally indeterminate, or very long terms subject to earlier release by the parole board. On the two types of statutes and a review of their origins, see Edward Lindsey, *Historical Sketch of the Indeterminate Sentence and Parole System*, 16 J. Crim. L. & Criminology 9 (1925). By 1926, forty-six states had parole systems. *See* Lawrence M. Friedman, Crime and Justice in American History 304 (1993). By 1937, thirty-nine states had indeterminate sentencing laws. Note, *Indeterminate Sentence Laws—The Adolescence of Peno-Correctional Legislation*, 50 Harv. L. Rev. 677, 678 (1937). Congress adopted the parole system in 1910. Stith & Cabranes, *supra* note 10, at 18–19.

[12] *See* Francis A. Allen, The Decline of the Rehabilitative Ideal 33–34 (1981) (noting critics who characterized rehabilitation as "a threat to the political values of free societies," "peculiarly vulnerable to debasement and the serving of unintended and unexpressed social ends," and ignorance about "how to prevent criminal recidivism by changing the characters and behavior of offenders."); Stith & Cabranes, *supra* note 10, at 30 (noting criticism that "the rehabilitative

deeply discretionary; but they were also powerful instruments of control."[13] The rehabilitative model might justify early release of a prisoner convicted of a grave offense, if the prisoner were deemed rehabilitated. On the other hand, a prisoner convicted of a minor crime might reasonably be judged a risk to the community for decades. Indeterminate sentencing meant punishing the offender on account of propensity to reoffend.[14] The law of course continues to hold recidivists responsible for their voluntary conduct. That seems both hypocritical and harsh.

Contemporaneous with fairness-based critiques of indeterminate sentences, retributivism gained fresh support.[15] Retributivists give different accounts of why criminals deserve punishment. They generally agree on the main objections to utilitarian theories. Retributivists generally criticized utilitarianism for permitting, in appropriate circumstances, (1) convicting the innocent[16] and (2) draconian punishments for minor crimes and slaps on the wrist for major ones.[17] Utilitarians, for the most part, retreated into so-called mixed theories, which prescribed punishments that pursue other goals, prominently including crime reduction, but only within limits set by retributive fairness.[18]

premise was too often a sham, and indeterminacy had the effect of increasing the average length of nominal prison terms meted out in court and the amount of actual time served.").

[13] FRIEDMAN, *supra* note 11, at 305.

[14] ANDREW VON HIRSCH, DOING JUSTICE: THE CHOICE OF PUNISHMENTS 128 (1976) ("Even if rehabilitation works, basing the sentence on the offender's 'need for treatment' falls afoul of the commensurateness principle, for much the same reason that basing the sentence on prediction would: the severity of the disposition is being determined, not by the gravity of what he *has* done and thus deserves, but by what he is expected to do in future if he successfully participates in the treatment program.").

[15] *See, e.g.*, TONRY, *supra* note 8, at 1 ("Interest in retributive theory in English-speaking countries revived in the 1970s. For at least a century before that, consequentialist ideas were overwhelmingly dominant.").

[16] *See, e.g.*, MICHAEL S. MOORE, PLACING BLAME 94–97 (1997). For a collection of sources pressing this objection to utilitarianism, see Russell L. Christopher, *Deterring Retributivism: The Injustice of "Just" Punishment*, 96 NW. L. REV. 843, 870 nn.138 & 139 (2002). As an important article points out, this criticism of the utilitarians detaches their theory of punishment from their broader commitments to political liberalism. Guyora Binder & Nicholas J. Smith, *Framed: Utilitarians and Punishment of the Innocent*, 32 RUTGERS L.J. 115 (2000).

[17] *See, e.g.*, IGOR PRIMORATZ, JUSTIFYING LEGAL PUNISHMENT 37–38 (1989) (noting that given the right factual conditions, utilitarians commit themselves to "very stiff sentences" for shoplifting or "six months in prison" for rape).

[18] *See, e.g.*, Norval Morris, *The Future of Imprisonment: Toward a Punitive Philosophy*, 72 MICH. L. REV. 1161 (1974); RICHARD S. FRASE, JUST SENTENCING (2013); ANDREW VON HIRSCH & ANDREW ASHWORTH, PROPORTIONATE SENTENCING: EXPLORING THE PRINCIPLES (2005). There is substantial variation in these positions. For example, compare FRASE, *supra*, at 24–80 (defending asymmetric limiting-retributivism model that caps maximum sentences according to retributive desert, but rejects retributive desert as a guide to minimum sentences) with VON HIRSCH & ASHWORTH,

The categorical prohibition of convicting the innocent and inflicting disproportionate punishments posed serious challenges for retributivists. First, no procedural system can avoid mistakes. How can retributivists justify a system they know is practically certain to convict the innocent? Second, while it is easy to condemn disproportionate punishments, it is much more difficult to say just what retributive proportionality means. With the *jus talonis* rightly consigned to the intellectual dustbin, just what moral metric should be put in its place?

Utilitarians who recognize side constraints against convicting the innocent and against disproportionate punishment face the same challenges. If utilitarianism can avoid its most sinister implications by adopting side constraints against convicting the innocent and disproportionate punishments, utilitarians, too, must decide just what these constraints mean in practice. With respect to sentencing, this means defining proportionality *as a constraint*, that is, in terms of some moral metric *more constrained* than the metric of marginal costs and marginal benefits.

Deferring the convicting-the-innocent issue to Chapter 8, we turn now to the problem posed by retributive proportionality. The concept is central to retributivist accounts and has generally been adopted as a limiting principle by utilitarians. What, however, are the necessary and sufficient conditions for classifying a punishment as proportionate to desert?

C. The Problem of Retributive Proportionality

Retributivists give quite different reasons for believing that criminals deserve to suffer on account of their crimes. The most popular theories say that the criminal deserves punishment because the crime was a bad choice, or reflected a bad character, or traduced the community's reciprocal bonds of self-restraint.[19] By whatever road they take, retributivists believe that more serious crimes deserve more severe punishment than less serious crimes.

supra, at 138 (rejecting asymmetry, arguing that culpability should determine the minimum as well as the maximum penalty).

[19] *See, e.g.*, Moore, *supra* note 16, at 548–88 (analyzing choice and character theories, defending choice against character); Richard Dagger, *Play Fair With Punishment*, 103 Ethics 473, 476 (1993) ("Punishment is justified, ceteris paribus, because the persons who disobey the law fail to meet their obligations to the other members of society.").

The gravity of crimes turns on two factors: harm and culpability. Some may count the harm actually inflicted but not intended or foreseen, and others only the harm intended or foreseen. However harm counts, harm is scalar. Murder by torture is worse than murder *simpliciter*. Ten homicides are worse than one; harm to a person is worse than harm to property. Culpability too is scalar. Intended harm is worse than accidental harm, even if a reckless or negligent actor may be held accountable for the accident.

Within the traditional *mens rea* categories, culpability is still scalar. The reckless driver who kills a pedestrian when speeding away from a drug deal and the driver who is speeding toward the emergency room are not equally culpable. Typical sentencing guidelines illustrate the wide menu of facts that aggravate and mitigate.

John Kleinig proposed the leading model for reasoned proportionality judgments in 1973: "In relating punishments to offences, we simply reserve the mildest punishment we can reasonably give for the least serious wrong, the most severe punishment for the most wicked deed, and scale other wrongs and punishments in between . . . ."[20] Kleinig immediately noted many difficulties attending this process: "No one is suggesting that assessments of responsibility, motives or intentions, and harm, or the relative weights to be given to each of these, is easy, or even that we shall always be able to determine them satisfactorily."[21]

A decade later, Jesper Ryberg published a systematic critique of the severity/culpability matrix.[22] Ryberg argued that each component of the matrix was problematic. The harm and culpability concepts behind the severity axis were subjective or indeterminate.[23] The mechanical expression of sentence severity in units of prison time ignored important realities about the impact of incarceration on different persons.[24] Above all, the seriousness of crime and the severity of punishment, however each is measured, are incommensurable. There is nothing but intuition to justify one type and the quantum of punishment for any given offense.[25] If the anchor points are mistakes (whether too punitive or not punitive enough), the whole system will generate consistently wrong results.

[20] John Kleinig, Punishment and Desert 124 (1973).
[21] *Id.* at 129.
[22] Jesper Ryberg, The Ethics of Proportionate Punishment (2004).
[23] *See id.* at 59–76.
[24] *Id.* at 102–9.
[25] *Id.* at 124 ("purely ordinal proportionality would not provide any guidance as to how a crime of certain degree of seriousness should actually be punished.") (footnote omitted).

These objections are quite powerful, and have been amplified since by distinguished critics.[26] Notwithstanding the difficulties, many US states and the federal government adopted sentencing guidelines that ranked offense severity on one axis and criminal history (thought to be a proxy for culpability) on another. Here, I use the Federal Sentencing Guidelines (FSG) to illustrate the force of the objections given by Ryberg and many others. I focus on the FSG not because they are representative; they are not. Their unique depth of detail, however, illustrates the practical relevance of the academic criticisms leveled at Kleinig's approach.

Begin with harm, which seems simple enough. What, however, of the FSG's reliance on the amount stolen to set the offense level for theft and fraud? The swindler who bilks a disabled accident victim out of a $100,000 insurance settlement faces a base offense level of 14, which would get a first offender fifteen to twenty-one months on the grid.[27] One who cons a billionaire out of $10 million in chump change earns level 26, calling for sixty-three to seventy-eight months for a first offender.[28]

The FSG set base offense levels for drug trafficking crimes based on the type and quantity of the drug. So a wholesale dealer arrested in possession of fifty grams of 99 percent pure heroin faces offense level 18.[29] If, however, the wholesaler avoids arrest and sells the heroin to a street dealer after converting the 50 grams pure into 250 grams of 20 percent purity, the street dealer, if

[26] *See, e.g.*, Chad Flanders, *Can Retributivism Be Saved?*, 2014 BYU L. Rev. 309, 312 ("The fact that retributivism places so much emphasis on proportionality (or fairness) in punishment, but cannot offer much illumination about what proportionality is—or how to achieve it—is a key insight that something has gone wrong with retributive theory, even on its own terms."); Vincent Chiao, *Proportionality and Its Discontents*, 41 Law & Phil. 193, 213 (2022) ("Proportionality merely recapitulates underlying moral judgments, meaning that your proportionality judgments will seem obvious to those who agree with you and baseless to those who do not."); Nicola Lacey & Hanna Pickard, *The Chimera of Proportionality: Institutionalising Limits on Punishment in Contemporary Social and Political Systems*, 78 Mod. L. Rev. 216, 219 (2015) ("The idea that appealing to proportionality as an abstract ideal can deliver limits to punishment . . . is a chimera: for while proportionality has a clear formal meaning . . . it only has substantive upshot where there is agreement about, or effective enforcement of, substantive criteria of equivalence or comparability."). Prominent retributivists admit that retributive theory thus far has no good metric. *See* Larry Alexander, *Proportionality's Function*, 15 Crim. L. & Phil. 361, 372 (2021) (summarizing challenges to retributivist proportionality, concluding that "we retributivists have a lot of unfinished theoretical business to conduct."); Douglas Husak, *Proportionality in Personal Life*, 15 Crim. L. & Phil. 339, 340 (2021) (adhering to retributive proportionality principle, but acknowledging "the immense difficulties" with the principle).

[27] FSG § 2B1.1(b)(1). Even with the two-level upward adjustment for inflicting "substantial financial hardship to one or more victims" per Section 2B1.1(b)(2), the offense level rises only to 16, yielding for a first offender a range of twenty-one to twenty-seven months.

[28] *Id.*

[29] FSG § 2D1.1.(c)

arrested with the stash, faces level 24 (and a "mandatory minimum" of five years if the government elects to charge it).[30]

The FSG are even more problematic with respect to culpability. The guidelines use criminal history as the horizontal axis of the grid.[31] The effect on a sentence can be dramatic. For example, if our street dealer facing offense level 24 has no criminal history, the prescribed range is fifty-one to sixty-three months. If, however, the defendant falls into Criminal History Category IV, the range rises to seventy-seven to ninety-six months. Other than a criminal record, the FSG allow limited consideration of individual offender characteristics. Yet the retributive case for using criminal history as a proxy for culpability is dubious.[32]

Another widely noted problem is how to weigh the roles of harm and culpability in determining the gravity of the crime. H. L. A. Hart asked: "Is negligently causing the destruction of a city worse than the intentional wounding of a single policeman?"[33] At each offense level between 12 and 26, the prescribed range for Criminal History Category VI is double that of the range for Category 1. Even assuming that criminal records provide some proxy for culpability, what reason is there for giving a prior record a roughly equal weight with harm?

Turning from offense seriousness to severity of punishment, the FSG prescribe months in prison without recognizing differences in offenders. Some offenders will be traumatized by incarceration, some more or less vulnerable to predation, some more or less in need of therapy, and so on. As Adam Kolber points out, for many defendants, the question of which prison is more important than the marginal length of the sentence.[34] The guidelines themselves do not speak to this question at all.

Ranking the seriousness of offenses based on harm and culpability and ranking the severity of punishment for different persons pose difficult challenges. The most daunting challenge of all is the moral metric problem.

[30] *See id.*; 21 U.S.C. § 841(b)(1)(B)(i).

[31] FSG § 5A (Sentencing Table).

[32] *See, e.g.*, Rhys Hester et al., *Prior Record Enhancements at Sentencing: Unsettled Justifications and Unsettling Consequences*, 47 Crime & Just. 209 (2018). *Cf.* Christopher Lewis, *Risk-Based Sentencing and the Principles of Punishment*, 112 J. Crim. L. & Criminology 213 (2022) (arguing that recidivism results from social disadvantage, making recidivists less rather than more blameworthy).

[33] H. L. A. Hart, Punishment and Responsibility 162 (1968).

[34] Adam Kolber, Punishment for the Greater Good 139 (2024) (discussing the "facilities challenge" to proportionality, stating: "Proportional harsh treatment requires a detailed examination not only of the duration of offenders' prison sentences but also of the conditions they will like face while incarcerated.") (footnote omitted).

The ordinal rankings make sense, but only if at least one cardinal judgment is made first. Even "if it were possible to arrange all crimes on a scale of relative seriousness, our starting point or base of comparison must be a crime for which a penalty is fixed otherwise than by comparison with others."[35]

The Sentencing Commission addressed this challenge by attempting—or at least claiming—to restate the existing sentencing practices of the judges in rule-like form, excluding the high and low outliers to minimize disparity.[36] The Commission consulted a database that includes more than ten thousand cases. The Commission, however, was not satisfied with the low anchor point shown by the data. "Even though the Sentencing Commission farmed this data, it immediately, and arbitrarily, without explanation then or now, jettisoned the nearly 50% of federal sentences where a defendant was given probation . . . ."[37] With the low anchor set where the median point had been in practice, the severity of federal sentences increased dramatically.

Now it might be that the noncarceral sentences ex ante were too lenient, so that the carceral sentences ex post were proportionate. The challenge to making reasoned proportionality judgments is *to give a reason* for one anchor or the other. After decades of thoughtful scholarship and well-intentioned reforms, that question still hangs.

The FSG show a final problem—and a ray of hope-for offense-gravity/sentence-severity rankings. Ultimately, sentences are determined by politics. Even if Kleinig's method permitted individuals to form coherent rankings, different people will rank crimes and punishments differently. As might be expected, the membership of the original Commission included advocates for both retributive and utilitarian first principles.[38] The Commission finessed this divide by cribbing and editing the collective practice of hundreds of judges, a sample that presumably included many with utilitarian and many others with retributive predispositions.[39] It is entirely possible

[35] HART, *supra* note 33, at 162.

[36] Stephen Breyer, *The Federal Sentencing Guidelines and the Key Compromises Upon Which They Rest*, 17 HOFSTRA L. REV. 1, 17 (1988) (Commission "decided to base the Guidelines primarily upon typical, or average, actual past practice. The distinctions that the Guidelines make in terms of punishment are primarily those which past practice has shown were actually important factors in pre-Guideline sentencing.").

[37] Mark Osler & Mark W. Bennett, *A "Holocaust in Slow Motion?" America's Mass Incarceration and the Role of Discretion*, 7 DEPAUL J. SOC. JUST. 117, 141 (2014).

[38] *See* STITH & CABRANES, *supra* note 10, at 51–53 (describing the just-deserts model favored by Paul Robinson and the cost-benefit model favored by Michael Block).

[39] *See* Breyer, *supra* note 36, at 17–18.

for a collective decision to approve a proportionality scale that everyone involved in the decision regards as suboptimal in some respects.

If the inability to agree on first principles is discouraging, a collective decision based on an overlapping consensus offers some ground for optimism. Indeed, recent proportionality scholarship is turning away from treating proportionality as a moral concept, and toward considering how these irreducibly intuitive judgments are—and might be better—structured by institutional design.[40]

D. The Obdurate Intuition that the Punishment Should Fit the Crime

Despite the hammer blows struck against proportionality rankings, no one—perhaps no one in history, and definitely no one in the current academic or policy conversations—proposes a single penalty for all the crimes in the code.[41] Kevin Reitz and Cecelia Klingele, the reporter and co-reporter,

[40] *See* Lacey & Pickard, *supra* note 26, at 219 ("What has been thought of a proportionality, in short, is not a naturally existing relationship, but a product of political and social construction, cultural meaning-making, and institution-building."); Matt Matravers, *Is Twenty-first Century Punishment Post-desert? in* RETRIBUTIVISM HAS A PAST: HAS IT A FUTURE? 31, 43 (M. Tonry ed. 2011) ("What is needed in the future is not only to think through what are the legitimate entitlements and expectations of liberal citizens in relation to their criminal justice system, but also to confront the problems that arise in the nonideal world in which we live.").

[41] Adam Kolber's *Punishment for the Greater Good* presents a sophisticated argument for basing the severity of sentences solely on consequences. *See* KOLBER, *supra* note 34. Consequentialism requires its own type of proportionality analysis. The more harmful the crimes we expect to prevent via deterrence and incapacitation, the more costly are the punishments justified by consequences. There is no reason to think that prosecutors are better at assessing the costs and benefits of incarceration than they are at assessing just deserts. There are, moreover, reasons to oppose basing sentences on unconstrained consequentialism. One is that without some fairness-based constraint, consequentialism might justify *any* sentence for *any* crime. *Id.* at 168. Kolber expresses more confidence than I share that unconstrained consequentialism would not lead to, for example, long indeterminate sentences for underclass teenagers caught jumping turnstiles. Given even modestly accurate predictions, each such sentence might well prevent multiple violent felonies. I find that risk all too real to abandon proportionality as a constraint on severity. Another reason to retain proportionality is that, practically speaking, we can't escape from it. The intuition that the punishment should fit the crime is reflected not just in the scholarly literature but also in surveys of popular opinion. PAUL H. ROBINSON & JOHN M. DARLEY, JUSTICE, LIABILITY, AND BLAME: COMMUNITY VIEWS AND THE CRIMINAL LAW 198 (1995) ("In sum, it is clear that our respondents are in accord with the general tendency in the legal codes to distinguish grades of offenses within and between offenses."). If democratic political processes, improbably, adopted statutes prohibiting considering just deserts in sentencing, socially motivated cognition by prosecutors, juries, and judges would lead to pseudo-utilitarian justifications for avoiding disproportionate sentences. Much more might be said about Kolber's admirably nuanced analysis, but I leave any further reflections for some other occasion.

respectively, for the American Law Institute (ALI) Model Penal Code–Sentencing, are worth quoting here:

> We know few people willing to complete the following sentence: "Disproportionately severe criminal punishments are justifiable, and should be recommended in model legislation, when . . . ." Or: "We are in favor of life sentences for people who don't deserve them when . . . ." If readers cannot comfortably fill in these blanks, or can think only of unreasonably extreme examples, then they are in substantial agreement with the MPCS that a proportionality constraint is needed whenever sentences are envisioned, threatened, imposed, or modified.
>
> The harder questions come in the implementation of the idea. How is proportionality to be defined (if it's even possible to do so) and who gets to define it?[42]

Commonsensical as this sounds, it equivocates on just what a right against retributively excessive sentences means.

The Model Penal Code–Sentencing provisions prioritize avoiding disproportionate punishment as a retributive constraint on utilitarian considerations. A utility-based proportionality doctrine would not constrain the operation of utilitarian reasoning. So mixed theorists, including the ALI drafters, need a retributive theory of proportionality that trumps other values.

Mixed theorists and retributivists alike face the problem that if the justice system must respect a categorical side constraint prohibiting disproportionate punishment, and proportionality itself is challenging to determine precisely, the system will be running the risk of disproportionate punishment in almost every case. Whatever our first principles, if we agree that we must never impose disproportionately severe punishments, and every system is practically certain to do just that, are we not under a categorical duty to forgo punishment altogether?

[42] *Model Penal Code–Sentencing—Workable Limits on Mass Punishment*, 48 Crime & Just. 255, 272 (2019).

PART III

PROPORTIONATE PUNISHMENT AS PROCEDURAL JUSTICE

8
Disproportionate Punishment and Convicting the Innocent

A. Procedural Justice and Convicting the Innocent

Recall that retributivists accuse utilitarians not just of countenancing disproportionate punishments but also of countenancing conviction of the innocent. Recall also that utilitarians respond that any criminal justice system is practically certain to do both, in at least some cases, and that the instances of mistake will be outwardly indistinguishable from cases in which a genuinely guilty offender receives a genuinely condign sentence. Retributivists have said little about the prospect of mistakenly imposing excessive punishment. They have, however, grappled with the risk of convicting the innocent.

Now, if retributivists cannot justify a criminal justice system because it is certain to make mistakes about liability, retributivists must either become anarchists or hypocrites or abandon retributivism. If, however, retributivists can justify a system that will accidentally convict the innocent, they can also justify a system that will accidentally inflict excessive punishment on the guilty. That equivalence is addressed in the next section. But first, let us consider the retributivist's assets in responding to the systemic risk of convicting the innocent.

No matter what their various forms, all such accommodations distinguish the abstract right to be free from unjustified state punishment from the procedures the accused can justly demand of the state. The issue for retributivists (and for mixed theorists too) is whether any normative case can be made for this distinction. Philosophers have offered various arguments, many of them by no means implausible.

An academic truism holds that there are as many theories as there are theorists. I do not here defend any particular retributive justification of fallible systems. Instead, the far-from-exhaustive illustrations that follow make two related points. First, to distinguish retributivism from anarchism, retributivists need some such theory of justified mistakes. Second,

Sentencing Discretion and the Constitution. Donald A. Dripps, Oxford University Press.
 DOI: 10.1093/9780197830390.003.0008

to distinguish a retributive theory of mistakes from unconstrained consequentialism, the retributive account must include special safeguards against false convictions. Mixed theories that subject consequentialist goals to retributive side constraints likewise need a theory of justified mistakes other than a mere surplus of benefits over costs, to distinguish mixed theories from anarchism on the one hand and unconstrained consequentialism on the other.

(1) The Doctrine of Double Effect

The doctrine of double effect (DDE) allows a person to perform an act for a good purpose even when the actor knows that this act will not only have harmful effects but also violate the rights of an innocent victim. Aquinas formulated the DDE as a solution to the problem of self-defense using deadly force.[1] The actor intends to save the actor's life, not to kill the attacker, even though the actor knows that shooting the attacker will do both. Another common example is a surgery necessary to save the life of a pregnant woman that cannot be performed without terminating the fetus.

In any given prosecution, the DDE does not apply because the police, prosecutors, and judges believe with good reason that the defendant is guilty in each case. These officials know, however, that in the total population of those convicted, there are certain to be some innocents. The point at which the DDE can enter is at the preliminary stage of establishing and operating such a system in the first place. Its designers and operatives intend it to punish the guilty, but know that it will sometimes convict the innocent.[2]

Even DDE proponents do not permit the actor to justify any means to a good end. The good and bad consequences of the act must be inseparable, and there must be a justifiable proportion between them.[3] This last criterion

[1] Thomas Aquinas, Summa Theologiæ, Second Part of the Second Part, Question 64, article 7 (1920), https://www.newadvent.org/summa/3064.htm#article7.

[2] *See* Michael Moore, Placing Blame: A General Theory of the Criminal Law 158 (1997) ("Agent-relative moral norms bind us absolutely only with respect to evils we either intend or (on some versions) knowingly visit on specified individuals.").

[3] *See id.*; Alison McIntyre, *Doctrine of Double Effect*, Stanford Encyclopedia of Philosophy (July 2, 2004, rev. July 17, 2023), https://plato.stanford.edu/archives/win2023/entries/double-effect/ (summarizing the elements of DDE at 3).

is not precisely defined. The strongest case is where the actor has a duty to bring about one result but also a duty to avoid the other.

In the surgery case, the doctor has a duty to save mother and baby; doing nothing violates both duties, and performing the surgery satisfies one. A mandatory retributivist could draw an analogy between the surgery case and the criminal justice system. Officials have a duty to punish the guilty, a duty not to punish the innocent, and both being duties rather than options, there is no incommensurability between the good and bad consequences.[4]

Indeed, most instances of punishing *the guilty* will injure innocent third parties. The offender's spouse loses a life partner, the children a parent. Utilitarians can accept this collateral damage as outweighed by the benefits of law enforcement. Retributivists can fall back on DDE. Those injuries really are inseparable from imprisonment. Per DDE, state officials foresee harm to an offender's family without intending it.

With respect to a justice system, DDE's inseparability requirement poses another issue.[5] In a system that "does all it can" to avoid convicting the innocent, convicting the innocent and convicting the guilty are indeed inseparable. If the state is doing less than what's feasible to avoid miscarriages of justice, false convictions are not inseparable from true ones. What do we mean by "all it can"?

If the irreducible risk of error were very high, the just and unjust convictions would still be inseparable. We might, however, then have doubts about whether the desired just convictions deserved priority over the foreseen but undesired false convictions. What, however, if the risk of error was very low, but might be made still lower at a very great expense? That reinforces the priority of the intended just convictions, but undercuts their inseparability, since there is still more the state can do to minimize the undesired but inevitable mistakes.

[4] *See* Larry Alexander, *Retributivism and the Inadvertent Punishment of the Innocent*, 2 Law & Phil. 233 (1983). Mandatory retributivism, understood to recognize agent-relative categorical obligations on state officials to punish the guilty, faces many objections. For example, mandatory retributivism appears to condemn granting one conspirator immunity in exchange for testimony against the other conspirators. My point here is that mandatory retributivists can accept some risk of error in the criminal process.

[5] Moore, *supra* note 2, at 158, insists on no criteria of reliability as a condition of moral freedom to injure "specified individuals." This is not the view taken by the positive law of criminal responsibility for advertent risk-running. The actor who, with awareness of a massive gap between risks and benefits, kills a person "unspecified" ex ante is (typically) guilty of manslaughter (if not murder). *See* Model Penal Code § 210.3(1)(b).

(2) Rights against Risks

Another, perhaps more promising, retributivist account holds that deontological rights against risks differ, either in their content or their "stringency," from rights against the harms that are risked. If this is so, then a retributivist could tolerate risks of punishing the innocent while maintaining an absolutist position against the actual conviction of the innocent.

Suppose we agree that we must never punish the innocent, and (miraculously) have a criminal justice system that convicts only one innocent person among every hundred accused. Assume also that this error rate is well-documented and that state officials know this. Is prosecuting one hundred persons morally equivalent to prosecuting one person the authorities know to be innocent? If the answer is yes, what about a procedure that runs a one-in-a-million chance of convicting the innocent?

Take the 1 percent error rate again. What if the jurisdiction is a small one and prosecutes only a dozen felony cases a year? Is the system justified for eight years but not nine? After all, the first person convicted might have been innocent. Indeed, the first three might have been innocent; it will just take thirty years for the statistics to normalize.

Intuitions may vary, but it would not be wholly eccentric to reject categorical rights against the imposition of all unconsented risks. The hypotheticals about subjecting your neighbor to Russian roulette are misplaced in at least two ways. The first is that the risks created by major public policy decisions are not aimed at any particular target. They are very widely distributed (as are the benefits, typically). Second, these sorts of institutional risks might be imposed, equally or nearly equally, *on the decision makers* and those close to them, as well as on everyone else. Under these conditions, no one is being used solely as a tool. All are treated as coventurers, not as means to another's ends.

The literature repeatedly rejects an absolutist deontological prohibition on risk because the absolutist fails to account for the benefits created by some types of unconsented risks. Nozick allows that running a railroad may impose unconsented risks comparable to some version of unconsented Russian roulette, but distinguishable by the benefits, which sounds, no matter the hypothetical state-of-nature apparatus, as nonabsolutist.[6]

[6] ROBERT NOZICK, ANARCHY, STATE AND UTOPIA 74 (1974).

More recent writers recognize the same irresistible tug of consequentialist balancing.[7]

Approving any particular criminal justice system as morally permissible still depends on some criteria for comparing the (ordinary) weight of consequentialist advantages with the (extraordinary but not absolute) priority of rights. A nonabsolutist retributivist might, for example, accept Hansson's current proposed resolution: "Exposure of a person to a risk is acceptable if and only if this exposure is part of an equitable social system of risk-taking that works to her advantage."[8] Our social system is a very long way from "equitable."[9] Any justification for accepting the risk of errors in criminal justice must account for those inequities.[10] With that accounting, however, a retributivist can accept some risk of error in criminal procedure.[11]

Consider an analogy to government-provided emergency medical services. The emergency medical technicians (EMTs) will transport nonresponsive accident victims to the hospital despite the absence of expressed consent. In a few cases, the ambulance will be involved in another

[7] Christian Tarsney et al., *Moral Decision-Making Under Uncertainty*, STANFORD ENCYCLOPEDIA OF PHILOSOPHY ARCHIVE: SPRING 2024 EDITION (Mar. 13, 2024), https://plato.stanford.edu/archives/spr2024/entries/moral-decision-uncertainty/ ("The non-consequentialist, even the absolutist, cannot plausibly claim that any action that carries a *risk* of violating a constraint is impermissible. . . . [E]ven if it's possible to be certain that you aren't violating a constraint (e.g., by simply doing nothing at all), the demand for such certainty is clearly excessive. It's permissible to drive your friend to the airport even though this entails *some* risk of hitting and killing an innocent pedestrian."); David McCarthy, *Rights, Explanations and Risks*, 107 ETHICS 205, 210 (1997) (defending deontological rights against risks but only because "we should reject the idea that rights are absolute."); Sven Ove Hansson, *Ethical Criteria of Risk Assessment*, 59 ERKENNTNIS 291, 295 (2003) (rejecting "probabilistic absolutism" of rights and duties because "such a strict extension of rights and prohibitions is socially untenable.").

[8] Hansson, *supra* note 7, at 305.

[9] *See, e.g.*, MICHELLE ALEXANDER, THE NEW JIM CROW 103 (rev. ed. 2012) ("What is painfully obvious when one steps back from individual cases and specific policies is that the system of mass incarceration operates with stunning efficiency to sweep people of color off the streets, lock them in cages, and then release them into an inferior second-class status.").

[10] It is hard to see how abandoning retributivism proportionality as a limiting principle would *reduce* social inequities. *See* Marah Stith McLeod, *Preventing Undeserved Punishment*, 99 NOTRE DAME L. REV. 493, 521 (2023) ("Utilitarian justifications for punishment are also at least as likely to be skewed by racial stereotypes."); Matt Matravers, *Is Twenty-first Century Punishment Post-desert?*, *in* RETRIBUTIVISM HAS A PAST: HAS IT A FUTURE? 30, 42 (Michael Tonry ed. 2011) ("It may well be that the background conditions of distributive injustice, or the capricious nature of those who police (in the widest sense) the criminal justice system, mean that greater injustice would be done by departing from proportionality than by sticking with it.").

[11] Absolutists can reach a similar result by defining categorical rights backwards from exceptions that have beneficial consequences. An absolutist retributivist might reject a right against false conviction in favor of a right to meticulously fair procedures. *See* Heidi M. Hurd & Michael S. Moore, *The Ethical Implications of Proportioning Punishment to Deontological Desert*, 15 CRIM. L. & PHIL. 495, 510 (2021) ("Our mode of reconciling the text-like character of deontology with the demand of punishments propositional to desert *is* thus to give up the former so as to preserve the latter.") (emphasis in original) ("propositional" probably should be "proportional").

accident, potentially killing the patient. I doubt that even the most committed libertarian would condemn this risk without consent as a categorical bar to transporting unresponsive victims to a hospital. If, however, the government agency did nothing to prevent accidents—didn't require sirens, or speed limits, or special training for drivers—the intuitions of many, not just libertarians, might come out differently.

(3) Imperfectly Constrained Consequentialism

Mixed theorists who qualify a consequentialist general justify aim with fairness-based side constraints face the problem of maintaining the constraint against convicting the innocent. If that prohibition is absolute, the constraint becomes the general, but nonjustifying, aim, because any real system will make mistakes. If retributivists can justify fallible systems by such arguments as just discussed, mixed theorists can appropriate those same arguments. Mixed theories predicated on consequentialism, however, may have justifications for fallible systems even if retributivists do not.

To see this, we need to distinguish between two concepts of side constraints. Nozick defends the familiar absolutist view. According to that view, we must never violate another's rights without consent.[12] He poses the issue in the context of a "tradition which holds that stealing a penny or a pin or anything from someone violates his rights."[13] Carried that far, this approach has the strikingly ironic result of denying everyone the freedom to do much of anything.

Depending on the risk and its benefits, the just response might be prohibition, compensation for casualties ex post, or compensation for risks ex ante.[14] Each of those responses, however, requires an enforcement apparatus. Nozick recognizes a right against being injured on account of an unreliable procedure.[15] Nozick does not, however, admit that even the best procedure is not perfect; the difference between risks of unjust conviction will be a matter of degree.

Hart, who never used the term "side constraint," saw the qualifications on the general justifying aim in a different way. Today, we would characterize

[12] Nozick, *supra* note 6, at 33.
[13] *Id.* at 75.
[14] *Id.* at 75–76.
[15] *Id.* at 105.

Hart's view as recognizing side constraints as "exclusionary reasons." Hart did not use that term either (it was adopted later by Joseph Raz). Exclusionary reasons are not exclusive reasons, not categorical imperatives. They are, however, stronger than ordinary utilitarian reasons. Hart clearly expressed this sense of privileged reasons, limiting the pursuit of the general justifying aim.[16]

Ronald Dworkin offered a detailed version of such an imperfectly constrained mixed theory.[17] Dworkin argued generally that rights trump ordinary utilitarian considerations. So, the most plausible way to read his account of criminal procedure is as a delineation of the rights that trump the public interest in crime control. This implies, although Dworkin was, so far as I know, never explicit about it, that he held a mixed theory of punishment in which the general justifying aim was utilitarian but subject to rights-based side constraints.

Dworkin begins his discussion of procedural rights by asking: "Does it follow, from the fact that each citizen has a right not to be convicted if innocent, that he has a right to the most accurate procedures possible to test his guilt or innocence, no matter how expensive these procedures might be to the community as a whole?"[18] Dworkin gives a negative answer, but also denies that criminal procedure should be based solely on utilitarian cost-benefit considerations.

Dworkin claims that because even accidental convictions of the innocent inflict, in addition to the "bare harm" of the punishment, additional "moral harm," procedure should be designed with greater tolerance for false negatives than for false positives.[19] While the individual right against false conviction requires the state to express this differential tolerance in its procedures, there is no fixed formula for defining the balance between the costs of procedural safeguards and the risk that this individual right would be violated.

[16] *See* H. L. A. Hart, Punishment and Responsibility 13 (1968) (in "extreme cases many might still think it right to resort to these expedients [vicarious punishment of an offender's family] but we should do so with the sense of sacrificing an important principle. We should be conscious of choosing the lesser of two evils, and this would be inexplicable if the principle sacrificed to utility were itself only a requirement of utility."); *id.* at 10 ("Just because the pursuit of any single social aim always has its restrictive qualifier, our main social institutions always possess a plurality of features which can only be understood as a compromise between partly discrepant principles.").

[17] Ronald Dworkin, A Matter of Principle 72 (1985).

[18] *Id.* at 72.

[19] *Id.* at 80.

Instead, Dworkin says that ordinary politics can be trusted to work this balance out, provided that the procedures adopted are the same for everyone accused. Only in this way, he says, can the state show all its citizens equal concern and respect.

Dworkin, it turns out, doesn't believe that you have a right against false conviction. He means that you have the right to procedures biased against false convictions to some unspecified degree, as long as you have the same access to these procedural safeguards as the social elite.[20] If you are innocent but mistakenly convicted by such procedures, you have no right not to be punished. What gives the state's officials the right to punish you is not your factual guilt but an acceptable process that concludes you are guilty.[21]

Now this is not a utilitarian account, because the procedures required by the minimize-false-convictions priority may cause more harm than they prevent. Such a position is consistent with constrained-utilitarian mixed theories. Its consistency with thorough-going deontology is another question. But it is at least possible that a retributive side constraint requiring minimization of false convictions might be consistent with the operation of fallible systems when retributive theories themselves are not.

On one point, Dworkin is clearly right. The legal rights we have in the criminal process run against the government. The question isn't whether a false conviction injures the accused; it certainly does. The question for the design of the legal system is whether the government has wronged the accused in the process that leads to the miscarriage.

B. The Moral Equivalence of Erroneous Judgments and Erroneous Punishments

If excessive punishment is morally equivalent to punishing the innocent, and retributivists can justify systems that run the risk of convicting the innocent,

[20] *Id.* at 92:

> people drawn into the criminal process do not have a right to the most accurate possible procedures . . . But they do have two other genuine rights: the right to procedures that put a proper valuation on moral harm in the calculations that fix the risk of injustice . . . and the related and practically more important right to equal treatment with respect to that evaluation.

[21] I bracket the painful question of whether an innocent person is morally justified in escape, or whether another person with percipient knowledge of the defendant's innocence, such as an alibi witness whose truthful testimony was not believed, is morally justified in assisting the escape.

it follows that retributivists can justify systems that run the risk of excessive punishment of the guilty. In what follows, I defend this moral equivalence.

In all versions of retributivism, there is some just punishment sufficient to satisfy the offender's negative desert. Past that, there is no desert-based justification for additional punishment. And retributivism forbids unjustified punishment.

In a widely quoted passage, Hegel says that the application of general law to particular cases leaves "room for considerable uncertainty. But fluctuations of opinion must be cut short, and a conclusion reached. Hence, inside of this limit a decision has the character of accident and caprice."[22] He then applies this notion of lawlessness-within-law to the problem of proportionate punishment:

> To whittle the universal down not only to the particular but to the individual case is the chief function of the purely positive in law. It cannot, for example, be determined by reason, or decided by any phase of the conception itself, whether forty lashes or thirty-nine, a fine of four dollars or three dollars and nine-nine cents, imprisonment for a year or three hundred and sixty-four or three hundred and sixty-six days, be the just punishment for a crime. And yet a lash, a cent, or a day too much or too little is an injustice.[23]

Readers of Hegel continue to disagree about his precise views on crime and punishment.[24] Whatever his precise views, this passage nicely captures how the problematic nature of proportionality presents retributivists with the same challenge as the problem of false convictions.

We cannot distinguish the risk of false conviction from the risk of excessive punishment by reference to the consequences for unlucky individuals. Say the police plant drugs on an innocent person, and the prosecutor and the jury believe the police. However, the judge has some doubts and imposes a sentence of probation. The probation conditions are burdensome and unjust.

[22] G. W. F. Hegel, Philosophy of Right 113 (Dover ed., S.W. Dyde trans., 2005).

[23] *Id.*

[24] *See, e.g.*, Thom Brooks, *Hegel on Crime and Punishment*, *in* Hegel's Political Philosophy: On the Normative Significance of Method and System 219–20 (Thom Brooks & Sebastian Stein eds., 2017) (challenging "consensus view" that "Hegel was a retributivist."). I know too little of Hegel to situate any particular passage in his comprehensive system. I quote him here for an intuition shared far more widely than his philosophy generally.

Compare, however, the case of a dealer who sells to an undercover officer and is promptly arrested. The (true) drug-dealing charge would ordinarily lead to a sentence of sixteen months in jail. If, however, the officer plants *a gun* on the (guilty) drug dealer, the sentence for the drug conviction balloons to sixty months. Both defendants have been treated unjustly, but it seems like the second case is a worse violation of rights than the first.[25]

One might say that trials are about binary verdicts dictated by historical facts, and sentencing is about scalar judgments informed by norms as well as by facts. This distinction is not tenable. Consider a homicide case where the defendant claims self-defense. Let's say that in this jurisdiction, the jury has three options: murder (punished by twenty-five to life), manslaughter (punished by fifteen to twenty-five), or not guilty by reason of self-defense.

Self-defense is justified when the defendant honestly and *reasonably* believes he must kill or be killed. Manslaughter is an unjustified killing where a reasonable person might have been provoked into a deadly rage, or subject to extreme mental or emotional disturbance for which there is "*reasonable* explanation or excuse." The jury's verdict may be based on norms as well as facts. It may also delineate not just the existence of liability but the severity of the punishment to be inflicted.

Indeed, it is quite common for trial verdicts to turn on disputed normative judgments, or to settle the grade of an offense rather than the existence of liability *vel non*. Negligent driving causing death is a tort; gross negligence is a serious crime. Possession of drugs is a crime, but possession with intent to distribute is a much more serious crime.

Take one more illustrative hypothetical. The defendant committed a minor felony, let's say low-level drug dealing. The defendant is sentenced to a three-year term, suspended on the condition of completing probation. The defendant, however, refuses to incriminate others. This refusal vexes the police, who now plant drugs on the defendant and arrest him for this new but fictitious drug offense. Does it make any difference whether the prosecutor proceeds to seek revocation of the probation, triggering imposition of the carceral sentence for the genuine drug offense or instead initiates a new but bogus felony charge which can be expected to end in imposition of an executed three-year sentence? Not, I think, to the defendant.

[25] For a similar example, see Christopher Lewis, *Risk-Based Sentencing and the Principles of Punishment*, 112 J. Crim. L. & Criminology 213, 252 (2022).

C. Skepticism about Error Bias

Retributivists and mixed theorists may not all agree with the precise ratio endorsed by Blackstone, that "it is better that ten guilty persons escape than that one innocent suffer."[26] These mainstream theorists, however, generally agree that criminal procedure should bias the distribution of errors against false positives. While the bias against false positives is generally accepted among scholars and is reflected in prevailing doctrine such as the reasonable-doubt standard, agreement is not unanimous.

Larry Laudan and Ron Allen maintain that minimizing false convictions short-changes public safety.[27] William Stuntz famously argued that systemic responses to pro-defense procedures actually promote harsher sentences and coercive trial penalties.[28] Dan Epps points out that if this is true, even innocent defendants may face coercive trial penalties and draconian sentences.[29]

These are substantial positions defended by substantial scholars. They are also vigorously challenged, even in the context of trial procedures.[30] My point here is not to revisit these debates but to distinguish sentencing discretion from trial verdicts and guilty pleas.

It may be true that optimal deterrence calls for penalties harsher than those consistent with retributive desert, or that failing to imprison felons causes a significant number of serious crimes. It by no means follows that sentencing discretion should be exercised by prosecutors rather than by judges. We begin with the crime-control critique and then turn to the systemic critique.

The premise of the crime-control critique is that pro-defense procedures prevent many justified convictions. That premise is absent in the sentencing context. Procedures at sentencing are not biased against the prosecution,

[26] 4 William Blackstone, Commentaries *353.

[27] Ronald J. Allen & Larry Laudan, *Deadly Dilemmas*, 41 Tex. Tech. L. Rev. 65 (2008); Larry Laudan, Truth, Error, and Criminal Law: An Essay in Legal Epistemology (2006).

[28] William J. Stuntz, The Collapse of American Criminal Justice 242 (2011) ("if the Justices did not cause the backlash, they made a large contribution to it.").

[29] Daniel Epps, *The Consequences of Error in Criminal Justice*, 128 Harv. L. Rev. 1065, 1110–15 (2015).

[30] Laudan and Allen assume a strong relationship between trial procedures and crime rates, when empirical evidence shows no such robust relationship. *See, e.g.*, Marvin Zalman, *The Anti-Blackstonians*, 48 Seton H. L. Rev. 1319, 1373–82 (2018). Stuntz's hypothesis, accepted by Epps, that pro-defense court rulings contribute to harsher sentencing practices is not implausible, but fails to explain the timing of the punitive turn or the uniformity of the punitive turn across jurisdictions. Stephen Schulhofer, *Criminal Justice, Local Democracy, and Constitutional Rights*, 111 Mich. L. Rev. 1045, 1075–76 (2013); Donald A. Dripps, *Does Liberal Procedure Cause Punitive Substance? Preliminary Evidence From Some Natural Experiments*, 87 S. Calif. L. Rev. 459, 472, 473, 492–93 (2014).

unlike those at trial. The judge resolves factual disputes under the preponderance standard, without a jury, without the hearsay rule, and without the constitutional exclusionary rules.[31]

Empirical evidence suggests that the deterrent influence of punishment depends more on certainty than on severity.[32] Even if more severe sentences are sometimes justified by their deterrent effect, prosecutors should not be trusted to say when this is the case. Depending on prosecutorial discretion, the punishment for criminal acts ranges from zero to the sum of the mandatory sentences provided by the code. Prosecutorial sentencing creates uncertainties that are inimical to deterrence.

The incentives created by prosecutorial sentencing are likely to be perverse rather than merely random. To the extent that savvy criminals know the system, their rational response to prosecutorial sentencing is to amass as much stock as possible to trade for a favorable deal in case they get caught. That means rising in the gang hierarchy rather than getting out of it.

As for incapacitation, even one who accepts the contested case for predictive restraint has no reason to think that prosecutors are better at predicting than judges or corrections professionals. Prosecutorial sentencing skews toward punishing the refusal to plead guilty, and toward rewarding assistance with ongoing investigations. What reason is there to think that defendants who refuse to plead guilty pose higher risks of reoffending than the gang bosses who benefit from cooperation deals?

As for the systemic critique, even if it is well-founded, it is misdirected at sentencing. Indeed, mandatory minimums exemplify the draconian legislation the skeptics attribute to backlash. Professor Stuntz, in fact, regarded judicial sentencing discretion after *Booker* as "a useful model for a kind of sentencing law that might push prison populations down rather than up."[33]

For innocent suspects, as long as prosecutors control trial penalties, shifting to a preponderance standard at criminal trials would be a catastrophe. A defendant must be bold or irrational to run the risk of prevailing

[31] *See, e.g.*, Brandon L. Garrett, *Accuracy in Sentencing*, 87 S. Calif. L. Rev. 499, 516–17 (2014); Brian Beaton, *Mistaking a Backdoor for No Door at All: Sentencing and the Exclusionary Rule*, 16 Harv. L. & Pol'y Rev. 217, 222 (2021).

[32] *See, e.g.*, Michael Tonry, *Learning From the Limitations of Deterrence Research*, 37 Crime & Just. 279, 280 (2008) ("There is some evidence, as Beccaria and Bentham believed, that certainty and promptness of punishment are more important than severity. Because there are differences in order of magnitude in the abilities of police and courts to alter the promptness of their behavior or affect would-be offenders' perceptions of risk, changes in police practices are more likely to achieve deterrent effects than are changes in sentencing policies and practices.").

[33] Stuntz, *supra* note 28, at 258.

trial penalties *even under the reasonable doubt standard.* Changing the standard of proof at trial without changing trial penalties would mean that fewer cases would survive motions to dismiss. Defendants who lost these motions would face the choice of pleading guilty or standing trial by juries instructed to convict on 51 percent to 49 percent confidence in guilt. Even innocent defendants with plausible defenses would be irrational to bet ten years of prison time on the decision of a jury following a preponderance-of-the-evidence instruction.

The previous section argued that punishment in excess of desert is morally equivalent to convicting the innocent. To the extent that skepticism about the Blackstone principle is persuasive, the case for biasing sentencing procedure in favor of shorter and against longer sentences is stronger than the case for biasing liability decisions against false convictions.

9
Proportionate Punishment as Procedural Justice

A. The Contingent Quality of Procedural Justice

Retributivists and mixed theorists, as we have seen, have plausible justifications for fallible criminal justice systems. If Chapter 8's claim that false convictions are morally equivalent to excessive sentences is correct, we can transpose justifications for fallible systems to the sentencing process. For example, retributivists who endorse double-effect arguments can meet Hegel's lash-counting problem by saying that if the judge mistakenly imposes forty lashes rather than the just sentence of thirty-nine, officials, including the judge, intend only the thirty-nine, even though they foresee that forty might be too many.

Even those who endorse the doctrine of double effect (DDE) in principle may not be satisfied by crocodile tears. If officials say, "[W]e don't intend to convict the innocent," or "we don't intend to inflict disproportionate punishments," they are not to be taken at their words without concrete demonstrations of good faith. Meticulously fair procedures are just such a concrete demonstration of good faith.

Likewise, the gains from a criminal justice system defeat deontological rights against risks, at least under certain conditions. Hansson's formulation of those conditions may not be perfect, but it captures very widespread intuitions about why officials acting in good faith do no wrong when they operate a fallible system. Meticulously fair procedures are essential to "an equitable social *system*" of risk-taking "that works to the advantage of all."[1]

One might also justify the existence of a system on utilitarian grounds, but qualify that justification by recognizing differences among persons in the risks of both factual error and excessive punishment. The benefits of the

[1] Sven Ove Hansson, *Ethical Criteria of Risk Acceptance*, 59 Erkenntnis 291, 305 (2003) (emphasis added).

Sentencing Discretion and the Constitution. Donald A. Dripps, Oxford University Press.
 DOI: 10.1093/9780197830390.003.0009

system are great, but are diffused among everyone. Those benefits, moreover, are not much reduced (if at all) by marginal changes in procedure to bias the process against false positives, whether by verdict or sentence. The costs of error are concentrated on unlucky individuals who are falsely convicted or punished excessively. Meticulously fair procedures reduce the risk that individuals will suffer catastrophic harm for the sake of the general welfare. As Dworkin points out, that doesn't mean doing everything possible, whatever the cost, to prevent injustices. It does mean, as he says, taking special account of the distribution, not just the quantity, of the harms inflicted by injustice.

Each justification of a system is contingent on the system taking steps beyond those dictated by costs and benefits to reduce the risk of false positives. Just what more is required is a difficult question.[2] We do not, however, ask that question so much in the abstract as at the margins of the present system. Even without a clear metric for superadding utility-reducing procedural safeguards to the criminal process, we can draw some strong conclusions about those practical questions. The system should add low-cost procedural safeguards that significantly reduce the risk of error. Failing to do so treats the offender as a means to be used, not as a person due punishment only as deserved.

Our procedure for establishing factual guilt is not infallible. This should come as no surprise when we remember the ubiquity of errors in other contexts. Even NASA cannot claim to safely return 99 percent of those who fly in space.[3] There are many exonerations, including many cases where the innocent accused pleaded guilty. The best guesstimate we have, however, comes from a survey of prison inmates, 6 percent of whom said they were convicted for crimes they didn't commit.[4] A retrospective study of DNA exclusions in Virginia came to a comparable estimate.[5] Some may have

[2] Dworkin's equal-access-to-procedural-safeguards approach depends either on public support for defense lawyers, investigators, and expert witnesses that matches what the wealthiest defendants can pay, or on limiting what the wealthy can spend to protect themselves from prosecutions that may be groundless. *Cf.* David Resnick, *Due Process and Procedural Justice*, 18 NOMOS 206, 226 (1977) ("If justice ought not to be for sale to the highest bidder, it would seem to follow that we ought to abolish the private practice of criminal law as we know it; [it] . . . not only provides less than equal justice for the poor, it provides more than equal justice for the rich.").

[3] *U.S. Human Space Flight Safety Record (As of 18 Dec. 2020)*, Fed. Aviation Admin., https://www.faa.gov/about/office_org/headquarters_offices/ast/regulations/media/HSF_Safety_Record_Data_with_footnotes_Final.pdf [https://perma.cc/9MEZ-2URE].

[4] Charles E. Loeffler et al., *Measuring Self-Reported Wrongful Convictions Among Prisoners*, 35 J. Quantitative Criminology 259 (2019).

[5] John Roman et al., Post-Conviction DNA Testing and Wrongful Conviction 6 (2012) (finding that "in Virginia Cases resulting in a convicted offender between 1973 and 1987 where

deluded themselves or lied on the survey, but it does set an estimate of the upper bound.[6]

By contrast, in our system, excessive punishment is far more common and may even be normal. Compared to practice in European nations, or in the United States before the 1980s, typical felony sentences are substantially more severe than those elsewhere, or hitherto, thought sufficient for the interests of justice.

B. Procedural Justice—Rawls's Taxonomy

John Rawls distinguished pure from impure procedural justice, and then perfect impure procedural justice from perfect impure procedural justice.[7] Pure procedural justice characterizes the definition of the correct result in terms of the outcome of a specified procedure. Gambling, says Rawls, is a case of this type.[8] If a rule provides that the team to have the ball first will be decided by a coin flip, the result of the coin toss is the right result, whether it comes up heads or tails, whether the toss was called by the home team or by the visitors.

Impure procedural justice characterizes the opposite situation, where the criteria of the right decision are prior to the procedure. The procedure then is instrumental, designed to reach a described outcome in particular cases. Rawls then distinguishes perfect impure procedural justice as a procedure that is practically certain to produce the desired result. Rawls gives the example of dividing a cake by appointing the last person to choose a slice as the cake cutter.[9]

More commonly, impure procedural justice is imperfect. "The characteristic mark of imperfect procedural justice is that while there is an independent criterion for the correct outcome, there is no feasible procedure

evidence was retained in an unbiased sample of 715 homicides and sexual assault convictions," the convicted offender is eliminated aa a "contributor for a probative evidence item, and that elimination is supportive of exoneration, in 5 percent [n=38] of convictions.").

[6] For the low estimate in the literature, see Paul Cassell, *Overstating America's Wrongful Conviction Rate? Reassessing the Conventional Wisdom About the Prevalence of Wrongful Convictions*, 60 Ariz. L. Rev. 815 (2018) (deriving a less-than-1-percent estimate based on estimates of the different rates of false conviction in trial cases and plea cases).

[7] John Rawls, A Theory of Justice 83–86 (1971).

[8] *Id.* at 86.

[9] *Id.* at 85.

which is sure to lead to it."[10] He cites criminal trials as an example of imperfect impure procedural justice.[11]

Rawls here is categorizing different relationships between procedures and outcomes to set up his famous veil-of-ignorance account of justice as fairness. He acknowledges the criminal trial as a species of impure and imperfect procedural justice but says nothing further about what conditions must be met for the outcome of a trial to be treated as authoritative. As with DDE arguments, an impure procedure might be imperfect, but irreducibly imperfect; that is, there is no way to reduce the likelihood of errors. It is also possible that a procedure might have room for improvement, but still makes errors extremely unlikely.

Rawls assumes that trials are solely about factual guilt and that this criterion is stipulated prior to trial. He does not consider the possibility of a procedure defined by reference to some normative criterion, such as the law's common direction to the jury to determine how a reasonable person would have behaved in similar circumstances. That is yet a fourth species of procedural justice—impure constructive procedural justice, where the procedure is designed to apply a general normative standard about which reasonable decision makers are likely to disagree even on undisputed facts. The criterion of decision is known ex ante, but defined in such a way that the decision turns on moral rather than historical judgment. Some potential decisions are clearly wrong, but there will be no consensus on the precisely right answer in each case.

C. Constructive Procedural Justice

Let's illustrate constructive procedural justice with an example almost as humble as Rawls's cake cutting. Suppose the coach sets the rules for a school's athletic team. The coach's rules include such things as being on time for practice, not cutting classes, keeping your grades above 2.7, not drinking alcohol during the season, observing a midnight curfew, and so on. The coach also sets a range of penalties for infractions.

The penalties include (1) morning laps; that is, running quarter-mile laps, early in the morning before first classes, no more than eight per

[10] *Id.* at 86.
[11] *Id.*

morning but with no limit on the number of mornings; (2) loss of playing time, measured in quarters of games, up to four quarters; and (3) suspension for a period of games. The coach's rules, however, provide that once the coach has determined that a player has violated a team rule, the penalty will be determined by the senior players (excluding a guilty senior player). The seniors are to select the penalty that "will be fair both to the team and the player." If the seniors are not unanimous, a simple majority suffices. If they are evenly divided, the lesser penalty will be imposed. The seniors, however, can only recommend the most serious penalty—a suspension—to the coach, along with a lesser penalty to be imposed if the coach rejects a suspension.

Now suppose that the coach has found a star player—a gifted but unpopular sophomore—to have been late for one practice by six minutes and to have missed another practice altogether. The seniors must now deliberate on the penalty. Consider some of the issues they might face:

(1) Biased tribunal—one of the seniors has lost almost all playing time to the delinquent and has made no secret of being unhappy about it.

(2) Desert-irrelevant consequences: there is only one game left in the regular season. A win in the next game means making the playoffs; a loss means missing them. Punishing the delinquent with reduced playing time—even if this did not, as it might, cause the delinquent to quit the team—would significantly reduce the team's chance of winning.

(3) Extrinsic good or bad conduct or character:

3.1. The delinquent is a talented but lazy and self-centered athlete, who is realizing far less of potential than any other player (but still better by far than any other);

3.2. The delinquent has been playing well all season, despite a painful injury.

(4) Extenuating circumstances: the delinquent's grandmother passed away a few days before the missed practice.

(5) Unwritten custom: The seniors know that in the past, the usual penalty for being late for practice has been one morning lap per minute late; and that the penalty for missing practice altogether has been eight laps and a one-quarter loss of playing time.

(6) Subjective experience of punishment: the delinquent's great passion in life is playing in games; the delinquent routinely rises early to run four miles (sixteen laps).

There is no rule or even standard about how these factors should influence the outcome in this case. Whatever the seniors do in each variation, they will be making normative judgments unconstrained and indeed unaided by the opaque directive to be fair to the player and to the team. This is constructive procedural justice. There is, in theory, a just outcome, but the tribunal is directed to determine on its own just what that just outcome is.

Suppose the seniors meet, and, with the delinquent's jealous rival participating, agree on a penalty of twenty-two laps over three mornings but no loss of playing time. They say that in their view, the loss of a quarter of playing time would be just, but it prejudices the team's chances of success. So instead of any loss of playing time, they doubled the customary number of laps for the missed practice.

In this scenario, the procedure was unfair because the biased rival participated in the decision. The result, however, is the same as if the jealous rival had not participated, because the penalty does not reduce the delinquent's playing time (the result that would benefit the rival).

Suppose, by contrast, the seniors meet, the jealous rival again participating, and impose a loss of three-quarters of playing time but no laps. The explanation is that the delinquent, who runs every morning anyway, wouldn't suffer from running laps. Ergo, there is no true punishment in requiring laps for either the missed practice *or the late practice.* Since the only meaningful punishment is lost playing time, the seniors impose two quarters of lost time for the missed practice and one quarter for the late practice.

Again, the process is unfair because of the biased rival's participation. Here, however, the sentence is just what the jealous rival wants. There is, therefore, an unfair procedure that may have led to a more severe sentence than was just. The sentence is disproportionate because it is more severe than the one that might have been imposed after fair (and low-cost) procedures. Note that while the in-the-eyes-of-God just sentence is unknowable, the output of a better process is easily accessible—exclude the biased player and see what the fairly constituted tribunal decides.

In our final variation, the biased rival is excluded from participating in the decision. The rest of the seniors convene and divide into groups subscribing to two somewhat different positions. The majority believes that although the morning laps are less onerous for a regular runner than for some other player, they are still unpleasant. The majority also believes that even though the laps are less onerous for this offender than for others, no deterrence will be lost by imposing the customary penalty, including both laps and lost playing time. Potential *future* offenders are not likely to enjoy running laps at the crack of dawn!

The majority also concludes that the benefits of the delinquent's playing time to the team call for remitting the usual two quarters of lost time to one quarter. Given that very few players miss even one minute of practice, the majority concludes that the customary penalty is harsher than necessary and if their decision changes the team's customs going forward, that's a feature, not a bug.

A substantial minority believes that there should be no disparity in punishment to improve the team's chances in a game. They therefore would impose the customary penalty, and they certainly would not reduce it because it seems to have been a practical success. The minority, however, believes the difficult circumstances of the missed practice count as substantial mitigation. They would not impose any loss of playing time, provided the delinquent is not even a minute late to any of the practices remaining before the big game. If, however, the delinquent is tardy again, no matter how slightly, they would then impose the full two-quarter loss of playing time.

Would the offender have just cause to complain about the imposition of the majority's penalty? The offender has been sentenced by the collective decision of a neutral body, based on factors many reasonable people regard as properly considered in proportioning penalty to offense. If the minority had prevailed, their going rate for the laps and suspended sentence for the playing time could claim the same justification.

How can two quite different penalties, one generally based on utility and the other on fairness, both be justified? What about other players, past and future, who will receive greater or lesser penalties for comparable delicts? The answer is that all offenders have received the same punishment, which is to be sentenced by a fair procedure.

As applied to criminal justice, constructive proportionality means that the output of the criminal process should be treated as proportionate sentences, *provided* that the government has observed meticulously fair procedures. Leaving aside exotic cases of self-imposed disability, *ought* implies *can*. The offender's right is not to a specific penalty dictated by a single and precise theory of justified punishment. The offender's right runs against the government, not against the universe.

The best characterization of the right against disproportionate severity is that the offender has the right to have official discretion over punishment exercised pursuant to meticulously fair procedures. The range of punishments will be set by the felt necessities of place and time, and relative rather than universal, just to that extent. The right to fair procedures for determining liberty or confinement can claim something at least close to social and temporal universality.

D. Constructive Procedural Justice versus Arbitrary Discretion

Centuries ago, Coke took from Littleton the maxim "*discretio est discernere per legem, qui sit justum*" (discretion is the selection of what is just by law). The exercise of judicial discretion "is, to discern by the right line of law, and not by the crooked cord of private opinion, which the vulgar call discretion."[12] This was the sort of mystification Bentham abominated. Judge-made law left the people ignorant of the law until they broke it: "When your dog does any thing you want to break him of, you wait till he does it, and then beat him for it. This is the way you make laws for your dog: and this is the way the Judges make law for you and me."[13] Mysterious legal technicalities served as a smoke screen to disguise the manipulation of the legal system by the elite social classes and the legal profession, a/k/a "Judge and Co."[14]

Yet when it came to sentencing criminals, Bentham himself could do no better than leave the punishment of most offenses to the "discretion of the tribunal." So how was the tension between legality and discretion to be mediated? In his *Specimen of a Penal* Code,[15] Bentham outlined a comprehensive code but gave only one illustrative example. "Simple personal injury" was defined, when perpetrated by commission as distinct from omission, causing "without lawful cause, or contributed to cause, a corporal pain, either light or weighty, which is not followed by any ulterior corporal evil." This would cover today's battery offenses, but include "aggravated battery" under the same head as "simple battery."

The punishments prescribed were fines, "At the discretion of the tribunal," imprisonment, "At the option and discretion of the tribunal," security for good conduct at "option and discretion," and in "very grave cases,"

[12] II First Institute 125 (J. H. Thomas ed. 1827) (1628).

[13] Jeremy Bentham, *Truth vs. Ashhurst*, *in* 5 The Works of Jeremy Bentham 231, 235 (J. Bowring ed., Edinburgh, William Tait, 1843).

[14] *See, e.g.*, Bentham, *Scotch Reform*, *in* 5 Works at 1, 3–16.

[15] Bentham, *Specimen of Penal Code*, *in* 5 Works at 164.

banishment "from the presence of the party injured, for a time or for ever. This also at option and discretion." The sentencing judge was thus required to impose some fine, however minimal, and was permitted to impose imprisonment without a set upper limit. Initially, this looks like legality has surrendered to discretion, but there is much more to be said.

First, note that Bentham vests sentencing discretion in "the tribunal," not in the party injured or any public prosecutor. Second, in *Specimen,* Bentham identified fifteen specific circumstances of aggravation, and two (provocation and excessive defensive force) of extenuation.[16] So it seems that an impartial tribunal was to exercise a discretion guided by exclusionary reasons identified ex ante by the legislature.

How to prevent the tribunal from abusing its discretion? For Bentham, the ultimate check was always publicity and democracy.[17] But we can glean a sense of the more immediate checks he had in mind from the *Constitutional Code.* Judges were required to make an oath-like undertaking abjuring partiality, venality, and neglect, and to affect the will of the legislature.[18] There was to be an inferior judicatory and an appellate one, so that the lower court would fear reversal.[19]

Judges were to be appointed by a Justice Minister.[20] The Justice Minister was to be appointed directly by the legislature, while other ministers by the Prime Minister, the chief executive.[21] Judges served for life, but were removable ("dislocatable") by the Justice Minister.[22] Officials generally could be removed only for a "justification cause" after a formal hearing at which evidence was taken.[23] In his discussion of life tenure, Bentham makes clear that the removal of judges was possible without a trial-type impeachment procedure.[24] He does not, however, clearly specify the grounds for removal.

So Bentham saw discretion as desirable in some situations, but he wanted discretion to be exercised pursuant to legislative guidance, by judges who did not stand for election, were neutral as to the parties, and were subject in the

16 *See id.* at 164–65.

17 *See, e.g.,* Bentham, *Constitutional Code, in* 1 WORKS at 158 ("To the pernicious exercise of power by the government it [public opinion] is the only check; to the beneficial, an indispensable supplement.").

18 *Id.* at 1, 533.

19 *Id.*, ch. XXII, at 585. *See also* Bentham, *Principles of Judicial Procedure, in* 2 WORKS at 1, 165.

20 Bentham, *supra* note 17, at 529.

21 *Id.* at 608–10.

22 *Id.* at 532.

23 *Id.* at 310–11. The only exceptions were for military officers.

24 *Id.* at 522–23.

first instance to appellate review. The end of the adjective law aims at is not whatever outcome the judge deems just but an outcome that is just according to exclusionary, albeit general, criteria applied impartially.

Even a statutory delegation to decide cases in the tribunal's "sole, plenary and unreviewable discretion" would not provide a defense to a bribery charge, or protect the judges from discipline for ethical violations such as conflicts of interest or ex parte communications. Every assignment of discretion assumes some background substantive norms, according to which at least some judicial choices are not just eccentric but erroneous.

In the United States, there is no doctrinally orthodox theory of punishment. A judge assigned discretion reasonably might consult retributive or consequentialist theories, or both. But a judge who imposed a discretionary sentence with an opinion stating "I am giving the max to D not because D is more blameworthy, or more dangerous, or a better deterrent example than other defendants, but because today is Wednesday and I'm always grumpy on Hump Day" would be, according to the view I am defending, doing something contrary to the authorizing statute. Likewise, a judge assigned discretion who automatically approved the prosecutor's (or the defendant's) recommendation would be transferring authority to a partisan.

This bounded view of discretion has at least one nonobvious but very important implication. One fear of judicial discretion is that eccentric judges may impose sentences much lower or much higher than the norm. Some criminals would suffer less, and others more, than deserved. Observers would be troubled by apparently arbitrary disparities.

Yet just as in Bentham's model, sentences based on reasoned application of general guidelines to particular facts can be reviewed on appeal. Appellate courts routinely apply the "abuse of discretion" standard of review. If there are concerns about undue lenience, undue severity, or disparity, the right of both prosecution and defense to challenge a sentence on appeal provides a powerful response.[25]

Now, those familiar with the modern US system might see this as very much a model for sentencing under advisory guidelines. This resemblance is genuine,

[25] *See* Arie Freiberg, *Prosecution Appeal Against Sentences*, Oxford Research Encyclopedia of Criminology 16 (2019), https://doi.org/10.1093/acrefore/9780190264079.013.649 ("If there has been an error, either in favor of the prosecution or the defendant, and the sentencing discretion has miscarried, that error should be corrected by an appellate court in a manner that treats both parties equally.").

but only after an executive selection of the offenses to be charged—a selection that looks far more like "dog law" than discretion.

E. The Indispensable Requirement of a Neutral Tribunal

If fair procedure is the test of proportionate punishment, just what does "fair procedure" mean? In a classic exposition, Judge Henry Friendly describes the range of individual interests at stake and the menu of procedural safeguards in order of their importance to fairness.[26] The most important individual interests call for the most painstaking procedures. Friendly ranked "an unbiased tribunal" as the first requirement of fair procedure, "a necessary element in every case where a hearing is required."[27] Friendly ranked deprivation of personal liberty as the "harshest action the state can take against the individual through the administrative process."[28] Capital cases excepted, it is also the harshest sanction imposed by the criminal process.

Fair procedure, of course, includes other elements. In the leading treatment of procedural justice in civil litigation, Professor Solum criticizes the justice system for trivializing personal participation in the process.[29] Transposed to the criminal process, that concern for participation seems misplaced. True, the actual processing of criminal cases resembles an assembly line. Nonetheless, all the key decisions made by the defense are the defendant's personal decisions.[30]

The criminal process revolves around the principle that the defendant personally must choose to plead guilty or stand trial.[31] If the accused elects trial, the accused attends personally and decides whether to testify.[32] If

[26] Henry J. Friendly, *Some Kind of Hearing*, 123 U. PA. L. REV. 1267 (1975).

[27] *Id.* at 1279.

[28] *Id.* at 1296.

[29] Lawrence B. Solum, *Procedural Justice*, 78 S. CALIF. L. REV. 181, 315 (2004).

[30] *See* Jones v. Barnes, 463 U.S. 745, 751 (1983) ("It is also recognized that the accused has the ultimate authority to make certain fundamental decisions regarding the case, as to whether to plead guilty, waive a jury, testify in his or her own behalf, or take an appeal.") (citations omitted).

[31] *Cf.* Gabriel J. Chin, *Pleading Guilty Without Client Consent*, 57 WM. & MARY L. REV. 1309 (2016) (recognizing, at 1315, that under *Barnes* "whether to plead guilty" is a decision under "the client's exclusive authority," but, at 1318, "tentatively" proposing "a legitimate and fair workaround in 'situations where there is overwhelming evidence of guilt and no defense' yet the client is unable to plead guilty.") (footnote omitted).

[32] *See, e.g.*, MODEL RULES OF PRO. CONDUCT r. 1.2 (AM. BAR ASS'N 1983) ("A lawyer shall abide by a client's decision whether to settle a matter. In a criminal case, the lawyer shall abide by the client's decision, after consultation with the lawyer, as to a plea to be entered, whether to waive jury trial and whether the client will testify.").

the accused elects to plead, the accused must personally hear the judge's admonitions and acknowledge guilt.[33]

Now Solum takes for granted a neutral tribunal, an assumption that makes sense in the civil context. It does not make sense in the criminal context. It seems odd that the criminal process should be long on the luxury item of personal participation and short on the essential requirement of official neutrality. Yet this is precisely the case.

[33] *See, e.g.*, Fed. R. Crim. P. 11(b)(1).

10
Implications

A. Vindicating the Procedural Baseline

Three steps determine the sentence imposed on an offender. The first step is code creation, the definition of offenses, and the specification of maximum and minimum penalties for each offense. The second step is charge selection, the choice of the particular offenses within the code maximum for which the defendant will be held responsible. Assuming a conviction, the third step is sentence selection, the choice of the precise penalty within the statutory range for each offense of conviction.

We are accustomed to thinking of code creation, charge selection, and sentence selection as, respectively, legislative, executive, and judicial responsibilities. Legislatures best reflect the polity's values. The executive knows best the available evidence, resource constraints, and the value of cooperation. Judges are familiar with how similar cases are treated, and essentially neutral in assessing where within a statutory range a given case belongs.

As we have seen, however, the combination of codes containing multiple overlapping offenses providing different penalty ranges for typical criminal conduct effectively abdicates the legislature's role as the voice of the community. Charge selection becomes the law, and is itself practically lawless (the pass given to marijuana legalization in the states is only the most blatant example).

The practical advantages of this sweeping delegation are probably too powerful to be reversed. In strict logic, the code as a whole falls afoul of the void-for-vagueness doctrine. There are, however, no plausible judicial remedies. No court is going to hold the entire criminal law void for vagueness, or that Congress must define lesser and greater offenses with no overlap.

So focus on the second and third steps, in reverse order. I will focus on federal sentencing for purposes of illustration. There are, of course, many variations in the states.

After conviction, the discretion delegated to the judge is confined to the statutory range and, within that range, is advised by detailed sentencing

Sentencing Discretion and the Constitution. Donald A. Dripps, Oxford University Press.
 DOI: 10.1093/9780197830390.003.0010

guidelines. Most convictions follow pleas, but even without a trial on the issue of guilt, there is a reliable process for finding the facts in each case. A corrections officer prepares a pre-sentence report.[1] Both parties have the right to challenge the report's findings,[2] and, if needed, to call witnesses at a hearing.[3] The defendant has the right to counsel,[4] and both sides have the right to appeal.[5] There is little criticism of the federal sentencing *process*, as distinct from the severity of the sentences that process produces.

Now those ranges are properly a legislative concern. The legislature, however, has passed that buck to the executive. Prosecutorial discretion, not legislation, defines the range of judicial sentencing discretion.

Truly mandatory penalties are imaginable. A statute might provide a single penalty (e.g., sixty months' imprisonment) for a specific offense (e.g., armed robbery). To make the sentence truly mandatory, however, the legislature would need to impose on the court an obligation to vacate any guilty plea or guilty verdict if the pre-sentence report shows conduct covered by the one-penalty statute. The prosecutor could bring a charge under the one-penalty statute, or nothing. Now that kind of statute would be a legislative *decision* about culpability rather than a delegation of sentencing power to the executive. To typical legislators, that's unthinkable—or at least, thus far, unthought of.

True, the prosecution must prove the selected charges beyond a reasonable doubt. In most cases, however, there is no reasonable doubt about the offender's guilt. After indictment, about 90 percent of federal cases end in a guilty plea, about 8 percent in dismissals, and of the 2–3 percent that go to trial, convictions outnumber acquittals by about four to one.[6] A defendant has better odds of having the district court's sentence reversed on appeal than of winning an acquittal at trial.[7]

[1] Fed. R. Crim. P. 32(c)(1).

[2] Fed. R. Crim. P. 32(f).

[3] Fed. R. Crim. P. 32(1)(2).

[4] Mempa v. Rhay, 389 U.S. 128 (1967) (holding that Sixth Amendment right to counsel applies at sentencing hear conduct weeks after conviction).

[5] 18 U.S.C. § 3742.

[6] John Gramlich, *Fewer Than 1% of Federal Criminal Defendants Were Acquitted in 2022*, Pew Rsch. Ctr. (June 14, 2023), https://www.pewresearch.org/short-reads/2023/06/14/fewer-than-1-of-defendants-in-federal-criminal-cases-were-acquitted-in-2022/ [https://perma.cc/K9YS-UBML].

[7] U.S. Sent'g Comm'n, *Fig. A: Type and Disposition of Appeals Cases, Fiscal Year 2023, in* 2023 Sourcebook of Federal Sentencing Statistics, https://www.ussc.gov/sites/default/files/pdf/research-and-publications/annual-reports-and-sourcebooks/2023/FigureA.pdf [https://perma.cc/GY5Y-CEHS] (8.8 percent of sentencing appeals resulted in reversal).

Since *Booker*, the scope of prosecutorial influence over sentences is less than it had been. No matter how high the statutory maximum, no matter how high the range prescribed by the Guidelines, the sentencing judge has discretion to impose a lower sentence. Raising the statutory maximum is not trivial because the sentencing guidelines continue to influence judicial discretion.

Raising the upper limit on judicial discretion, however, can't require a sentence exceeding what a neutral tribunal would choose. Mandatory minimums are different. They are "mandatory" on the court, not on the prosecutor. Where a conviction carries a mandatory minimum, the minimum is either above or below what the judge would have selected if unconstrained. If below, the charge hasn't influenced the sentence. If above, the charge not only influences the sentence—it controls it. If the argument for treating proportionate punishment as procedural justice is correct, a sentence higher than called for by retributive principles as applied by a neutral tribunal is disproportionately severe.

We should never inflict disproportionately severe punishments. The best we can do to avoid excessive punishment is to delegate discretion to be exercised only through fair and reliable procedures. The first requirement of fair procedure is a neutral tribunal. It follows that prosecutorial discretion over minimum sentences is contrary to a fundamental principle of criminal justice.

B. The Proposed Doctrine

So closely are the proportionality and baseline problems intertwined that only a few further words are necessary. The baseline for assessing the voluntariness of guilty pleas should be the defendant's right against disproportionate punishment. That right should be understood in terms of procedural justice. No conception of procedural justice, however minimal, permits partisan control of outcomes.

Given those premises, due process permits prosecutors to come down, but not to go up, from the sentence reflecting the defendant's culpability as determined by fair procedures.[8] As long as the judge can come down from

[8] Assuming retributive proportionality should set a minimum, that wouldn't preclude prosecutorial concessions for public advantage unless one accepts a strong version of mandatory retributivism. For such a view, see ANDREW VON HIRSCH & ANDREW ASHWORTH, PROPORTIONATE

the statutory maximums, prosecutorial charging decisions will not impose sentences disproportionate to culpability in the sense of procedural justice.

Contrition ex post at least arguably reduces culpability for the prior offense. The downward departure for acceptance of responsibility reflects this judgment and suffices to motivate guilty pleas in many cases. Insofar as plea bargaining depends on imposing more severe sentences on defendants convicted by trial rather than by plea, the baseline for distinguishing threats and offers is the sentence set by fair procedures. Proposing a reduction in the potential maximum is an offer. Proposing a binding increase in the minimum is a threat.

The criminal justice system might move toward procedural justice in different ways. Legislatures should repeal mandatory minimums, as they often have before. The Model Penal Code–Sentencing (MPCS) proposes a very cogent and politically feasible reform—authorizing appellate courts to police sentencing, including the power (now enjoyed by prosecutors but not judges) to reduce minimum sentences set by previous statutes.[9] The MPCS arrangement would ensure that no offender's sentence exceeds a neutral determination of desert.

Perhaps surprisingly, one step that might help considerably is to facilitate *prosecution* appeals of sentences. Federal prosecutors have that option now, but rarely use it.[10] Prosecutors in the local office regularly appear in front of the district judges and may be reluctant to call out a judge on outlying sentences. A reform statute might provide for centralized review of sentences for potential appeals in a national office in the Justice Department. Excessive lenience is less of a concern than excessive severity, but it *is* a concern.[11] It may also be, politically speaking, the major obstacle to curtailing prosecutorial sentencing power.

Sentencing: Exploring the Principles 138 (2005). If prosecutors make such concessions by bringing a less serious charge, the judge has no power to compel prosecution under statutes with more severe maximums.

[9] Model Penal Code: Sent'g § 10.10 (Am. L. Inst. 2023).

[10] *See* U.S. Sent'g Comm'n, *supra* note 7, at n.1 ("Of the 6,555 appeals cases, 184 were excluded because the type of appeal was 'unknown'. Of the remaining cases, 6,340 involved an appeal by the individual sentenced, 24 involved an appeal by the government, and seven involved a cross appeal.").

[11] *See* Model Penal Code: Sent'g § 7.09 cmt. c (Am. L. Inst., Proposed Final Draft 2017):

> Subsection (2) affords parallel rights to appeal sentences to the government and defendant. . . . Where societal interests necessitate a punishment more severe than that imposed by the trial court, either on utilitarian grounds or grounds of disproportionate lenity, errors in favor of the defendant should be correctable under law.

Turn now to constitutional law. A procedural justice understanding of proportionality vindicates the constitutional requirement of a sentencing hearing. It also reinforces the *Booker* line of cases. Quite aside from the Sixth Amendment, due process requires that legislative delegations of sentencing discretion conform to basic requirements of procedural fairness.

There are at least two different ways to implement this principle without reinventing the criminal justice system. One is for legislatures to adopt the ALI's MPCS proposal to authorize an appellate court to modify a disproportionately severe sentence, even when the sentence was the minimum authorized for the offense of conviction.[12] The other is for courts to follow the *Booker* remedial opinion.[13] The minimum term should be severed from the maximum, with the minimum declared unconstitutional and the offense definition and the statutory maximum still in force.[14]

At least two further issues would need to be worked out. The first is retroactivity. One way the issue might come up is in a trial case, like *Bummer*, where the defendant rejected the offer and was sentenced to a mandatory minimum upon conviction. In those cases, the *Booker* remedy enables the vindication of due process without reversing the conviction.

The other way to raise the issue is by motion to vacate a plea induced by the threat of a mandatory minimum. The defendant can waive almost anything, but not the right to freedom from coercion. If the mandatory minimum is unconstitutional, threatening one is coercive. Again, following *Booker*, the remedy should be to vacate the plea. In the new negotiations, the prosecution would be free to bring charges carrying higher maximum sentences against

[12] *Id.*, § 7.09(5)(b) ("The appellate courts may reverse, remand, or modify any sentence, including a sentence imposed under a mandatory-penalty provision, on the ground that it is disproportionately severe. The appellate court shall use its independent judgment when applying this provision."). Adopting the MPCS would satisfy due process, but I claim here only that due process requires sentencing by neutral tribunals. Jury sentencing would be neutral, but is undesirable because of each jury's ignorance of the outcomes of other cases. Nonetheless, jury sentencing, as long as the jury is not instructed that it must impose a minimum term, satisfies the constitutional neutrality requirement.

[13] United States v. Booker, 543 U.S. 220, 259 (2005):

> [W]e must sever and excise two specific statutory provisions: the provision that requires sentencing courts to impose a sentence within the applicable Guidelines range (in the absence of circumstances that justify a departure), and the provision that sets forth standards of review on appeal, including *de novo* review of departures from the applicable Guidelines range. (citations omitted)

[14] The severability question is much easier than in *Booker* because most of the important mandatory minimums were added to preexisting statutory offenses. The suggestion that Congress, had it known that mandatory minimums are unconstitutional, would have preferred the outright repeal of the laws against drug trafficking, child pornography, or the use of a gun during a felony is implausible.

defendants who insist on a trial. Because higher maximums subject to judicial discretion cannot exceed what the neutral tribunal sees as proportionate, there would be no coercion from the standpoint of the procedural baseline.

These two types of cases differ in one important respect. Under the Court's retroactivity doctrine, new rules of criminal procedure do not apply to prisoners whose convictions have become final on direct review.[15] By contrast, a new constitutional rule of substantive criminal law does apply, no matter how long ago the sentence was imposed.

The law of pleading is procedural. The law of sentencing is substantive. A prisoner who pleaded guilty to avoid the threat of a mandatory minimum could not vacate the conviction. A prisoner actually serving a term that was increased by a mandatory minimum could vacate the sentence, but not the conviction. That would be a significant, but manageable and one-time-only charge on judicial resources.

The second follow-on issue would be noncarceral sentences.[16] If two statutes cover the same conduct, and one has a minimum fine higher than the other, prosecutorial discretion over which charge to bring amounts to prosecutorial sentencing. Procedural due process is distinct from the Eighth Amendment's Excessive Fines Clause. Compensating a judge by a percentage of the fines imposed clearly violates due process.[17] Substituting a prosecutor who isn't neutral in the first place for a judge whose neutrality is compromised doesn't solve the due process problem.

Collateral consequences present another issue. If the statutory scheme, as many do, gives prosecutors discretion to treat common conduct as either a misdemeanor or a felony, and a felony conviction carries mandatory post-conviction disabilities, the felony conviction is categorically more serious even if there is no minimum prison term. If this implies a constitutional requirement of an individualized assessment of appropriate post-conviction disabilities, that's a feature, not a bug.

If the argument here is correct, *Bordenkircher* is inconsistent with the right-to-a-hearing-at-sentencing cases. If those later cases are right, *Bordenkircher* is wrong, at least on the plausible assumption that the neutral sentencing tribunal (the jury, in that case) would have imposed a sentence

[15] *See, e.g.*, Edwards v. Vannoy, 593 U.S. 255 (2021).
[16] If the prison abolition movement eventually succeeds, all sentences would be noncarceral. My account of proportionality as procedural justice would still be indispensable. The principle of retributive proportionality applies to *any* punishment that can be graduated.
[17] Tumey v. Ohio, 273 U.S. 510 (1927).

below the minimum required by the recidivism statute. The threat of raising *the maximum* to twenty-five years would have provided a strong incentive indeed for Hayes to plead guilty. But if he did not, a neutral tribunal, not the prosecutor, should have had the final say on a sentence below the maximum for the offenses of conviction.

Current constitutional law generally reflects this principle. But there's a blind spot in the constitutional cases. While the Court insists that under statutory maxima, fair hearings must inform judicial discretion, the Court has yet to apply these principles to the discretionary selection of charges from the range authorized by the code maximum.

There are reasons to be guardedly optimistic for changes in constitutional doctrine. Experience after *Booker* shows that the costs of principle need not be high, and judges of many political persuasions have shown no love for mandatory minimums. Even raising the prospect, suggested in a concurring opinion or two, of overruling *Bordenkircher* and similar cases likely would prompt legislative reconsideration of either the more notorious mandatory minimum statutes, or of the ALI proposal to subject current minimums to proportionality review by the courts.

The obvious conflict between the judicial sentencing cases and the prosecutorial sentencing cases has persisted for decades. The likely explanation is that legislators and judges believe that prosecutorial power over sentencing is indispensable to effective law enforcement. We engage pragmatic considerations in our final chapter. Prosecutors and judges both play essential roles in the criminal justice system. They ought, however, to play different roles.

11
Engaging Objections

A. Anticipated Objections

The long argument concluded here can be restated simply.

The descriptive claim is that legislatures delegate sentencing discretion to prosecutors. The normative claim is that this delegation violates the right to have proportionate sentences determined by neutral tribunals. The doctrinal claim is that, once the theory of procedural justice vindicates the procedural baseline in the judicial sentencing cases, prosecutorial sentencing violates the due process clauses of the Fifth and Fourteenth Amendments.

The author of a thesis is not always the best judge of what might be said against it. With that caveat, I can see three possible contrary arguments. First, it might be said that while prosecutors have jurisdictional power over sentencing, they have not been delegated sentencing discretion, because prosecutors operate, or at least might be made to operate, within institutions and traditions that effectively constrain their discretion. Second, it might be conceded that prosecutors control sentences and are not encumbered by tradition or practice, but it is argued nonetheless that prosecutors *ought* to control sentences. Third, it might be conceded that prosecutors do control sentences, and that this is bad, but that legislatures, rather than courts, should be the exclusive avenue of reform.

B. Ministers of Justice?

There can be no denying that prosecutorial charge selection can determine individual sentences. Yet it might be possible that prosecutors exercise this discretion according to norms and constraints that make prosecutorial sentencing less partisan than it sounds. There is some truth to both institutional norms and judicial constraints—but not enough.

Sentencing Discretion and the Constitution. Donald A. Dripps, Oxford University Press.
 DOI: 10.1093/9780197830390.003.0011

Whatever the institutional norms governing prosecutors have been, we cannot take those norms for granted. We should not design legal institutions for a society of angels, but instead supply, "by opposite and rival interests, the defect of better motives."[1] Prosecutors are not devils, but they are not angels either.

We can be grateful that prosecutors generally have tried to act like ministers of justice. If they did not, to a considerable extent, succeed, our criminal justice system would be far worse than it is. Admit this, however, and what follows? If prosecutors are acting like judges now, nothing is lost by returning sentencing discretion to real judges. There is a fundamental contradiction in saying that when it comes to sentencing, the prosecutor sheds the trial lawyer's suit for imaginary judicial robes, and saying that pragmatism justifies prosecutors setting sentences differently than judges.

Judges, of course, can push back against perceived overcharging.[2] Yet at best, this again shows that nothing would be lost by giving up mandatory minimums. If prosecutors are doing what judges would do, then we might as well ask the judges in the first place.

The mechanisms of judicial pushback are somewhat sketchy, in both senses. The judge can remonstrate (there are some on-the-record colloquies of that sort). A judge's practical power, however, comes from an unmentionable source—the power to rule unfairly against the prosecution on other issues or even in other cases. If that power is never exercised, the idea of judicial pushback is an illusion. If it is exercised, important cases will be decided not by the facts and the law but by the institutional equivalent of a blood feud.

The normative issue is whether sentences should be controlled by prosecutors subject to judicial influence, or whether sentences should be controlled by judges or parole boards subject to prosecutorial influence. The former arrangement is wrong on principle. It unsurprisingly turns out to be wrong in practice.

[1] The Federalist No. 51, at 319 (James Madison) (Clinton Rossiter ed., 2003).

[2] *See, e.g.*, David A. Sklansky, *The Nature and Function of Prosecutorial Power*, 106 J. Crim. L. & Criminology 473, 482–84 (2017) (noting distinction between decisional authority and influencing how that authority is exercised).

C. Institutional Competence—Prosecutors and Judges

(1) Why Prosecutors Should Not Make Sentencing Decisions

Up to a point, the prosecutorial discretion cases rest on plausible grounds of institutional competence. Police and prosecutors have the information and incentives to allocate enforcement resources rationally. Judges don't know the strength of the evidence or the value of cooperation.[3] When, however, charging decisions determine not just who is to be punished, but *how severely* they are to be punished, the case for unreviewable discretion becomes problematic.

Prosecutors are more punitive than judges. If prosecutors were not more punitive than judges, mandatory minimums would never have been entrusted to prosecutors. The Sentencing Commission's statistics on variances confirm the comparative punitiveness of prosecutors versus judges. Federal judges vary downward from the guidelines range in about 40 percent of cases, about evenly divided between variances sponsored by the prosecution and those that are not. Upward variances are exotic.[4] In other words, the ratio of judges being less, as opposed to more, punitive than prosecutors is on the order of twenty to one.

The case against *prosecutorial* sentencing discretion, however, does not depend solely on the relative propensities of prosecutors and judges. After all, in a great many cases, these are the same people, holding different offices at different points in their careers.[5] Yet even if the polity decides that more

[3] For the classic exposition of these considerations, see *Wayte v. United States*, 470 U.S. 598, 607 (1985) ("Such factors as the strength of the case, the prosecution's general deterrence value, the Government's enforcement priorities, and the case's relationship to the Government's overall enforcement plan are not readily susceptible to the kind of analysis the courts are competent to undertake.").

[4] *See* U.S. SENT'G COMM'N, 2024 SOURCEBOOK OF FEDERAL SENTENCING STATISTICS 58 tbl.29 (2024), https://www.ussc.gov/sites/default/files/pdf/research-and-publications/annual-reports-and-sourcebooks/2024/Table29.pdf [https://perma.cc/U28A-UUG4]. Judges imposed a sentence under the guidelines range, without government sponsorship, in 19.4 percent of cases. In 3.4 percent of cases the court imposed a sentence above the guidelines range, but the Commission does not even have a category for upward variances not sponsored by the government. In these cases the court was as punitive as the prosecution, not more so.

[5] Brian A. Sutherland, *Whether Consent to Search Was Given Voluntarily: A Statistical Analysis of Factors That Predict the Suppression Rulings of the Federal District Courts*, 81 N.Y.U. L. REV. 2192, 2212 (2006) (stating that twenty-six of seventy-six judges selected in a sample were former prosecutors); *Why Public Defenders Are Less Likely to Become Judges—and Why That Matters*, SPLINTER (Mar. 18, 2016), https://splinternews.com/why-public-defenders-are-less-likely-to-become-judges-a-1793855687 (stating that 41 percent of President Obama's judicial nominees had experience working as prosecutors).

severe sentences are the right response to rising crime, that policy choice could be implemented without trusting the executive branch with particular sentences. Maximums could be raised; guidelines could be tightened.

Prosecutorial sentencing promotes not just harsher sentencing across the board, but selective severity that at best is arbitrary and more predictably perverse. Arbitrary would be neutral in a bad way. Prosecutorial incentives, however, align in positively perverse opposition to prevailing theories of justice in sentencing. Judges want efficient dispositions. They too want the guilty to plead, but have no institutional stake in severe outcomes. Prosecutors have an incentive to threaten catastrophic trial penalties in cases where they perceive irrational obstinacy or, worse, some colorable defense.

Some defendants will hazard these, perhaps against the advice of counsel. Then, to paraphrase an aphorism from Holmes, the office must keep its promises. John Gleeson, a federal district judge in Brooklyn, New York, says prosecutors "routinely threaten ultraharsh, enhanced mandatory sentences that *no one*—not even the prosecutors themselves—thinks are appropriate."[6] A study by Human Rights Watch found that "prosecutors often charge or threaten to charge mandatory minimums not because they result in appropriate punishment, even in the view of the prosecutor, but to pressure defendants to plead guilty and to punish them if they do not.[7] *Bordenkircher*, *Angelos*, and *Bummer* are illustrative.

The key justification for *prosecutorial* power over catastrophic sentencing consequences is not a generalizable preference for severity. That would counsel across-the-board increases in severity, not discretionary ones. The real utility, for law enforcement, of discretionary mandatory minimums is not visiting harsh consequences on the worst criminals. The real utility results from pressuring the guilty to confess and encouraging cooperation.

The result is not just unconnected to basic criminal law principles, but positively antagonistic to them. The offenders with the most stock to trade are the worst offenders,[8] such as those who have orchestrated major conspiracies

[6] Erik Eckholm, *Prosecutors Draw Fire for Sentences Called Harsh*, N.Y. Times (Dec. 5, 2013) (quoting Judge Gleeson), https://www.nytimes.com/2013/12/06/us/federal-prosecutors-assailed-in-outcry-over-sentencing.html.

[7] Jamie Fellner, Hum. Rights Watch, An Offer You Can't Refuse: How Federal Prosecutors Force Drug Defendants to Plead Guilty 31 (2013).

[8] *See, e.g.*, United States v. Brigham, 977 F.2d 317, 318 (7th Cir. 1992) ("Mandatory minimum penalties, combined with a power to grant exceptions, create a prospect of inverted sentencing. The more serious the defendant's crimes, the lower the sentence—because the greater his wrongs, the more information and assistance he has to offer to a prosecutor."); Stephen J. Schulhofer, *Rethinking Mandatory Minimums*, 28 Wake Forest L. Rev. 199, 211 (1993) ("Defendants who are most in the

or those who have murdered by their own hands.[9] *They* have a lot of information to trade, and good lawyers to help them negotiate. The street dealers,[10] lookouts,[11] and significant others[12] may have no such stock. Yet, to reward the worst wrongdoers, it is necessary to set a baseline for the little fish sufficiently high to overcome both the perverted loyalty and the physical fear that inhibit cooperation. Investigation has subverted adjudication.[13]

(2) Why Judges Should Not Make Charging Decisions

The literature has not yet recognized the fundamental contradiction between the Supreme Court's cases on charging and sentencing. Commentators have discerned the disturbing scope and consequences of unregulated prosecutorial discretion. The legal literature on prosecutors is rich and surprisingly consistent. Society asks prosecutors to act as both partisans and arbitrators.[14]

know, and thus have the most 'substantial assistance' to offer, are often those who are most centrally involved in conspiratorial crimes.").

[9] *See, e.g.*, United States v. Winberry, 393 F. App'x 295 (6th Cir. 2010). Winberry beat the victim to death with a laundry iron, then set fire to her home. He pleaded guilty to arson and conspiracy to commit murder for hire. The latter conviction carries a mandatory life sentence, which, on the government's motion, the district court reduced to 360 months. Winberry later testified that Billy Johnson, one of the victim's sons, had paid him to do the murder. United States v. Johnson, 443 F. App'x 85 (6th Cir. 2011).

[10] *See, e.g.*, United States v. Davies, 469 F. Supp. 3d 175, 178 (S.D.N.Y. 2020) (granting compassionate release to defendant sentenced to five-year mandatory minimum for participating in a "serious" drug conspiracy in a "low-level role, as a street seller . . . [whose] participation in the crime was motivated by his desire to fund [his] deep heroin addiction . . .").

[11] *See, e.g.*, *Brigham*, 977 F.2d at 317.

[12] *See, e.g.*, Sarah L. Swan, *Conjugal Liability*, 64 UCLA L. Rev. 968, 995 (2017)

> the negligible role these women play in drug crimes can end up being part of the reason they may actually face harsher sentence than the primary wrongdoers: the state often threatens female intimate partners with severe criminal sanctions in the hopes that they will then offer up information about their partner's drug activities in exchange for leniency. Unfortunately, if they are not a significant part of the drug activities, these women generally they have little to no knowledge to give, and are thus unable to have valuable information that they could trade for lighter sentencing deals (footnotes omitted).

[13] *See, e.g.*, *Brigham*, 977 F.2d at 318 ("meting out the harshest penalties to those least culpable is troubling, because it accords with no one's theory of appropriate punishments."); Schulhofer, *supra* note 8, at 211 ("This result makes nonsense of the intuitively plausible scale of punishments that Congress and the ordinary person envisage when they think of sentences linked to drug quantity or other hallmarks of the most serious criminal responsibility.").

[14] *See, e.g.*, United States v. Agurs, 427 U.S. 97, 110–11 (1976) ("For though the attorney for the sovereign must prosecute the accused with earnestness and vigor, he must always be faithful to his client's overriding interest that 'justice shall be done.' "); Eric S. Fish, *Prosecutorial Constitutionalism*, 90 S. Calif. L. Rev. 237, 244 (2017) ("The professional ethics of the American prosecutor reflect two starkly different ideals. One ideal views the prosecutor as a partisan lawyer who must try to convict criminal defendants. The other ideal views the prosecutor as an unbiased minister of justice who

In coping with this "tension"[15] or "schizophrenia[,]"[16] "all prosecutors are subjected to influences which naturally steer them to a conviction psychology and an advocate's role."[17] The literature then divides where the road to reform forks toward seeking reform from prosecutors themselves[18] or seeking external oversight, either by judicial review[19] or reinvigorated grand juries.[20]

One approach proposes prosecutorial guidelines, without external oversight. Judicial participation would be kept to a minimum, perhaps to the point of judicial decisions compelling promulgation of the policies, but not extending to judicial review of individual cases for consistency with the new guidelines.[21] The other approach calls for promulgation of guidelines, but, as in administrative law generally, backed up by judicial review of individual decisions.[22]

Prosecutors have every incentive to write the guidelines in a way that doesn't seriously restrict their discretion in individual cases.[23] The Justice Department's changing policy on bringing charges that carry mandatory minimums illustrates the difficulties. At a time when few federal statutes

must ensure fairness to criminal defendants."); Sklansky, *supra* note 2, at 500 ("The prosecutor is a kind of 'impartial party,' with a 'dual role as an advocate for the government and as an administrator of justice'" (footnotes omitted)).

[15] Angela J. Davis, *Prosecution and Race: The Power and Privilege of Discretion*, 67 FORDHAM L. REV. 13, 52 (1998).

[16] Kenneth J. Melilli, *Prosecutorial Discretion in an Adversary System*, 1992 BYU L. REV. 669, 698.

[17] *Id.* at 703.

[18] *See* Maximo Langer, *Rethinking Plea Bargaining: The Practice and Reform of Prosecutorial Adjudication in American Criminal Procedure*, 33 AM. J. CRIM. L. 223, 266–67 (2006) ("The first option would be to eliminate prosecutorial adjudication.... The second avenue for reform would not entail eliminating prosecutorial adjudication, but improving it."). For arguments pursuing the second path, see, for example, David A. Sklansky, *The Progressive Prosecutor's Handbook*, 50 U.C. DAVIS. L. REV. ONLINE 25 (2017); and Stephanos Bibas, *Prosecutorial Regulation Versus Prosecutorial Accountability*, 157 U. PA. L. REV. 959 (2009).

[19] *See, e.g.*, KENNETH C. DAVIS, DISCRETIONARY JUSTICE: A PRELIMINARY INQUIRY 207–14 (1969).

[20] *See, e.g.*, Joshua Kleinfeld et al., *White Paper of Democratic Criminal Justice*, 111 NW. U. L. REV. 1693, 1700–01 ("grand juries should be given the information, authority, and responsibility necessary to engage in genuine and substantial supervision of prosecutors' charging decisions.").

[21] *See, e.g.*, James Vorenberg, *Decent Restraint of Prosecutorial Power*, 94 HARV. L. REV. 1521, 1564 (1981) (noting reluctance to adopt guidelines that create "new defenses based on the asserted failure to comply," and that "even unenforceable" guidelines would be useful to defense counsel in plea negotiations).

[22] *See, e.g.*, John F. Pfaff, *Prosecutorial Guidelines*, *in* 3 REFORMING CRIMINAL JUSTICE 101, 117–18 (Erik Luna ed., 2017) (distinguishing binding from presumptive guidelines, favoring binding ones).

[23] Donald G. Gifford, *Equal Protection and the Prosecutor's Charging Decision: Enforcing an Ideal*, 49 GEO. WASH. L. REV. 659, 706 (1981) ("Judicial consideration of guidelines would encourage prosecutors ... to draft nonspecific provisions and to include open-ended exceptions"); Vorenberg, *supra* note 21, at 1564–65 ("Few prosecutors' offices ... will promulgate guidelines that limit their freedom in a significant way, and courts are unlikely to require standards in the absence of legislative direction.").

carried mandatory sentences, Attorney General Civiletti promulgated the guiding principle that if a case merited federal prosecution, prosecutors should bring "the most serious offense that is consistent with the nature of the defendant's conduct, and that is likely to result in a sustainable conviction."[24]

Thirty years later, Attorney General Holder qualified this standard by adding that "the charges always should reflect an individualized assessment and fairly represent the defendant's criminal conduct." According to this new policy, prosecutors were not to allege drug quantities that trigger mandatory minimums against nonviolent, low-level dealers with limited criminal histories. Attorney General Sessions countermanded the Holder policy, and then Attorney General Garland established a policy that went further than Holder's in limiting charges with mandatory minimums.

Garland's memo states that "in selecting the appropriate charges, prosecutors should consider whether the consequences of those charges for sentencing would yield a result that 'is proportional to the seriousness of the defendant's conduct, and whether the charge achieves such purposes of the criminal law as punishment, protection of the public, specific and general deterrence, and rehabilitation.'"

Because the "proliferation of provisions carrying mandatory minimum sentences has often caused unwarranted disproportionality in sentencing and disproportionately severe sentences," the memo directs special care in bringing such charges. Charges carrying mandatory minimums may not be brought without the approval of a supervising prosecutor ranking no lower than "section chief or equivalent." Decisions to bring charges carrying mandatory minimums must be documented and reported to the main Justice, there to be entered into a nationwide database.

The Civiletti principles prohibited considering the defendant's race, religion, sex, national origin, or political beliefs. Also excluded were the prosecutor's "personal feelings" about the defendant or the victim, and possible ramifications for the prosecutor's "own professional or personal circumstances." Garland added something new and potentially dramatic. Garland's 2022 policy further provides that: "Charges or statutory sentencing enhancements may not be filed, nor the option of filing charges

[24] U.S. Dep't of Just., Principles of Federal Prosecution 16 (1980). Additional charges might be filed when "necessary" to ensure that the indictment "adequately reflects the nature and extent of the criminal conduct," to provide "the basis for an appropriate sentence under all the circumstances of the case," or to " significantly strengthen the government's case. . . ." *Id.* at 17–18. This language continues under the new Garland policy. *See* U.S. Dep't of Just., Just. Manual § 9-27.320 (2023).

or enhancements raised, simply to exert leverage to induce a plea or because the defendant elected to exercise the right to trial."[25]

Since the election in 2024, we can expect a return to a policy similar to the Sessions policy. The difference between the Garland and Sessions policies, however, while important, is less dramatic than might be supposed. The Sessions policy presumptively required, while the Garland policy presumptively prohibited, the more severe charge. Both rules, however, are default rules, from which departures can easily be justified.

Even the Sessions policy acknowledged "circumstances in which good judgment would lead a prosecutor to conclude that a strict application of the above charging policy is not warranted." Even the Garland policy says only that charges carrying mandatory minimums "ordinarily" should be reserved for violent criminals. As long as the prosecutor has additional reasons for threatening more severe charges, such as encouraging cooperation or making more evidence admissible at trial, the threat would not be "simply" to exert bargaining advantage.

Regardless of their content, since their inception, the Department of Justice's policies explicitly authorize the local US Attorney's Offices to depart from them, only requiring notice to the main Justice if the departures are to become standard procedure rather than ad hoc exceptions.[26] Likewise, since their inception, they have expressly disclaimed creating any right whatsoever enforceable in court.[27] So not only are the DOJ's policies on charge selection mere default rules that can be set aside in specific cases. They don't demand compliance from the offices, and they aren't enforceable in court.

Caseload pressures have led to minimal oversight within prosecutors' offices.[28] We can expect any Court-ordered guidelines to ratify broad discretion.[29] With senior management lacking the capacity or the motivation to police new regulations, only judicial review at the behest of defendants could practically implement the administrative law model.

[25] U.S. Dep't of Just., Just. Manual § 9-27.260 (2023).

[26] U.S. Dep't of Just., *supra* note 24, at 3.

[27] *Id.* at 4.

[28] *See* Adam M. Gershowitz & Laura R. Killinger, *The State (Never) Rests: How Excessive Prosecutorial Caseloads Harm Criminal Defendants*, 105 Nw. U. L. Rev. 261, 267 (2011) (urban prosecutors regularly handle "hundreds or even thousands of felony cases per year."); Melilli, *supra* note 16, at 683 (one reason "charging policies tend to have little impact" is that decisions "must often be made spontaneously and instinctively with infrequent opportunity for serious internal review.").

[29] Melilli, *supra* note 16, at 683 ("Office guidelines tend to be broad and flexible, in part to avoid defense motions claiming violations of internal guidelines.").

Guidelines and judicial review could go together, as they do in administrative law generally.[30] Prosecutors might promulgate charging guidelines similar to sentencing guidelines.[31] Guidelines offer a benchmark for judicial review.[32] The basic idea is that charging has become sentencing, so charging should be made neutral in the interests of fairness.

The decades-old dates on some of the literature suggest the political obstacles to administrative-law-type reforms.[33] The dates suggest something else, equally important. Scholars advanced the administrative law model for prosecutorial charging decisions when judicial sentencing decisions were just as unconstrained by ex ante criteria and ex post review.[34] That has changed. The administrative law model now governs sentencing decisions.[35] Charging guidelines intended to regulate sentence severity would be redundant with advisory sentencing guidelines except insofar as some charges carry mandatory minimums.

If charging did not control sentencing outcomes, charge selection would still influence the strength of the case, as charging a firearms offense in a domestic violence case can avoid calling the victim as a witness. No one proposes regulating prosecutorial charging selection to improve the tactical judgment of prosecutors about such choices. Reformers want to regulate

[30] Langer, *supra* note 18, at 267 ("These two avenues of reform are not incompatible . . . one could introduce reforms to reduce the scope of prosecutorial adjudication, while at the same time improving these due process rights in remaining prosecutorial adjudication practices.").

[31] *See, e.g.*, Vorenberg, *supra* note 23; Gifford, *supra* note 23, at 704; Richard S. Frase, *The Decision to File Federal Criminal Charges: A Quantitative Study of Prosecutorial Discretion*, 47 U. Chi. L. Rev. 246, 292–96 (1980) (discussing the virtues and drawbacks of prosecutorial guidelines that require prosecutors to offer written reasons subject to review for their discretionary decisions to charge); Ronald F. Wright, *Reinventing American Prosecution Systems*, 46 Crime & Just. 395, 401 (2017); Ronald F. Wright, *Sentencing Commissions as Provocateurs of Prosecutorial Self-Regulation*, 105 Colum. L. Rev. 1010 (2005).

[32] *See, e.g.*, Charles P. Bubany & Frank F. Skillern, *Taming the Dragon: An Administrative Law for Prosecutorial Decision Making*, 13 Am. Crim. L. Rev. 473, 510 (1976) ("with the promulgation of standards, judicial review could be limited to the issue of abuse of discretion, the defendant being required to make at least a colorable claim that his prosecution violated an established policy of the prosecutor.").

[33] This is not to deny that many states have taken limited steps toward judicial review of charge selection. For a comprehensive assessment of how state judges might, and to some limited extent already do, supervise charging decisions, see Andrew Crespo, *The Hidden Law of Plea Bargaining*, 118 Colum. L. Rev. 1303 (2018). Further movement in that direction would collide with the genuine distinctions in institutional competence between prosecutors and judges.

[34] *See, e.g.*, Marvin E. Frankel, Criminal Sentences: Law Without Order (1973).

[35] In addition to the federal guidelines, dozens of states have sentencing guidelines. *See, e.g.*, Kelly Lyn Mitchell, Robina Inst. Crim. L. & Crim. Just., Sentencing Commissions and Guidelines by the Numbers (2017). Other states have adopted statutes guiding sentencing discretion and providing for appellate review. *See, e.g.*, People v. Shenouda, 192 Cal. Rptr. 3d 725 (Ct. App. 2015) (rejecting challenge to trial court's imposition of "middle sentence" provided by Determinate Sentencing Law, because trial judge was not "arbitrary or irrational").

charging decisions because charging decisions have so much impact on sentences.

Charging decisions can influence sentences in two ways. They can raise or lower both the minimum and the maximum. Under the maximum, sentences are determined by judicial discretion constrained by advisory guidelines. The maximum matters—but the maximum is *already* regulated, not at the front end but at the back end.

Prosecutorial control over the minimum is now unregulated. The real point of these various reform proposals is to close that gap. However, unlike judicial regulations of sentences under a discretionary maximum, judicial regulation of charging decisions fixing a mandatory minimum is a daunting proposition.

What would be gained if prosecutorial guidelines were mandatory and enforceable in court? The nebulous nature of the federal charging policies shows why turning to prosecutorial guidelines as the baseline for coercion claims is doomed to fail. The guidelines will permit so many different charges on similar records that it would be very hard to say that any particular case was being treated as an outlier.

Next, consider resource demands. If overcharging claims could be waived in plea agreements, the guidelines would be just as unenforceable as ever. If waivers were not permitted, overcharge claims could be raised in many—maybe most—of the 95 percent of cases that now end in pleas. If judicial review for compliance with charging guidelines added even 1 percent to the cost of processing 95 percent of cases, the systemic costs of adjudicating the cases that currently plead would nearly double.

Would judicial oversight produce better charging decisions? Prosecutors, rather than judges, have the institutional competence to evaluate plea deals. They know when to worry about witnesses refusing to testify, and about what benefit to expect from a defendant's cooperation.

Not only would judges be out of their depth if they second-guessed charging decisions. Hands-on involvement in charging decisions would threaten judicial neutrality.[36] A judge who rejected an overcharge claim might end up trying a case, or sentencing in one, after approving the charges

[36] *See* Inmates of Attica Corr. Facility v. Rockefeller, 477 F.2d 375, 380 (2d Cir. 1973) (absent "statutorily defined standards governing reviewability, or regulatory or statutory policies of prosecution, the problems inherent in the task of supervising prosecutorial decisions do not lend themselves to resolution by the judiciary. The reviewing courts would be placed in the undesirable and injudicious posture of becoming 'superprosecutors.'").

as reasonable. At the least, judges trying cases would know that some other judge had rejected an overcharge motion.

(3) Prosecutors, Judges, and the Void-for-Vagueness Doctrine

"As generally stated, the void-for-vagueness doctrine requires that a penal statute define the criminal offense with sufficient definiteness that ordinary people can understand what conduct is prohibited and in a manner that does not encourage arbitrary and discriminatory enforcement."[37] The cases generally treat constraining official discretion as more important than fair notice.[38] The Court's most recent vagueness decisions reject prosecutorial sentencing by holding that due process permits judges, but not prosecutors, to apply vague sentencing enhancements.

Johnson v. United States[39] applied the doctrine to statutes increasing sentences even when the statute defining the forbidden conduct is very clear. Samuel James Johnson, a white supremacist suspected by the government of plotting terrorism, pleaded guilty to a felon-in-possession-of-a-firearm charge. Standing alone, the firearms charge carried a maximum sentence of ten years. The government, however, asked the district court to sentence Johnson under the Armed Career Criminal Act, a statute providing a mandatory minimum term of fifteen years and a maximum of life when, *inter alia*, the defendant has a record including three or more violent felonies.

In addition to forcible crimes such as attempted murder or robbery, the act enumerates some specific serious crimes (e.g., burglary) as violent felonies. At the end of this list, Congress added a residual clause to include any crime that "otherwise involves conduct that presents a serious potential risk of physical injury to another."[40] Johnson's resume included three violent felonies only if a state conviction for possessing a sawed-off shotgun qualified under the residual clause. Justice Scalia's majority opinion overruled precedent by holding the residual clause void for vagueness.

Now, Johnson had notice that being a felon in possession of a firearm is a crime. The Court, however, began by noting that the vagueness doctrine condemns "a criminal law so vague that it fails to give ordinary

[37] Kolender v. Lawson, 461 U.S. 352, 357 (1983) (citations omitted).
[38] *See id.*; Smith v. Goguen, 415 U.S. 566, 574 (1974).
[39] 576 U.S. 591 (2015).
[40] *Id.* at 593–94.

people fair notice of the conduct it punishes, *or* so standardless that it invites arbitrary enforcement."[41] The vagueness doctrine applies "not only to statutes defining elements of crimes, but also to statutes fixing sentences."[42] The majority ruled that the residual clause was void for vagueness.

A subsequent case, *Beckles v. Unites States*,[43] arose when the sentencing guidelines advised, but did not require, judges to select a high sentence under the statutory maximum. Superficially, the case of Travis Beckles resembled Johnson's case in many ways. Both men were convicted of being a felon in possession of a firearm, and the issue in each case was whether possessing a sawed-off shotgun was a crime of violence. The differences, however, were more important than the similarities.

In *Beckles*, the crime of conviction was possessing a sawed-off shotgun, triggering a ten-year maximum. Beckles's criminal history, however, clearly qualified him for sentencing under the Armed Career Criminal Act, triggering a fifteen-year minimum and a maximum of life. The district court sentenced Beckles pursuant to Sentencing Guideline Section 4.B.1, which increases the sentence for recidivists provided that the offense of conviction is a violent felony. The Guidelines defined violent felony in the same language as the Armed Career Criminal Act, including the residual clause struck down in *Johnson*.

Pursuant to Guideline Section 4.B.1, the district court had sentenced Beckles to thirty years, double the statutory minimum. Beckles made the logical argument that if the residual clause was unconstitutionally vague when it triggered the higher minimum and maximum penalties under the Armed Career Criminal Act, the same language should be unconstitutionally vague when it had the effect of imposing a sentence above the fifteen-year minimum in the Act itself. The court of appeals rejected this argument because the Sentencing Commission's published comments on Section 4.B.1 explicitly included possessing a sawed-off shotgun as a crime of violence.[44]

The Supreme Court, however, upheld the sentence on a broader ground. According to the majority, the sentencing guidelines can *never* be void for

41 *Id.* at 595 (emphasis added) (citation omitted).
42 *Id.* at 596 (citation omitted).
43 580 U.S. 256 (2017).
44 Beckles v. United States, 616 F. App'x 415 (11th Cir. 2015) (per curiam).

vagueness, because, since *Booker*, the guidelines are only advisory. The pre-guidelines cases approved standardless sentencing discretion as long as neutral tribunals exercised it.[45] A statute imposing a mandatory minimum trumps judicial discretion, but judicial discretion trumps the advisory sentencing guidelines.

Justice Thomas wrote for the majority: "Unlike the ACCA, however, the advisory Guidelines do not fix the permissible range of sentences. To the contrary, they merely guide the exercise of a court's discretion in choosing an appropriate sentence within the statutory range. Accordingly, the Guidelines are not subject to a vagueness challenge under the Due Process Clause."[46]

Beckles, therefore, held that sentencing guidelines cannot be void for vagueness as long as they satisfy *Booker*'s requirement of judicial discretion.

The Court repeatedly has referred specifically to "prosecutors" as among the agents the vagueness doctrine is supposed to constrain.[47] The Court's decisions on prosecutorial discretion, however, impose minimal practical constraints on charge selection. The result is that prosecutors now do what *Johnson* prohibited judges and juries from doing (i.e., imposing increased punishment without comprehensible criteria).

The executive branch has always had the power to limit the discretionary *maximum*. Even in the days of private prosecution, the executive could file a *nolle prosequi* before trial or indulge in clemency after. Charge selection has, and should continue, to set the upper limit on an offender's punishment. What the sentencing cases condemn unequivocally is the partisan and harsher exercise of sentencing discretion.

[45] In pre-*Furman* cases approving discretionary capital sentencing, or guilty pleas induced by the risk of capital punishment, discretion over the death penalty was exercised not by judges but by (equally neutral) juries. *See* Brady v. United States, 397 U.S. 742, 743 (1970); Parker v. North Carolina, 397 U.S. 790, 792 n.1 (1970); North Carolina v. Alford, 400 U.S. 25, 27 n.1 (1970); McGautha v. California, 402 U.S. 183, 185 (1971).

[46] *Beckles*, 580 U.S. at 263.

[47] Sessions v. Dimaya, 584 U.S. 148, 156 (2018) (plurality opinion) ("[T]he doctrine guards against arbitrary or discriminatory law enforcement by insisting that a statute provide standards to govern the actions of police officers, prosecutors, juries, and judges."); Kolender v. Lawson, 461 U.S. 352, 358 (1983) ("Where the legislature fails to provide such minimal guidelines, a criminal statute may permit 'a standardless sweep [that] allows policemen, prosecutors, and juries to pursue their personal predilections'" (quoting Smith v. Goguen, 415 U.S. 566, 575 (1974)). *See also* Chicago v. Morales, 527 U.S. 41, 65 (1999) (O'Connor, J., concurring) ("A criminal law, however, must not permit policemen, prosecutors, and juries to conduct 'a standardless sweep . . . to pursue their personal predilections'" (quoting *Kolender*, 461 U.S. at 358)).

D. Pragmatics

Three pragmatic concerns, rarely voiced but certainly felt, explain the persistence of mandatory minimums. The first is that lenient judges short-changed public safety, and that mandatory minimums in executive discretion solve this problem.[48] The second is that discretion to impose mandatory time is necessary and sufficient to induce the guilty to plead guilty.[49] The third is that this discretion is necessary and sufficient to induce the complicit to cooperate.[50] This section speaks to these concerns.

(1) The Specter of Judicial Lenience

Today, the alternative to prosecutorial sentencing is not individual and potentially eccentric judicial discretion but judicial discretion regulated by sentencing guidelines or determinate sentencing laws. If some jurisdictions still retain discretionary sentencing, they have guidelines as an alternative to mandatory minimums. Even without mandatory minimums, prosecutors have discretion to raise the maximum, with a corresponding effect on the guidelines range. Downward departures or variances are public decisions supported by reasons and subject to appellate review.

Given the empirical finding that increasing certainty of punishment has more deterrent power than increasing severity,[51] mandatory minimums are unlikely sources of marginal deterrence. The empirical evidence shows that mandatory minimums produce disparity rather than certainty.[52]

[48] *See* Erik Luna & Paul G. Cassell, *Mandatory Minimalism*, 32 CARDOZO L. REV. 1, 10–12 (2010) ("Without mandatory minimums, proponents thus claim, judges might issue undeservedly lenient sentences for these violent offenders.").

[49] *Id.* at 12 (proponents argue that the "threat of long, obligatory sentences tends to encourage plea bargaining").

[50] *Id.* ("[T]he possibility of a long sentence provides a powerful incentive for members of a criminal group to provide information to law enforcement . . .").

[51] *See, e.g.*, Mirko Bagaric, *Consistency and Fairness in Sentencing—The Splendor of Fixed Penalties*, 2 CALIF. CRIM. L. REV. 1, ¶ 35 (2000) ("General deterrence works: there is a general connection between the existence of a criminal sanction and the crime rate. Natural social experiments concerning the effects of police strikes reveal that absent the threat of criminal punishment a far greater number of people would commit criminal offenses. However, studies have failed to establish the validity of marginal deterrence: the claim that there is a link between higher penalties and the crime rate."); Michael Tonry, *Learning From the Limitations of Deterrence Research*, 37 CRIME & JUST. 279, 279–80 (2008) (reviewing studies reaching similar conclusions).

[52] *See, e.g.*, Paul J. Hofer, *Review of the U.S. Sentencing Commission's Report to Congress: Mandatory Minimum Penalties in the Federal Criminal Justice System*, 24 FED. SENT'G REP. 193, 197 (2012) [hereinafter Hofer, *Review*] ("[A] fair reading of the evidence shows that mandatory minimums are the greatest source of unwarranted disparity in federal sentencing today.").

Judges and parole boards have access to the same risk assessment tools as prosecutors. They do not share the incentive to reward the worst villains with shorter sentences. When the mandatory minimums for drug trafficking and firearms offenses take a dealer out of circulation, new ones step forward in response to the same incentives as their predecessors. At the back end of long sentences, society pays for prison space better devoted to career criminals earlier in their criminal trajectories. Unsurprisingly, empirical research has yet to prove that these laws are more effective than discretionary guidelines.[53]

The standard arguments for mandatory minimums contradict one another. To encourage pleas and cooperation, the prosecution must waive the "mandatory" sentences. Sophisticated offenders know this ex ante. The worst offenders have the most information to trade. From the standpoint of deterrence, incapacitation, or retribution, it simply can't be true that the only just sentence is the minimum *and* that the prosecution should routinely waive the minimum for guilty pleas and/or cooperation.

(2) Inducing Pleas and Cooperation

The theory that accepting responsibility after the crime reduces the blameworthiness of the offender gives plea incentives at least a patina of principle. Prosecutors have the right information and incentives to weigh the values of guilty pleas and offers to cooperate. They are the wrong agents for assessing culpability and allocating corrections assets. They are the right agents for balancing the value of cooperation against risks to public safety. Prosecutors should have authority to come down from the baseline set by fair procedure, but not to go up by selecting charges with higher minimums.

Recommending a discount for accepting responsibility is only one way to do this. The more dramatic way is by forgoing charges that would raise the maximum and the guidelines sentence along with it. Under the proposed doctrine, defendants who elect trial and lose the discount face only their

[53] *See, e.g.*, Michael Tonry, *The Mostly Unintended Effects of Mandatory Penalties: Two Centuries of Consistent Findings*, 38 Crime & Just. 65, 101 (2009) (reviewing studies, concluding: "No matter which body of evidence is consulted—the general literature on the deterrent effects of criminal sanctions, work more narrowly focused on the marginal deterrence hypothesis, or the evaluation literature on mandatory penalties—the conclusion is the same. There is little basis for believing that mandatory penalties have any significant effects on rates of serious crime.").

neutrally assessed liability—but that might be considerably more severe than the sentence imposed, under the lower statutory maximum, on defendants who plead guilty. Defendants who lose at trial can rightly complain if deals are offered and withheld for invidious reasons, but they have no due process objection against their sentences as long as neutral proportionality assessments set those sentences.

Experience shows that mandatory minimums are not necessary to induce guilty pleas. The federal guilty plea percentage is not perceptibly lower in theft, embezzlement, or antitrust cases, where mandatory minimums rarely apply, as in drug cases, where they usually do.[54] *Booker*, in effect, eliminated many mandatory minimum sentences without producing a surge in trials.[55] Mandatory minimums play an exceptionally limited role in Wisconsin,[56] yet only about 3 percent of Wisconsin cases end in trials rather than pleas.[57] When the prosecution has a strong case, and the sentencing consequences are reasonably clear, defendants advised by competent counsel act rationally.

Some evidence suggests that mandatory minimums are not required to pressure gangsters into the despised and dangerous game of cooperation.[58] There is also a legitimate way to add pressure on reluctant witnesses. Rather than prosecutors imposing harsh sentences because they believe (not always correctly) that the defendant has important information, courts could impose harsh sentences for willfully refusing to cooperate.

[54] *See Table D-4–U.S. District Courts–Criminal Statistical Tables for the Federal Judiciary*, U.S. CTS. (June 30, 2018), http://www.uscourts.gov/statistics/table/d-4/statistical-tables-federal-judiciary/2018/06/30 (showing 1,205 convictions for larceny/theft, 1,166 by plea; 313 convictions for embezzlement, 309 by plea; 76 convictions for antitrust, and 70 by plea).

[55] From 2005, when *Booker* came down, through 2009, the guilty plea percentage in federal courts actually rose. *See* Paul J. Hofer, *Has* Booker *Restored Balance? A Look at Data on Plea Bargaining and Sentencing*, 23 FED. SENT'G REP. 326, 327 fig.1 (2011).

[56] Michael O'Hear, *Wisconsin Sentencing in the* Walker *Era: Mass Incarceration as the New Normal*, 30 FED. SENT'G REP. 125, 125–26 (2017).

[57] *See Wisconsin Measures*, MEASURES FOR JUST., https://app.measuresforjustice.org/portal/WI?c=2 [https://perma.cc/B3LR-2B65] ("Felony Cases Resolved with a Trial Verdict" tab). As noted by O'Hear, *supra* note 56, at 126, "[T]he elected judiciary operated in the same punitive political environment as the legislators, which helped to ensure steadily lengthening prison sentences even without rigorous legislative mandates."

[58] *See* Hofer, *Review*, *supra* note 52, at 209 ("We know from Commission statistics that cooperation is routinely obtained in cases that do *not* carry mandatory minimums. In 2010, the rate of substantial assistance departures in drug trafficking cases was 24.6 percent. The rate was comparable or higher in many kinds of cases that do not carry mandatory minimums: 50 percent in antitrust cases, 22.7 percent in arson cases, 32.3 percent in bribery cases, 23.7 percent in kidnapping cases, 24.5 percent in money laundering cases, and 22.2 percent in racketeering/extortion cases" (footnote omitted)).

(3) Taking Contempt Seriously

When the prosecution has completed its investigation against a low-level gangster, it can obtain an immunity order trumping the defendant's privilege against self-incrimination. Immunized defendants who refuse to cooperate can be held in contempt. Typical sentences for criminal contempt are relatively short, but there is no maximum in the federal contempt statute.[59] The Sentencing Commission has declined to promulgate any guidelines for contempt cases.[60] That helps to explain why *Beckles* came out as it did. Were it not a delegation to judges exercising traditional sentencing discretion, the contempt penalty would be manifestly void for vagueness.

In rare cases, contempt is severely punished.[61] For example, in *United States v. Leyva*, the defendant, following his conviction on heroin trafficking charges, was given immunity but refused to testify.[62] The district court imposed a thirty-five-year sentence for contempt, which the appellate court reduced to two years.[63] Part of the reason for reducing the sentence was the potential for abuse by judges imposing summary convictions. That genuine risk can be countered by requiring indictment, trial by jury, and sentencing under new guidelines.[64]

Defying the court order is culpable (otherwise, we would not punish contempt criminally at all). The question of *how culpable* has received little attention. Arguably, refusing to testify should not be punished more seriously than obstruction of justice or perjury. These comparisons, however, are inapt. Different lies in the same proceedings can support multiple counts

[59] 18 U.S.C. § 401 ("A court of the United States shall have power to punish by fine or imprisonment, or both, at its discretion, such contempt of its authority . . .").

[60] U.S. SENT'G COMM'N, GUIDELINES MANUAL ANN. § 2J1.1 n.1 (2024) ("Because misconduct constituting contempt varies significantly and the nature of the contemptuous conduct, the circumstances under which the contempt was committed, the effect the misconduct had on the administration of justice, and the need to vindicate the authority of the court are highly context-dependent, the Commission has not provided a specific guideline for this offense.").

[61] *See* State v. Price, 820 A.2d 956 (R.I. 2003) (defendant sentenced to twenty-five years, fifteen suspended, consecutive to extortion sentence); People v. Geiger, 30 N.E.3d 1206 (Ill. App. Ct. 2015) (after state supreme court vacated sentence of twenty years for refusing to testify at murder trial, appellate court upheld ten-year sentence).

[62] *See* United States v. Leyva, 513 F.2d 774 (5th Cir. 1975) (reducing thirty-five-year sentence for contempt to two years).

[63] *See also* United States v. Brady, 168 F.3d 574, 580–81 (1st Cir. 1999) (eighty-seven months); United States v. Papadakis, 802 F.2d 618, 622 (2d Cir. 1986) (five years); United States v. Jones, 278 F.3d 711, 716–18 (7th Cir. 2002) (seventy-six months).

[64] *See* Bloom v. Illinois, 391 U.S. 194 (1968) (holding defendant sentenced to two years for contempt had constitutional right to jury trial).

of perjury.[65] Different acts of obstruction likewise can support multiple counts.[66] A refusal to testify is only one contempt. Comparing the sentence for criminal contempt with the sentences for perjury and obstruction therefore does not justify a low limit on sentences for contempt.

States by statute, and the federal Sentencing Commission by guideline, should provide that refusing to testify without a good claim of privilege is a crime almost as serious as the offenses under investigation. The elements to be proved would be the existence of the court order, the defendant's knowledge of the order, and the defendant's refusal to testify.[67] Sentencing should be based on the most serious crime the grand jury has found probable cause to investigate within the scope of defendant's knowledge.[68]

This approach would punish people, guilty or not of serious crimes of their own, for protecting major criminals. It would bring extremely serious pressure to bear on the low-level conspirators now threatened with grossly exaggerated sentences for their actual crimes. The contempt procedure could be threatened without being used.

The prospect of threatening to imprison domestic violence victims, or the spouses of drug dealers, unless they rat out their partners, is disquieting. If such pressures were deemed sufficiently unsavory, returning to the traditional spousal privilege, vesting the right to claim the privilege in the target spouse, would be an honest step to mediate the dilemma.[69] As things are now, complicity and conspiracy doctrine expose the dealers' lovers and children to punishment theoretically as harsh as that faced by the dealers

[65] The line between distinct and repetitive false statements can be hard to draw, but it is often drawn. *See, e.g.*, United States v. Clarridge, 811 F. Supp. 697, 703 (D.D.C. 1992) ("The precedents do not formulate a precise and exhaustive formula for determining whether perjury and false statement allegations are multiplicitous. However, in the view of this Court, the appropriate test is this: each count must set forth a separate lie or false statement, and in cases where the facts present a close question of whether separate lies exist, it is relevant to inquire into the degree to which the second statement impaired the body before which it was made.").

[66] *See, e.g.*, United States v. Berkowitz, 700 F. Supp. 1526 (N.D. Ill. 1988) (holding that defendant could be held liable for two counts of obstruction, one for stealing incriminating documents and the other for destroying them).

[67] *See, e.g.*, United States v. Trudeau, 812 F.3d 578, 587–88 (7th Cir. 2016) ("The essential elements of a finding of criminal contempt under 18 U.S.C. § 401(3) are a lawful and reasonably specific order of the court and a willful violation of that order" (citation omitted)).

[68] Under *Booker* this could be done by a preponderance of evidence at sentencing, as long as the contempt guidelines were advisory.

[69] The Supreme Court adopted the traditional view in Hawkins v. United States, 358 U.S. 74 (1958), then overruled Hawkins in Trammel v. United States, 445 U.S. 40 (1980). The traditional view can be modified by recognizing an exception for cases where the witness spouse is the victim of the charged offense.

themselves.[70] The significant others, however, are less likely to have information of substantial value to the prosecution.

Just as now, when negotiating plea agreements, underlings would factor in punishment for not cooperating. A street dealer might plead guilty in exchange for dropping a gun charge, or for agreeing not to compel cooperation. The prosecution might be willing to agree to one or the other. The prosecution's contempt option would provide as much leverage as the mandatory minimums give now, without countenancing prosecutorial sentencing.

E. Procedural Justice and Mass Incarceration

It is tempting to focus on prosecutorial discretion as a driver of mass incarceration. Prosecutors contributed to mass incarceration by filing more serious charges than they had before.[71] It seems to follow that constraining prosecutorial sentencing would make a major contribution to reversing mass incarceration.

A contribution, yes, but not a decisive one. A prison commitment depends on multiple antecedents, each necessary but not independently sufficient.[72] The legislature must define the offense and fix a range of penalties. Less conspicuous but practically more momentous are funding decisions. The number and length of carceral sentences depend on prison capacity.

Police must arrest a suspect. Prosecutors must decide to file charges. The accused must be convicted, generally by plea but occasionally by trial. The conviction must authorize a carceral sentence. If the offense of conviction carries no statutory minimum, the judge must decide to impose a prison term.

Of all these off-ramps, the only one that would be opened by abolishing mandatory minimums is judicial discretion. That would make a difference, but less of a difference than might be supposed. In the federal practice, where

[70] *See supra* note 12.

[71] *See* John F. Pfaff, Locked In: The True Causes of Mass Incarceration and How to Achieve Real Reform 127 (2017) [hereinafter Pfaff, Locked In] (during the 1990s and 2000s, "the probability that a prosecutor would file felony charges against an arrestee basically doubled, and that change pushed prison populations up even as crime dropped.")

[72] *See, e.g.*, Jeffrey Bellin, Mass Incarceration Nation: How the United States Became Addicted to Prisons and Jails and How It Can Recover 95–164 (2022).

prosecutorial sentencing is pervasive, only 16 percent of convicted offenders were subject to mandatory prison time in fiscal year 2023.[73]

Without mandatory minimums, even this group of offenders would receive a guidelines sentence that would probably, but not always be, below the current mandatory minimum. True, in about 20 percent of federal cases, the judge grants the defendant a downward variance from the guidelines sentence. That's a significant but modest share of cases. In those cases, moreover, the defendant is typically sentenced to prison, but for a shorter term than the guidelines prescribe.

In many states, judges are elected or subject to recall. Wisconsin's minimal reliance on mandatory minimums didn't prevent mass incarceration.[74] Abolishing mandatory minimums would make a difference, but not one that should exhilarate reformers or frighten conservatives.

Without the threat of mandatory minimums, the balance of advantage in plea bargaining would change. Judges are conscious of caseload pressures,[75] but the risk of a discretionary trial penalty is quite different than the certainty of a catastrophic one. Either more cases would be tried, drawing resources away from processing other cases, or prosecutors would offer deals that reduce sentences below what would be expected from the judge after a trial conviction. We should expect some combination of these responses. This change in plea bargaining dynamics probably would do more to reduce incarceration rates than the direct effect in cases formerly subject to mandatory minimums.

Without the mandatory minimum, the Sentencing Commission and its state counterparts would be free to take two more reforms. The first is to rewrite the guidelines for offenses now carrying mandatory minimums. As it stands, the high end of the guidelines range must be at least as long as the mandatory minimum. Unchained from the statutory minimum, the guidelines range for many offenses could come down significantly.[76]

[73] U.S. Sent'g Comm'n, Quick Facts on Statutory Mandatory Minimum Penalties (2024), https://www.ussc.gov/sites/default/files/pdf/research-and-publications/quick-facts/Quick_Facts_Mand_Mins_FY23.pdf [https://perma.cc/W7XX-M3EQ]. About 30 percent of convictions include some mandatory prison term, but in about 40 percent of these cases the mandatory minimum is not actually imposed, either because of the safety valve, a cooperation deal, or both. The 2023 numbers were very similar to those for the previous four years.

[74] O'Hear, *supra* note 56.

[75] For a discussion of trial penalties imposed by judges, see, for example, Carissa Byrne Hessick, Punishment Without Trial 44–46 (2021).

[76] Luna & Cassell, *supra* note 48, at 60.

The second step the Commission might take is to limit trial penalties. The Commission might do this by itemizing hallmarks of a case presenting *bona fide* trial issues. For example, if the jury convicted only after the judge prodded an apparently deadlocked jury with a "dynamite charge," it would be a clear sign that the accused put the prosecution to its proof for reasons better than fantasy or spite.

Defendants convicted at trial lose, at the least, the acceptance-of-responsibility (AOR) discount. If we believe that a significant number of trials have systemic benefits, as a distinguished American Bar Association task force recently declared,[77] the Commission should create a colorable defense discount equal to the AOR discount.[78] Presently, any such move would invite the prosecution to bring charges carrying mandatory minimums.

F. Institutional Competence—Courts and Legislatures

History shows that periodically legislatures adopt "mandatory" minimums, thereby delegating sentencing authority to prosecutors, because their political incentives make this nearly ineluctable. Perhaps that's the best foundation for the Court's prosecutorial discretion cases. The problem all along has been legislative delegations to the executive, and over time, legislatures generally have undone those delegations. Why not trust that process once again?

A powerful but nonobvious response is that the public-choice dynamics haven't changed. There will be new crises provoking new moral panics, in turn provoking the old logic of acting tough by delegating to the executive branch.[79] It is *possible* that the overdue and modest-but-welcome legislative reaction against mass incarceration announces a brave new world of legislative indifference to popular passion. It was equally *possible* after Prohibition and after the Boggs Act. Indeed, the Court decided *Bordenkircher* after the repeal of the Boggs Act but before the advent of the crack cocaine epidemic.

[77] Thea Johnson, ABA Crim. Just. Section, Plea Bargain Task Force Rep. 10 (2023).

[78] *Cf.* Daniel Givelber, *Punishing Protestations of Innocence: Denying Responsibility and Its Consequences*, 37 Am. Crim. L. Rev. 1363, 1400 (2000) ("We could set the range of punishments at the level currently applied to the vast majority of all defendants, and treat the frivolous decision to insist upon a trial as a basis for enhancing that sentence.").

[79] *See, e.g.*, Pfaff, Locked In, *supra* note 71, at 220 ("One major problem with relying on legislative reforms to end mass incarceration . . . is that any victory can be easily undone in the future, as we saw with Congress and drug mandatories.").

We have seen the results. Should we leave the door open to going through that again?

A second response acknowledges the role of politics in constitutional law. Over time, the Supreme Court has created new constitutional law not in the spirit of platonic guardians but in response to social movements that made the status quo as questionable as change. With respect to sentence severity, we have seen such political successes in the very recent past.[80]

Yet a third response points to the use of artificial intelligence in sentencing. The machines can learn how to sentence, but they must learn *from* something. If, as seems probable, the future of sentencing is delegation to machines that have learned the records and outcomes of many thousands of cases, the content of the cases that teach the machines will be critical.[81] Today, a database of judicial sentencing decisions will reflect the prior decisions of prosecutors.[82] Do we want the machines to sentence like prosecutors, or to sentence like judges?

The decisive response comes from the very start of this book. Suppose a legislature did directly what almost all do indirectly—delegate sentencing discretion to prosecutors. How would the judges react to *Prosecutorial Sentencing*? Would they say that this is a legislative innovation and probably wrong, but we trust the same legislature that passed the statute to repeal it? Or would they say, as they have said in cases where statutes delegated prosecutors the power to issue warrants, or permitted judges to charge fees for imposing fines, that when the violation of due process is as plain as punch, the legislature, with all respect, must look for constitutional solutions to our many and serious social problems?

If you agree with me that the courts, giving elected legislatures due deference, would hold the statute hypothesized by *Prosecutorial Sentencing* unconstitutional, we have traveled together to the end. *Prosecutorial*

[80] *See, e.g.*, *Remarks by President Trump at Signing Ceremony for S. 756, the "FIRST STEP Act of 2018" and H.R. 6964, the "Juvenile Justice Reform Act of 2018,"* White House (Dec. 21, 2018), https://trumpwhitehouse.archives.gov/briefings-statements/remarks-president-trump-signing-ceremony-s-756-first-step-act-2018-h-r-6964-juvenile-justice-reform-act-2018/ [https://perma.cc/4S8F-K6NV].

[81] *See, e.g.*, Jesper Ryberg, *Criminal Justice and Artificial Intelligence: How Should We Assess the Performance of Sentencing Algorithms?*, 37 Phil. & Tech. art. 9 (Jan. 2024) (rejecting the criterion of results indistinguishable from human decisions but noting the absence of a normatively theorized alternative).

[82] This point is distinct from the common argument that algorithms adopt human biases about race and class. For example, a tool that absorbed the records and sentences in the cases of Scott Bummer and Tony Amato would learn that refusing to plead guilty "should" roughly double the sentence.

Sentencing is patently unconstitutional—and there is no distinction between *Prosecutorial Sentencing* and *229 Degrees.*

G. Conclusion

Meticulously fair procedures can produce a sentence that offends the intuition of the great majority of observers. Yet for legal purposes, that's the proportionate sentence, just as a conviction after trial on weak evidence is deemed correct until set aside by further proceedings. Defendants have no right in either law or morals to perfect outcomes. They can claim no more than the right to meticulously fair procedures about both guilt *and* punishment.

That may sound like no more than common sense, but there is nothing commonplace about common sense. This book adds something nonobvious and momentous to professional thinking about both the substantive criminal law of sentencing and the procedural law of plea bargaining. Defendants, as is widely believed, have no right to anything more than the outcome produced by fair procedures. To this I add: They do have the right to nothing less.

Index

For the benefit of digital users, indexed terms that span two pages (e.g., 52–53) may, on occasion, appear on only one of those pages.